Exploring Maths through Stories and Rhymes

This practical book is packed with tried-and-tested activities which draw on popular stories and rhymes, and use everyday materials and objects to help young children develop their understanding and enjoyment of mathematical concepts.

By relating ideas of number, shape, size and pattern to everyday contexts, stories and experiences, *Exploring Maths through Stories and Rhymes* improves confidence, increases understanding and develops children's desire to engage with maths. Offering a range of creative and exciting activities to encourage hands-on learning and discussion, the chapters of this book:

- include a range of step-by-step activities which are easily adapted to varying needs, ages and abilities;
- use popular stories and nursery rhymes as a way of engaging children with mathematical thinking;
- show how inexpensive, everyday materials can be used to encourage learning;
- include full colour photographs, photocopiable materials, vocabulary lists and key questions to help the reader get the most out of the ideas described.

This practical text will be a go-to resource for early years practitioners and students looking to adopt a creative approach to early years mathematics.

Janet Rees is an independent mathematics consultant who has a wealth of experience working with children, parents and teachers.

Exploring Maths through Stories and Rhymes

Active Learning in the Early Years

Janet Rees

Routledge
Taylor & Francis Group
LONDON AND NEW YORK

First published 2019
by Routledge
2 Park Square, Milton Park, Abingdon, Oxon OX14 4RN

and by Routledge
52 Vanderbilt Avenue, New York, NY 10017

Routledge is an imprint of the Taylor & Francis Group, an informa business

© 2019 Janet Rees

The right of Janet Rees to be identified as author of this work has been asserted by her in accordance with sections 77 and 78 of the Copyright, Designs and Patents Act 1988.

All rights reserved. The purchase of this copyright material confers the right on the purchasing institution to photocopy pages which bear the photocopy icon and copyright line at the bottom of the page. No other parts of this book may be reprinted or reproduced or utilised in any form or by any electronic, mechanical, or other means, now known or hereafter invented, including photocopying and recording, or in any information storage or retrieval system, without permission in writing from the publishers.

Trademark notice: Product or corporate names may be trademarks or registered trademarks, and are used only for identification and explanation without intent to infringe.

British Library Cataloguing-in-Publication Data
A catalogue record for this book is available from the British Library

Library of Congress Cataloging-in-Publication Data
Names: Rees, Janet, author.
Title: Exploring maths through stories and rhymes : active learning in the early years / Janet Rees.
Description: Abingdon, Oxon ; New York, NY : Routledge, 2019. | Includes bibliographical references and index.
Identifiers: LCCN 2018060186 (print) | LCCN 2019002993 (ebook) | ISBN 9780429452222 (eb) | ISBN 9781138322189 (hb : alk. paper) | ISBN 9781138322196 (pb : alk. paper)
Subjects: LCSH: Games in mathematics education. | Mathematics—Study and teaching (Early childhood)—Activity programs. | Rhyming games. | Mathematical recreations. | Educational toys.
Classification: LCC QA20.G35 (ebook) | LCC QA20.G35 R4375 2019 (print) | DDC 372.7/044—dc23
LC record available at https://lccn.loc.gov/2018060186

ISBN: 978-1-138-32218-9 (hbk)
ISBN: 978-1-138-32219-6 (pbk)
ISBN: 978-0-429-45222-2 (ebk)

Typeset in Bembo
by Apex CoVantage, LLC

Printed and bound in Great Britain by
TJ International Ltd, Padstow, Cornwall

Contents

Acknowledgements vi

Maths through stories: engaging young learners in maths 1

1 Teddy bears 14

2 Houses and homes 52

3 Big and little 93

4 Dinosaurs and dragons 122

5 Bags, boxes and baskets 153

6 Minibeasts and woodland animals 179

Resource sheets 216
References and bibliography 259
Index 262

Acknowledgements

I would like to thank both Carole and Anna Bean for their contributions to this book. Carole, for sharing her ideas, to Anna, for the illustrations in Goldilocks and the Three Bears, Little Red Riding Hood, The Elves and the Shoemaker, Jack and the Beanstalk and The Three Little Pigs.

I would also like to thank the many children who helped by letting me use their pictures and writing, especially Oliver, Henry, Jack, William, Sophie, James, Stephen and Thomas.

And last but not least, my husband Phillip, who dealt with me sensitively and with patience (mostly!) whilst I was writing. He also took the photos.

Maths through stories
Engaging young learners in maths

Introduction

This book presents maths through a thematic approach, and themes are set in the familiar context of stories. Each chapter aims to introduce children to a way of working that may impact on different areas of their lives. Children will be engaging in creative and exciting activities, all of which are centred on definite mathematical concepts. There will be many opportunities for children to take part in group and whole-class discussions where each child can have ownership of their own ideas and feelings and where each child engages in 'real life' communication with their peers as well as with adults.

Techniques used in this book

Throughout this book, meaning is established through thematic, integrative approaches, as well as through visual clues.

The book will give ideas and suggestions of how to develop children's understanding of mathematical concepts through both familiar an unfamiliar stories, practical everyday materials and strategies of total engagement. It will be suitable for children in the early years as well as Key Stage 1 and older children working at lower levels.

The book has three aims:

1. To introduce maths as an exciting and challenging subject in a non-threatening environment.
2. To develop confidence of teacher and child.
3. To involve both teacher and child in making and using ideas, thoughts and resources appropriate to each story.

'Teacher' in this sense refers to any adult working with a child, which covers:

- playing and exploring;
- active learning;
- creating and thinking critically.

This book can also be used as the basis of a parent evening, home/school links and parent/carer education. Stories include:

- early counting, addition/subtraction;
- shape, space and measures;
- storytelling;
- technology ideas;
- listening and attention;
- speaking, reading and writing;

- problem-solving;
- developing appropriate mathematical vocabulary through working in the non-threatening environment of stories.

The book shows how children can acquire language through extended listening experiences and negotiation of meaning through a relevant, meaningful context, which is necessary for effective language acquisition. It demonstrates how children can acquire language through a focus on meaning rather than on grammar, and it encourages children to involve many senses in the acquisition process.

The importance of mathematical language

I have, throughout this book, used mathematically correct language. However, it is important that, initially, all children are allowed to develop their own language in their own ways to describe what they have done or learnt. Encouraging discussion will help them do this. There is a comprehensive list of appropriate vocabulary to facilitate such discussion at the beginning of each chapter.

Acquiring language, especially mathematical language, when one word can mean different things (for example, volume, take away or table) can be challenging for the learner. This book identifies correct mathematical vocabulary and gives examples of where it can be used. Thus, the book addresses the issue of children failing to show mathematical ability because they do not understand the spoken or written instructions, are not familiar with mathematical vocabulary or are confused about mathematical terms. I believe that mathematical language is crucial to the development of children's thinking. If children do not have the vocabulary to talk about grouping or numbers, they may not make progress in understanding these areas of mathematical knowledge.

Throughout this book learners will experience situations that allow them to see relationships between mathematical concepts as well as relationships between home and school activities. They will draw connections from the real world and begin to understand how these connections can be made.

The teacher will see how a story can enhance children's learning and open the door to later learning. Children will start their academic learning journey by developing essential skills for later life.

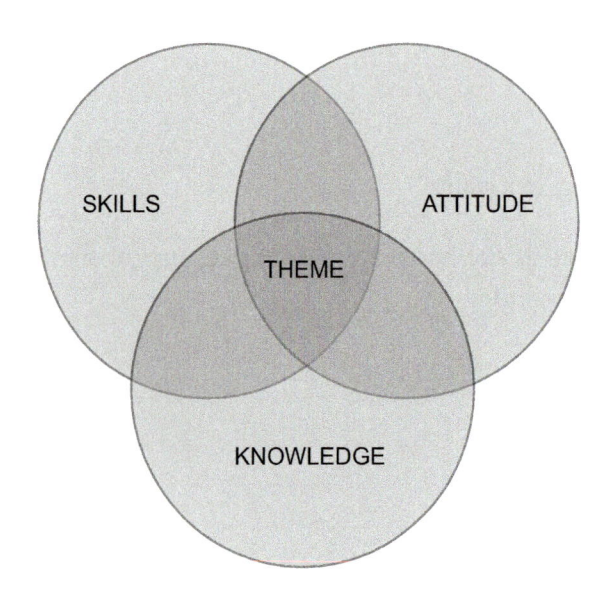

Using a thematic approach

Mathematics has traditionally been presented as a series of disconnected, abstract ideas. A thematic approach allows young children to explore ideas, both adult-led and child-initiated, in a context that allows connections to be made between these ideas.

Mathematics is a set of interrelated ideas: it is not made up of separate elements that are often taught in isolation from one another. When interest is allowed to develop, most children will want to pursue that interest rather than change course. A thematic approach allows the learner to extend their interest and thus maximises learning.

Maths in context

In the adult world, learning almost always arises as a result of some need within a specific context. This book looks at mathematics learning that happens in a way that is not abstract or disconnected from children's experiences. A wealth of evidence shows that self-initiated and -structured work leads to better motivation and understanding among pupils.

> *Mathematics is important because of its real world context. On the inverse, without context, it is often hard to identify with the beauty and power of mathematics.*
> (Marcus, Posted February 19, 2016 in Calculate Blog, Teacher PD)

Watanabe and Ischinger (2009)[1] categorise contexts as follows:

Personal contexts – of direct personal relevance to the learners.
Educational and occupational contexts – scenarios that learners might confront while at school.
Public contexts – situations experienced in everyday life.

Some authors also classify questions according to the purpose of the context. For instance, Vappula and Clausen-May (2006)[2] argue there are two purposes for contexts. The first purpose is getting the story across rather than supporting the acquisition of mathematical knowledge. The second purpose is to provide a model for the learner to think with.

Activity-based learning

I selected the themes in this book because, in my extensive work on the early years, I found them to stimulate children's interest and provide excellent opportunities to explore basic mathematical concepts. The activities suggested in this book encourage creativity and ingenuity, both of which are essential parts of learning mathematics. The development of mathematical processes by children is as important as the gaining of skills and knowledge. Processes such as collecting and displaying data, estimating, asking and answering questions, making hypotheses and testing ideas are at the heart of learning mathematics. It is through these activities that children will discover the real power of maths.

This begs the question of how to balance child-initiated and adult-led learning. Adult-led activities are based on our own understanding of what we should teach our children and what experiences they should have. We feel we are in control! However, we cannot control what children *learn* through this way of teaching.

I usually go with about a third of adult-led and a third of child-initiated activities, with the other third reserved for child-initiated activities that are then supported by an adult. But we must remember to be flexible. No watching a clock to make sure our timing is fixed. The individual needs of each child must be taken into account.

Each of the stories and subsequent activities included in this book allow this balance naturally.

Child-initiated play

Child-initiated play helps children develop ideas and take control of their learning. It is where the child approaches an idea and engages in activities of their own choice. It enables them to learn through first-hand experiences, allowing them to choose how to use resources to do so. When we take children away from their own choice of activity, we may actually be impeding their learning.

Child-led activities may start out as an adult-initiated activity; however, by allowing the child space and time, the child may extend the resources and ideas provided to create their own experience. It is important to strike a balance between adult-led and child-initiated activities to produce the best outcomes.

Adults play an important role in child-initiated play. They provide a safe environment for the child to explore and test out their ideas. They may also use the child's interests or next steps to develop play. It is important for the adult to understand the needs of the child. This can be done through observations and by building a solid relationship with the child in order to learn about their likes and dislikes.

Adult-led play

There are many reasons why early years settings provide adult-led play. At times it allows higher risk activities such as cooking or using equipment such as knives or scissors. At other times it allows children to carry out activities that otherwise they would not be able to manage by themselves. In these types of activities adults should also teach children how to use the equipment safely. Adult-led play is also beneficial when teaching new skills and concepts, such as playing a new game. It can also help children's language development.

However, there are also some possible disadvantages. Sometimes the learning is not very effective if children have not had time to solve problems or practice skills or develop their own ideas. There may not be an opportunity for the child to ask questions or to do things their own way. This prevents children from showing their independence.

Children working as a group

In learning together, children are encouraged to share ideas and the reasons for them. They can express their ideas orally, which will help them to communicate what they think and 'see'. It is often the process of explaining that fosters understanding. Misconceptions can be explored and learning from one another becomes a possibility. Successful group work depends on the teacher's ability to encourage children to take responsibility for themselves and others. In this way they can work as independently as possible.

Children working as individuals

Children are encouraged to ask their own questions and to follow their own lines of enquiry so that they can link their own learning to their current understanding. This book provides challenges for all pupils, although outcomes may differ from child to child. In this way, no child can fail! This is an extremely important aspect of maths that will build confidence and self-esteem.

The importance of stories

In every language in every part of the world, story is embedded in the history of the people. By telling stories we learn about ourselves, our cultures, our beliefs and our histories. We learn about make-believe and facts. In some cultures without written language, storytelling was the only way to convey a society's cultures, values and history (Egan 1986).

> *Stories have this crucial feature, which life and history lack, that they have beginnings and ends and so can fix meanings to events.*
>
> (Egan 1986)[3]

The story, Egan says, reflects a basic and powerful form in which we make sense of the world and experience. He suggests that children learn a great deal from stories and fantasy, and further, that this learning is fairly abstract. While the child may not be able to articulate abstractions, he or she uses them in making sense of stories. Egan explores how a teacher can use children's conceptual abilities to present school content in the form of stories.

In listening to stories, children internalise the features of the words being used. They can also be asked to contribute their own emotions and ideas.

Using different types of stories

Christopher Booker's *The Seven Basic Plots: Why We Tell Stories*[4] outlines the following story plots:

1. Overcoming the monster. For example, The Three Billy Goats Gruff, The Three Little Pigs.
2. Rags to riches. For example, Aladdin, Cinderella, The Elves and the Shoemaker.
3. The quest. For example, Jack and the Beanstalk.
4. Voyage and return. For example, Goldilocks and the Three Bears, Peter Rabbit.
5. Comedy. For example, Chicken Little, The Hare and the Tortoise, The Gruffalo.
6. Tragedy. For example, Little Red Riding Hood, Snow White and the Seven Dwarves.
7. Rebirth. For example, Beauty and the Beast, The Frog Prince.

Although not everyone agrees with his ideas, I do find them useful when planning different story sessions in different early years settings. This approach helps young children experience different emotions and gives them different problems to solve.

How can we use them?

By developing children's responses to the stories that they hear, they can develop a critical and creative way of thinking. For example, asking *what do you think happens next?* will give various responses from different children based on their knowledge and understanding so far in their development.

Discussing questions asked by the children will develop logical thinking and understanding.

Making a 3D model, collage or map illustrating the story will show understanding of the story, and being able to sequence the story is an important mathematical concept.

Making a class version of the story, altering the order of events or discussing possible outcomes develops communication skills, which are important in problem-solving.

Learning the language of maths through a story is a non-threatening way of learning new words. In maths, in particular, words and phrases, such as 'table' and 'take away', can mean something entirely different than in everyday conversation.

The structure of the book

The chapters of this book cover the following topics:

Teddy bears;
Houses and homes;
Big and little;
Dinosaurs and dragons;
Bags, boxes and baskets;
Minibeasts and woodland animals.

Each chapter follows a similar format:

A brief overview of the chapter explaining the rationale behind it;
A theme diagram;
Examples of children's work;
Questions and discussion points;
Mathematical activities linked to the story, which cover playing and exploring, active learning, creating and thinking critically;
References to the resource sheets section.

The first story in each chapter has extension activities related to a set of pictures. But the ideas given can be used for every other story in the chapter. Ideas are shown as photographs or diagrams. Examples of children's work are included. Vocabulary and questions are an integral part of the content.

The bibliography includes more stories relating to each theme.

Each chapter offers advice on how to use role play, maths trails, home/school links, easy-to-create resources, games and the outdoor environment to support mathematical learning. Additional guidance on planning for these types of activity is given in the following sections.

Role play

Role play gives children the opportunity to express themselves creatively and engage in storytelling. Children vocally enact the role that they are playing, which enhances their language development and communication.

In the role play area, whether inside or out, we aim to develop five basic skills:

Communication skills: speech, movement, creative activities, touch;
Motor skills: manipulation of self, materials and resources;
Discrimination skills: classifying, identifying, quantifying and causality;
Social skills: self-discipline, independence and interaction;
Attention skills: concentration, perseverance.

Such play is crucial to the development of young children. It allows them freedom to explore and make sense of the world around them. It can also allow problem-solving to develop, set new challenges and revise and consolidate previous learning. Children are allowed to follow their natural curiosity in whatever direction it takes. This can be unique for each child.

Play is most effective when children are provided with good, effective stimuli.

For further ideas, go to 'A Corner to Learn' by Neil Griffiths,[5] which is packed with ideas. There are further ideas for reading in the Bibliography.

Maths trails

A maths trail encourages both children and adults to look for, see and use maths in the school environment, village or town. Children gain first-hand knowledge of how maths is used to interpret the world in which we live. A trail can provide a variety of contexts in which maths ideas can occur and help children to use and apply the maths already learnt. They can also:

- allow children to familiarise themselves with their school. This is particularly important for children new to the school, either in the early years or after moving to the area;
- encourage children to work together, where they can discuss ideas and findings;
- encourage children and parents or carers to work together in a non-threatening environment;
- show that maths is more than just 'sums'. This is just as important for the children as for teachers and parents/carers;
- emphasise that maths is a whole and not a series of disconnected topics. We are now being encouraged to view maths not only as a subject in its own right but also to look for connections with other subject areas and within maths itself;
- emphasise the practical application of maths.

The purpose of trails

Maths trails can:

- encourage children to see how maths is used to interpret the world we live in;
- help children to see the relevance of maths outside the classroom;
- help children to see their school from a different viewpoint;
- encourage children to see maths in their own environment;
- introduce children to the wonder of mathematics.

By following a trail, children are encouraged to follow instructions, gather information through words or pictures, observe a variety of mathematical examples (both natural and man-made), solve problems and make decisions.

Writing a trail will take time, but I think you will find it to be worthwhile. For the younger children, make sure that there are enough helpers available. These can be older children, adults or parents and carers. This is a good opportunity to develop home/school links.

For the younger children it might be worth putting markers at key points, STOP labels or numbers/colours relating to the numbers/colours in the trail.

The best maths trails have a variety of activities, including those that can be solved on the spot, be extended later in the classroom or at home or involve recognition.

The trail should not be too long, as the interest and stamina of the younger children will begin to wane.

Developing a maths trail

Careful planning of a maths trail can enable children to engage with mathematical experiences which complement and extend those on offer in the classroom. The following practical ideas, based on the key areas of maths – *number and quantity, pattern, shape and space and measurement* – are offered as starting points for planning.

Developing a maths trail, either inside or outside the school building, puts mathematics where it belongs – in the real world! The trail need not be an extensive one; one set just within the confines of the classroom can be rewarding. Children can be given opportunities to see the importance of maths, and how it is used, within an environment with which they are familiar. However, it is possible to widen the trail to include the whole school (both buildings and people), the grounds and the larger community. Trails can be man-made, natural or a combination of the two.

Developing home/school links

Not only is developing home/school links possible, but it is essential! It is now widely recognised that the more involved parents are in their child's education, the better the pupil will perform at school. Greater parental engagement often motivates children to do well.

The UK Government first set out its strategy for securing parental engagement in a White Paper published in 1997 entitled 'Excellence in Schools'. The Paper suggested that there were three key points to improving the school-home partnership: providing parents with information; giving parents a voice; and encouraging parental partnerships with schools.

Remember, parents and teachers are equal, but not identical, partners. Parenting and teaching are two very different but closely related responsibilities. Generally, they are quite distinct, but there are also aspects of them which blur into each other. It is essential, therefore, that there be understanding and mutual respect between teacher and parent.

There are potential rewards for teachers, parents and children, in terms of trust and confidence building, if the process is openly negotiated, properly planned and carefully coordinated. Parental involvement does not present a threat to teacher professionalism, but provides an opportunity for teachers to demonstrate to parents the expertise, dedication and skill that has often been unseen and therefore unrecognised outside the four walls of the early years classroom.

Making and using split books

A split book is a book where the pages are cut enabling the pictures to be split.

For the best effect and to give your books a longer life you will need access to a laminator and a spiral binder. However, this is not essential. You can use bulldog clips to keep the edges together instead of a spiral binder. Many stationery shops offer a laminating service, so it is worth asking.

For this example, I have used Goldilocks and the Three Bears, but most stories can be made into similar books.

Use the pictures in the resource sheets section at the back of the book, colour and cut them out and glue them onto stiff paper or cards. You may also wish to add words to support the pictures.

The pictures can be made into split books where, in this example, the chairs and the beds can be matched to the bears.

Hint: When putting the book together, do not match them so that all the ones that go together are on the same page. This will cut down on discussion opportunities.

1 Using three sheets of A4 card, divide each sheet into three as shown below. Use daddy bear, his chair and bed to determine the width of each division. **Do not cut the pages at this stage**.

Daddy Bear	Chair	Bed

2 Stick the coloured pictures onto the card. Place one of the bears on the left-hand side of each sheet.
3 Put the chairs into the centre division and finally the beds on the right-hand side of each sheet.
4 You now have three sheets, each with a bear and its corresponding chair and bed.
5 If you like, you can also add words at this point.
6 You will also need pieces of card for the front and back covers, which can have the title of the story and appropriate pictures drawn by the children.
7 Now is the time to laminate the pages, if possible.
8 Place the pages onto the comb binder, if you have one, and punch the holes across the top.
9 Cut each of the pages along their marked lines.
10 Using the comb-binding machine, follow the instructions to bind the book. Or clasp the pages together with small bulldog clips.

Using puppets to help learning

Many young children love puppets. They use them to make everyday objects come to life through their play. Toys and dolls take an active role in children's play; they laugh and talk and argue. Young children will often use waste materials such as kitchen roll middles, cardboard boxes or packaging as a 'talking' partner. I have seen children talking to their fingers, toes and even knees as part of their play.

This section aims to give any adult who is privileged enough to be invited to join in with children's play some ideas to extend the thinking, vocabulary and play opportunities offered by puppets.

Puppets provide an ideal play situation for children who are withdrawn, or who have poor knowledge of language. Puppets provide a means of developing speaking and listening skills, especially when used in a paired situation, where the language can be modelled by another child or adult.

Puppets can be experienced through the senses of sight, touch and sound, as well as perhaps taste (with mouthing children) and smell (depending on what the puppets are made from). All children can participate in puppet sessions whatever their race, gender, disability or ethnic background.

Making puppets helps to develop both fine and gross motor skills and gives a purpose to 'gluing and sticking'.

Hint: Try leaving the puppets out, with maybe a few appropriate props, so that children can begin to develop their own stories. Resist the 'tidy up time' syndrome. Allow children to come back to the story they have started without having to start from the beginning again. This also allows others to become involved and offer support and suggestions.

Using characters from well-known stories may get them started. Familiar stories will give the children a structure, where they develop the story and join in with familiar phrases. With little or no adult interference, the children will be free to explore both the puppets and the story.

Be led by the children and their ideas and a whole new experience could open up for you all!

Simple stick puppets

Even small children can make these puppets. All you need are some small garden canes and something for a head. This could be a potato, a sponge, a cheese box, a stuffed sock or a ball. The stick can be attached as a central rod under the head and any arms or legs can be attached to the stick. They make excellent flying puppets such as fairies or butterflies. Allow the children to create their own unique characters.

Finger puppets

Finger puppets are very good for early language and finger rhymes. Children can make puppets that go with a story or a set of puppets for their own story. They can be drawn straight onto their fingers, or drawn onto cardboard tubes. If old gloves are available, the fingers can be cut off, or the whole glove can be used, giving the child five puppets to work with.

You may want to let the children play with a set of ready-made puppets before you offer the opportunity to make their own. In this case, do not interfere too much with their chosen story line. It may be very different from the original, but it is their story, not yours. (You could always make a story of your own!)

Sock puppets

A sock is a wonderful thing and can become lots of different characters. What the sock becomes depends on the child. By adding hair, eyes, ears and even hats, an old sock can become anything a child wants them to be.

Let children have ownership of the whole project and watch them develop. What started as a simple idea can become a whole world of make believe, engaging and motivating even the youngest child.

Developing games

We all know that children enjoy playing games. Experience tells us that games can be very productive learning activities.

Oldfield[6] (1991) says that mathematical games are 'activities' that:

- involve a challenge, usually against one or more opponents;
- are governed by a set of rules and have a clear underlying structure;

- normally have a distinct finishing point;
- have specific mathematical learning objectives.

But what are the benefits?

Davies[7] (1995), in a review of the literature to date at the time, summarised the advantages of using games in a mathematical programme:

- Meaningful situations – games create opportunities to apply mathematical skills;
- Motivation – children freely choose to participate and enjoy playing;
- Positive attitude – games provide opportunities for building self-concept and developing positive attitudes towards mathematics, through reducing the fear of failure and error;
- Increased learning – in comparison to more formal activities, greater learning can occur through games due to the increased interaction between children, opportunities to test intuitive ideas and problem-solving strategies;
- Different levels – games can allow children to operate at different levels of thinking and to learn from each other. In a group of children playing a game, one child might be encountering a concept for the first time, another may be developing their understanding of the concept, a third consolidating previously learnt concepts;
- Assessment – children's thinking often becomes apparent through the actions and decisions they make during a game, so the teacher has the opportunity to carry out diagnosis and assessment of learning in a non-threatening situation;
- Home and school – games provide 'hands-on' interactive tasks for use at both school and home;
- Independence – children can work independently of the teacher. The rules of the game and the children's motivation usually keep them on task.

One very important advantage to children playing games is that there will usually be very little, if any, language. The basic structures of some games are common to many cultures, and the procedures of simple games can be quickly learnt through observation. Children who are reluctant to participate in other mathematical activities will often join in a game and so gain access to the mathematical learning as well as engage in structured social interaction.

Exploring the outdoor environment

Being outside offers children unique opportunities and experiences. Mathematics is one of them. The environment plays a key role in supporting and extending children's learning and development. The school grounds, whether they comprise acres of land or more manageable plant pots, can provide the stimulus for a wide range of mathematical investigations and activities.

Careful planning of outdoor provision allows children to engage in mathematical experiences which complement or extend those on offer in the early years classrooms, and which build on their everyday experiences. But be aware that many opportunities for mathematical development arise from children's own interests and actions.

When we work with young children, we need to be aware of the role we play in supporting and extending children's mathematical understanding as well as knowledge. Introduce relevant mathematical vocabulary: *heavy, heavier than, light, lighter than* (see the vocabulary lists within individual chapters). Comment on their actions, such as 'you went **under** the slide', 'you're at the **top** of the ladder', 'you've made a lovely **pattern** with those pebbles'. Ask questions that encourage children to think mathematically and solve problems, such as 'do you think the crate will be high enough for you to reach the top of the wall?'

Look at patterns of bricks on the school wall, or how the windows fit together, or how paving slabs are used. Do not be afraid to use the correct mathematical words whenever possible (words such as 'tessellate' when looking at paving or bricks). Explain what it means and show an example. Allow children to choose their own objects to count: bikes, people on the slide, pebbles. Discuss what they find out together.

If you have basic outside equipment, think about how the basic activity (for example, riding a bike) can be enhanced. Maybe make a garage or number parking places. Or look at what happens to wheels as they go around.

Make a chart of your equipment such as the one in Table 0.1 and use it to lead discussion with others in your setting or with parents during an open day.

Table 0.1 Basic and enhanced play

Equipment	Basic use	Enhanced use
Slide	Climb the ladder and come down the slide.	Use material, scarves or curtains to cover the top and it can be Rapunzel's tower. Or hide underneath to make a cave or a dungeon.
Toy car	Ride round and round the outdoor space.	Develop a repair area, a parking lot with numbered spaces or a taxi rank; number the cars to match the parking spaces.
Skipping rope	Skipping.	Add balls, skittles and hoops and make an exercise area. Set time challenges so everyone has a turn with every piece.

Use the seasons and explore new growth in spring, flowers in the summer, leaves in autumn and animal tracks in the snow in winter.

On a sunny day, have a shadows challenge. Measuring needs to be done throughout the day, so normal activities may be disrupted. Use string or chalk to record what you find out.

Using bird food, measure how much will be put out (using non-standard measures for the younger children) in the morning. Note when it has all gone or measure it again later. Using words such as 'more', 'less', 'the same as' and 'none left' will enhance the learning.

Using balance scales to weigh amounts of different things such as apples, bread or seeds will be useful.

Reminding children to take care, draw minibeasts that can be found outside. Discuss the drawings when you are back in the classroom. Symmetry can be seen in all minibeasts.

Become shape detectives. Look for different shapes, using correct vocabulary, in the outdoor area. These can be natural or man-made shapes.

And finally . . .

As you go through this book, add notes of your own, things that worked and did not work so well. Be reflective; think about what you did or said or the resources that were available to the children.

But most of all, I hope you and the children you are working with enjoy and learn something new with every story.

Chapter 1: Teddy bears

Why bears?

A teddy bear is a type of toy that looks like a bear, normally a cub or baby bear. Teddy bears are found all over the world. In Russia, bears were used as children's toys for many years before they became popular in the United States. The teddy bear in Russia has been the subject of folklore or stories for many years. Teddy bears are often toys for children, but they are also used to comfort people or show love and affection. Teddy bears may often have human-like features, and they are usually small and soft. Early-twentieth-century teddy bears were made from mohair, the hair of goats. Now they are usually made from synthetic fabrics.

The teddy bear is often a theme or topic in early years classrooms, and they have been found to comfort and support children. The teddy bear can also be also used to teach children about different places. In a story, the bear can travel and send postcards to the readers, a theme exemplified by the story of Paddington Bear and his adventures with the Brown family. There are books, films, games, songs and a wealth of other material built around bears. Teddy-bear books help children learn to read and also hold fond memories for parents and grandparents.

Thanks to Sophie for her mummy bear (with fidgit spinner!)

Chapter 1: Teddy bears

Mathematics

Sorting, ordering by height, length and weight

Matching

Comparing

Number 3

Counting, understanding and using numbers

Ordinal numbers

Cardinal numbers

Discussing

Exploring capacity

Exploring volume

Calculating simple addition and subtraction problems

Describing shapes and measures

Problem-solving

Passage of time

Estimating

Sharing equally

Sequencing

One-to-one correspondence

Representing and interpreting data

Using logic

Shape: triangle, circle, hexagon

Mathematical processes

Choosing appropriate equipment

Being systematic

Presenting results

Selecting materials

Simplify a problem

Recording systematically

Classifying

Communicating

Talking about work in hand

Explaining how a procedure works

Thinking logically

Ordering

Predicting

Discussing with others

Generalising

Recognising patterns

Completing a task

Looking for patterns

Estimating

Vocabulary

Counting numbers

Count one, two, three . . .

Comparing and ordering numbers

First, second, third, compare, match, most, least, more than, less than, the same as, how many. . .?, enough, count, more, less, too many, too few

Adding and subtracting

More, altogether, make, take away, how many are left?

How many have gone?

Solving problems

Reasoning about numbers or shapes

Pattern, count, sort, group, sort, same, different, list

Problems involving 'real life' or money

How much, how many, buy, sell

Money, coin, penny, pence, cost, spend

Measures

Measure, size, compare, guess, enough, not enough, too many, too few, just over, just under

Length

Length, width, big, bigger, biggest. Tall, taller than, tallest

Small, smaller than, smallest, short, shorter than, shortest. Middle size, long, too long, too short, taller, shorter, height

Mass

Lighter, lighter than, light, heavy, heavier than, weigh, balances, scales, grams

Capacity

Full, empty, holds

Time

Morning, night, before, after

Exploring patterns, shape and space

2D shapes

Triangle, circle, hexagon, pattern

Position, direction and movement

In, out, under, behind, in front, beside, on top, inside, outside, next to, over, between, through, under, back, front, on, off, below' above

General

What do you think?

Why do you think that?

What comes next?

Goldilocks and the Three Bears

Chapter 1: Teddy bears

Many children have a teddy bear, and we tell lots of stories about bears.

The story of Goldilocks and the Three Bears gives a wonderful opportunity to introduce mathematical ideas about sorting and ordering, matching and comparing, using vocabulary appropriately as well as to introduce early number work.

Getting to know the story

A small bear, a middle-sized bear and a great, huge bear live together in a house in the woods. Each of these bears has their own porridge bowl, chair and bed. One day they make porridge for breakfast, but it's too hot to eat, so they take a walk in the woods while their porridge cools. While they are out, a young girl called Goldilocks comes to their house. She looks through a window, peeps through the keyhole and lifts the latch. She calls out, but no one is there so she walks in. Goldilocks is very hungry and is pleased to see the bowls of porridge, but the only one she can eat belongs to baby bear. As she sits on the small chair, it breaks. Goldilocks goes upstairs and sees the three beds. She lays on them each in turn but falls asleep in the smallest bed. When the bears come back they find Goldilocks still in the small bed. She wakes, sees the bears, jumps out of the window and runs all the way home. She is never seen again.

Developing a bear environment

As this is the first story about bears, prepare a section of the room as a bear-only environment. This can be a large or small space, but it needs to be where the children can take part in activities and become involved in the life of a bear. A large cardboard box on its side will do.

Cover surfaces with material or wrapping paper showing bears, start a collection of different types, sizes and colours of bears, and use old birthday cards as a background display.

Display a selection of story books that include bears.

As you work through the three bears, add plates, bowls, cups, cutlery and a table cloth. Display children's work and any books they make.

If possible, add three chairs of different sizes and a table.

Improvise if necessary, using junk materials, remnants of material or dough objects. (See the dough recipe in the resource sheets section.)

Discuss the display with the children. *'What can you see? Which bear do you like the best? Tell me about your favourite bear. Are the bears all the same as each other? Show me two that are not the same. Can you find me a taller bear or a shorter bear? Have you ever seen a real bear on the television or in a zoo? Tell us about the bears you have seen'*.

Developing a prop box

When setting up a play corner, a prop box is a useful starting point. But what is a prop box?

A prop box contains objects or resources that make a connection to a specific role play focus or a series of linked activities. But, in fact, the box can be a bag, a plastic open box, a closed box, a small suitcase or part of (or an entire) vegetable rack. On the whole, having the same container makes life easier over time. Boxes, clearly labelled, can be stacked so that in the future when you approach that particular role play theme, a box will be ready and waiting for you. Over time, you may need to throw away and replace some of the pieces and even introduce new ones.

It is also useful to clearly label the boxes with a list of the contents.

Remember that focusing on a theme for a prop box does not mean that activities are restricted. They are there for children to use or not. *They* make the choice. But for some children, the fact that they have a starting idea allows them to develop and add to it.

In each box think about what will be useful to both you and the children. For example, include relevant books (fiction and non-fiction), maths and writing resources, songs and rhymes on cassette/CD, labels, banners and blank paper of different colours and shapes.

Other cultures, languages, traditions and artefacts should be in your boxes as much as possible. Children with special needs also need to be considered, as they have a right to access all of the activities. For example, use resources that link with the senses, such as noisy toys and books; musical instruments, such as bells and tambourines; and tactile materials and surfaces, such as velvet, sandpaper and faux fur fabric. Use sand and water when it naturally fits with the story. For snacks, after checking for allergies and medical conditions, children can be offered different types of honey on different types of bread or toast.

I have also found that, when working with parents or carers, it is useful to have a list of appropriate mathematical vocabulary that can be used during play or in discussion later in the day.

It is important to remember that children should be invited to add to the list of props and care for the equipment in the boxes. At some points during or after play, the contents need to be checked and put away. A pictorial list can help children in 'ticking off' the items as they are packed away.

Developing a role play area: Cottage Corner

This corner can be an area designed for a week (or more) of use. Or it can be a large cardboard box on its side. A table will do just as well, covering the top with material that gives the impression of a cave underneath. Allow free play in the Cottage Corner at first. Then introduce some ideas such as setting the table. Have lengths of material (the right size for each bear) to act as beds. Involve children in the measuring activity. This can be as simple as laying each bear on top of or beside the length offered to see if it is *too long, too short* or *just right*. Using non-standard measures would be suitable for older children. Have the right number of cups, plates and bowls. Match each cup, plate and bowl to each bear to encourage counting to three. Add a table cloth that will be the right size to cover the table. Offer different cloths and ask the children to choose the one they think is the best fit. The Cottage Corner will allow children to sort all sorts of items such as food, cutlery and cushions into sets of three.

Start sharing food between the three bears (things like grapes, small biscuits or small pieces of cheese). This can be part of snack time. Try sharing a bunch of nine grapes equally between three dishes. How many does each bear have? This is an early introduction to repeated subtraction leading to division.

Ask children to draw or paint pictures of three bears to decorate the inside of the box or hang on a wall in Cottage Corner.

And at the end of a session or a day, tidying the Cottage Corner can be another sorting and counting activity.

Sorting the bears

Choose a bear to be the mummy bear.

Ask the children to find a bear that is *taller* and a bear that is *shorter*.

Name them 'daddy bear', 'mummy bear' and 'baby bear'. You can use labels or dress them in appropriate clothes.

Talk about one bear being *taller than* or *shorter than* another bear. But there is a problem about mummy bear, because she is *taller than* the baby but *shorter than* daddy. Discuss how she can be both taller and shorter at the same time.

Exploring the story

Ask the children if they know the story of Goldilocks and the Three Bears. Ask them to tell you what they already know. Can they sequence the story? Can they tell you what happens *before* or *after* an event? What comes next?

Read the story of Goldilocks and the Three Bears using the three bears from the previous activity. Hold each bear up as they are mentioned in the story or give three children a bear each and ask them to hold them up when they are mentioned. This will increase concentration as the story is read. As the children become more familiar with the story, ask them to make the sound of each bear growling instead of holding up the bears. (Audience participation!) Do all bears make the same sound? Will baby bear have the same growl as mummy or daddy bear?

Developing practical understanding of capacity and volume

Put the three bears' cups and bowls in a sand and/or water tray. Allow free play before you ask the children to find which cup/bowl holds the *most/least*. Order the cups/bowls according to capacity. Encourage the children to check their guesses by filling one container with water or sand and pouring this into a different cup/bowl. This can also be done with other containers such as a jug or plastic pencil pot.

Making beds for the bears

Encourage children to choose a bear and make a bed for it. Use vocabulary to introduce the idea or relative size. *Is this bed too long for the bear? Find a bear that will fit in this bed. Find a bear that is too short for this long bed.*

Children can choose a bear or bring one in from home. Let the children experiment with ways of making a bed for their bear. They can use blocks, bricks, LEGO, cardboard boxes or cut strips of paper and glue them together. Allow them free choice, even if you think that their choice may not work too well. Children can always change their minds and start something new.

Discuss the bears and beds. Use words such as *big enough, long enough, too short, too long, too wide*.

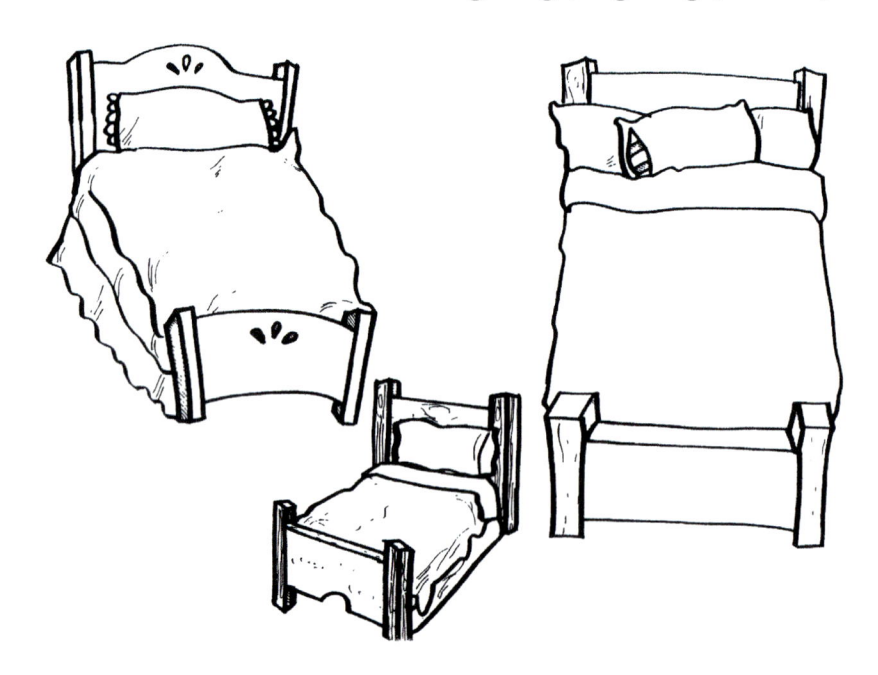

After the children have made their beds, discuss the size of pillows and sheets. Have three different sizes of pillows and sheets. Once the beds have been made, challenge the children to find the 'right' bear for each bed. (Be aware that some children may try to squash daddy bear into baby bear's bed just because they like the colour of the sheet.) Allowing children to change their mind if they need to can facilitate learning. It is even better if they can give you a reason for the change.

Ordering weight

Choose two bears and compare their weights. Simple balance scales will be ideal. Label the bears '*heavy*' and '*light*'. Use vocabulary such as *heavier than* and *lighter than*.

Add more bears to the weighing queue and compare their weight to the two already weighed. Can children make a line of four or five bears going from the lightest to the heaviest?

Ordering height

Choose three bears of different heights and ask the children to put them in order of height.
Which is the smallest? Which is the biggest? Which is the tallest? This bear is the smallest. He will be the first in our line. This bear is the tallest. He will be the third in our line. Where should this bear go? It is taller than this bear, but shorter than this bear.

This can be done several times with different sets of bears. One bear that was the tallest can become the shortest within a different set. And the shortest can become the tallest in another set. Discuss what is happening with the children. How can a bear be both tall and short?

Or they can compare the heights of all the bears. For example, a child can choose any bear from the selection and then collect all the bears that are *shorter than* or *taller than* their bear.

The number 3

Playing in and around the three bears' cottage is essential for children to make sense of the number 3, which is shown in different ways: bowls, plates, cups, chairs, beds made from different lengths of fabric on the floor. Initially allow free play but gradually introduce more structured play; for example, set the table and put the right bear on the right bed. Link these activities with other sorting of items into three. These can be pencils, paint brushes or blocks. Collect natural materials from outside as well, such as fir cones, sticks and leaves. As the children are playing in the 'house', introduce the idea of matching using one-to-one correspondence. '*Are there enough bowls for each bear? What if baby bear brings a friend for tea? How many bowls will we need?*'

Encourage the children to collect as many examples of '3' as they can find for an interest table.

Discuss ways of making three. For example, 1 + 1 + 1, 1 + 2, 2 + 1, 3 + 0, 0 + 3. Use and display both the words and the numbers to show 1, 2 and 3. This can be developed as a home/school link.

Have children look around their home or garden and collect sets of three. Encourage adults to ask the children about their sets. Use both ordinal and cardinal numbers, such as *one, two and three* and *first, second and third*. Maybe parents can come into school, with their child, to talk to other children about the sets that they have made at home. Bring photos or drawings or the sets themselves.

Hint: A set of three live chickens doesn't work out too well!!

Being creative with paint

Encourage children to mix their own colours in order to paint a picture of a bear. This may be messy, but children will be learning early ideas about ratios. Encourage children to think about quantities of colour that are going to be mixed. For example, *if I put a spoonful of this colour in and a spoonful of this colour, I think that . . . will happen. Let's try it and see. What do you think will happen if you put more blue in this pot? What do you think will happen when you mix in some white?* You may want to limit the number of colours you provide. Remember, to a child, not all bears need to be brown.

Ideas for using the pictures

You will find photocopiable pictures in the resource sheets section.

Attach hook-and-loop fastener or magnetic tape to the back of each picture to illustrate the story. Compare the size of the bears. Sequence the story. Ask children to tell the story using the pictures. Emphasise mathematical vocabulary within the story such as *big, bigger, biggest, small, smaller, smallest*.

Discuss other words which could be used to describe the sizes of the bears, such as *little, short, small, tiny*.

Sequence the events in the story. This can be done as a group using larger pictures or by individuals or pairs with smaller pictures. Give smaller pictures to each child so they can make their own story book.

As the children are playing, encourage language development by counting and ordering the bears, chairs and beds: *one two three, first second third*.

Begin simple addition by using the bears sitting at a table: one bear is at the table, one more sits down. *How many now?*

Similarly introduce subtraction by having three bears sitting down for tea. Baby bear needs to go to bed. *How many bears are left?*

Vocabulary for positioning can be used through play situations such as: mummy bear is *next to* baby bear. Daddy bear is *next to* mummy bear. Baby bear is *between* daddy and mummy bear.

Making a split book

Make a split book described on pages 9–10 in the introduction.

Chapter 1: Teddy bears   23

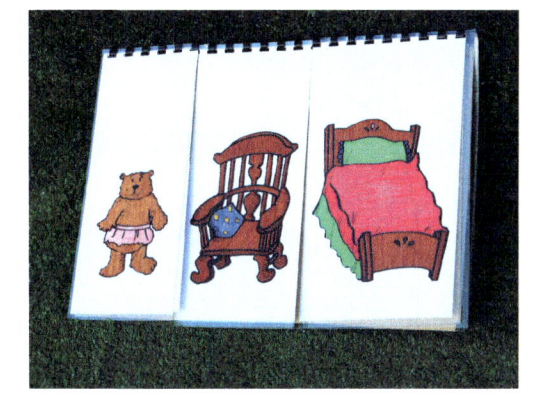

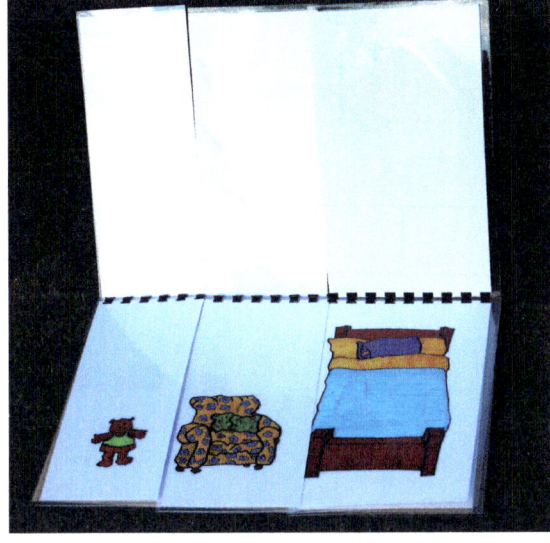

Ask children to sort the pages so that the correct bear is shown with their own chair and bed. Remember: at the beginning, many children will sort according to what they think or want the combinations to be. Although you may have a plan for the 'correct' answer, that may turn out not to be every child's plan. Ask them to tell you why they sorted the pictures in the way that they did.

Put the books in the book corner, the prop box or in Cottage Corner so that children can have free access to them. Many children I have worked with have used them to tell stories to the bears or to their friends.

Designing and developing games

Use any of the pictures to create board games of Goldilocks' route through the forest to the bears' cottage. The rules can reflect the skills to be developed, such as counting or colour recognition. The game shown next has no numerals, which may confuse younger children, and the players can go either way round the board. Give a few simple rules at the beginning but make them more complex as time goes by.

After playing the games, allow children to design and make their own. They can play their game with a friend and tell the rest of the class about it. Or take it home to play with siblings and adults.

A full-size version of the game can be found in the resources sheets section.

Developing trails

Develop a trail through the forest, which can be a tabletop, across the floor, outside drawn in chalk or an actual forest if you have one! Use 3D models to represent trees, bushes or flowers. Include some mini beasts made from paper plates or cups.

Use outdoor play equipment to develop a cottage: *under* the slide, *in* a shed or using large blocks or wooden bricks. Even old tyres will work. Remember to use the children as a source of ideas. It will be more relevant to their learning if they choose and make their own cottage.

Home/school links

Many adults at home want to help with children's learning but are perhaps not very confident about how. Write a short pamphlet for children to take home with the pictures to make a split book or story sequencing. Make sure that the instructions are very clear. Add illustrations if necessary. Give ideas of what can be done with it, using correct mathematical language. Include questions to ask such as '*Which bear do you think this is? Why do you think that? Let's look at the other bears. Do you want to change your mind?*' Do the same sort of thing with the beds and chairs.

Shape

The notion of learning about shapes in a practical context is not new, but some children are still being taught the name of shapes without looking at their properties. This leads to confusion later, such as the age-old question of 'Is a square a rectangle?' Look at the properties of both and that will give you the answer. I have worked with young children who will turn a triangle the 'right way up' to make it become a triangle!

Why does this happen? I think there are several reasons.

First, especially with triangles, a child sees them in books, on worksheets and even in maths dictionaries as the 'right way up' and this is never questioned. Allow children plenty of free play with shapes, pointing out properties as well as names. A triangle is always a triangle, whichever way it is presented. A square *is* a type of rectangle, however much you do not want it to be.

Second, when triangles are drawn by adults, many will be drawn in the conventional way. How about drawing a triangle like this? ▽ Or this? ▷ Or this? ◁ Count the corners and sides each time to reinforce the properties as well as the name of the shape.

Third, how many early years settings have all types of triangles within their shape boxes? The equilateral triangle seems to be the most common, but there are others which can be investigated.

Circles can be a bit tricky. We all want the children to become as independent as possible when working and playing, but anything that involves scissors and paper, for most young children, will not result in a circle. It will give a child's representation of a circle. And that is not the same thing.

When developing ideas and knowledge of circles, I tend to use actual circles. We can talk about corners (none), straight sides (none) and possibly even angles (none). We can look around the classroom and outside to find examples of circles. We can investigate what circles do and how/why they are used. We can plan shape trails where we just look for circles. We can use pre-gummed shapes to make circle designs and we can make puppets that show circles being used as parts of the puppet.

Puppets

Making bear puppets so that children can develop their own storytelling techniques or maybe devise a play or performance is a wonderful experience. Have your camera ready!

To make a very simple one, start with a paper bag, a plate or saucer to draw around, and a pair of eyes and a bobble for a nose (a circle of felt would do). Try to use different textures for the bear's head, eyes, ears and nose. It adds a certain something to the puppet. Remember, a child may want a bright green bear with purple ears. Go with the flow!

Unaided bear

Aided bear

An alien bear, Henry, age 4

A happy bear, William, age 2 (almost 3!)

Or use the very humble kitchen roll middles. The addition of wiggly eyes makes them seem more 'alive', but they are not necessary. Tall bears, short bears, fat bears and thin bears can all be included.

Using your imagination

Best of all, ask children to write a story about their own bear.

The teddy can walk.
The teddy can walk

hItoyismiskut e b...anbonsot

he has eyes
he is hard

the ted is mes is disrl fm ted is muın adrs ne nted is munrus den mteau mu teddus mın sat mau tre is rts cend

Add some more illustrations to show a day in the life of your bears and track through the events in order as the story likens itself to the Three Bears and their day. Ask questions such as '*What do you think would happen if you went into your bedroom and saw someone asleep in your bed? How would you feel? What would you do?*'

Do you like porridge? Data handling

Have you ever eaten porridge? Did you like it?

In your setting make two or three different types of porridge. One bowl has porridge made with milk, one has porridge made with milk with a small amount of sugar added,

Chapter 1: Teddy bears   27

and the last one is porridge made with water. Check for allergies or special diets beforehand, and then give each child their own spoon. Once the porridge has cooled, ask the children to taste a small portion of each type of porridge. Rinse each spoon after tasting each type. Give each child a piece of paper for them to draw a picture of their face, with a big smile. Design a chart with each type of porridge showing. Children stick their face picture on the chart according to the porridge they like the best.

If possible, use three different coloured bowls.

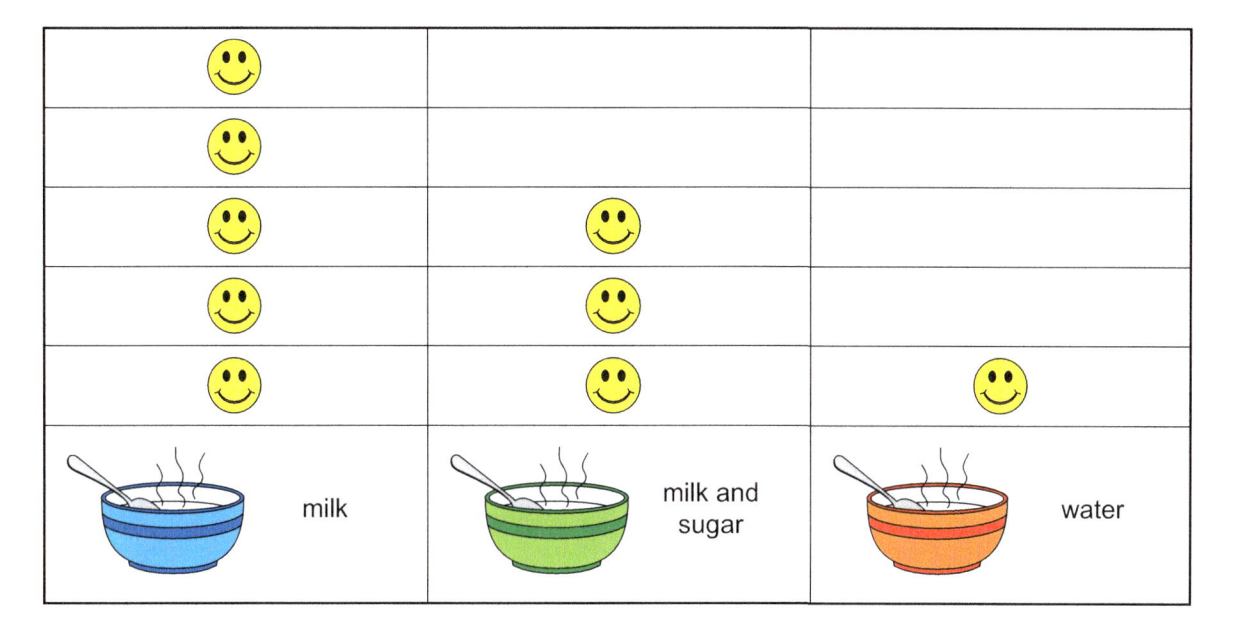

milk	milk and sugar	water
😊		
😊		
😊	😊	
😊	😊	
😊	😊	😊

Talk about the results. Ask questions such as '*Which did you like the most? Which didn't you like? Can you tell me why? Which porridge was liked the most in our class? How do you know? Which porridge was liked the least? How do you know? How many children liked the porridge made with milk/milk and sugar/water?*'

The ideas from this first story can be adapted and used for the other bear stories in this chapter. Remember, children usually have a wealth of ideas. Do not dismiss them; encourage them!

Mr Brown's Fantastic Hat by Ayano Imai
Published by Michael Neugebauer

'Who needs friends?' thinks Mr Brown. 'I can suit myself and wear my smart hat all day long'. Try as he might, however, Mr Brown is lonely. But when a woodpecker decides Mr Brown needs some company, his life is transformed.

Getting to know the story

'Mr Brown had no friends and he didn't want any'. So begins the tale of a reclusive bear who finds that his hat becomes a home to a great number of birds. As time passes, he grows fond of their company – a bird nestles in a teacup; a tiny tree grows out of the dining table.

This story about friendship will lead to a lot of discussion with children about friends. Read the story to the children. Discuss what it means to be a friend and to have a friend. '*Who is your friend? What do you do with your friends? How would you feel if you didn't have friends? Why do you think Mr Brown didn't want friends?*'

'*Did you like this story? Which part did you like the most? Do you think Mr Brown was happy with his new friends? Would you like a hat like Mr Brown's? If you could choose, what animal would you have living inside your hat?*' Discuss the possibilities and the pros and cons of each. Too big? Too heavy? Too noisy?

Which hat?

Develop a hat guessing game. Use clues such as:

1. I wear it to keep my head warm in wintertime.
2. A princess, a prince, a king or queen would wear this.
3. I wear one when I ride my bike.
4. I wear it to keep my head dry.
5. I wear it when I put out fires.
6. There are several colourful ones in the circus. Who would wear a colourful hat?
7. A space man wears one.

This could be linked to pictures so that younger children have visual clues as well as the spoken words.

As an extension, choose two cards and weave them into a story. Demonstrate the idea first so that the class can see how the activity develops. Then ask children to choose two cards and make a story that has both hats in it. They can tell their story to their friend, or they can take the cards home and tell the story to someone there.

Role play area

Allow the hat from the story to inform the role play area just as the number 3 did with the Three Bears. Set up a hat shop in a corner of the area.

Talk about hats in general. '*Why do we wear hats? What kind of hats do we wear in the summer? What kind of hats do we wear in the winter? What hats are worn to protect our head? When you ride your bike, what do you wear? Tell me about other hats that you have seen or that you know about.*'

Over the years I have gathered a huge collection of hats. When I am involved in developing this story in an early-years setting, I make sure that I wear a different hat each morning as we start the day.

Each hat that I wear goes into a 'hat shop corner' to boost the number of hats for sale. In this corner I try to have a hat number line which can be added to when introducing new numbers, a variety of hats (charity shops are very good sources of these), a till, real money for spending and giving change, paper, pads and pencils, old mobile phones, phones with a handset, links and tape-measures for measuring around heads. These tend to be a bit safer than string or ribbon. A book of hat designs made from cut-out pictures from magazines is a nice resource and can be added to at any time. These design books are made by the children so sometimes half of the hat may be missing as cutting skills still need to be enhanced.

Allow children to explore freely in the role play area before giving specific tasks. Try to include hats that could be worn at a wedding, when going shopping or to a sports centre.

Developing a prop box: making paper hats

Hats can be very difficult things to store. You may need to invest in a row of hooks or only use collapsible ones. Paper hats are easy to make and can be sent home with the children at the end of this particular topic.

So, how do you measure around your head? How can you make a hat that fits if you do not know how big your head is?

Start with a simple hat.

Making a paper cone

Choose paper that is twice as tall as the hat you want to make. Pick a colour that works for the type of hat you are making. For example, grey for a soldier hat, pink for a princess hat, black for a witch hat.

Draw a semicircle on the paper using a plate. This needs to be twice as tall as you want the hat to be. Draw a semicircle along one edge of the paper. This way the straight edge will be even.

Cut around the curved edge of the shape. Decorate it with paint, markers, stickers or glitter. Do not put anything too heavy on the paper and give enough time for everything to dry.

Roll the paper into a cone and secure the seam. This can be done with tape, staples or glue. Curl the straight edges of the paper together until they meet, then overlap them until you get a cone. The more you overlap the edges, the narrower the cone will be.

Let the hat dry before you wear it!

This next hat can be for a pirate or a sailor.

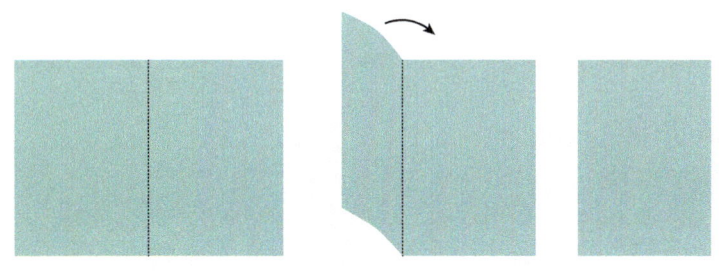

Fold the paper vertically.

Open the paper and fold it horizontally, then unfold again.

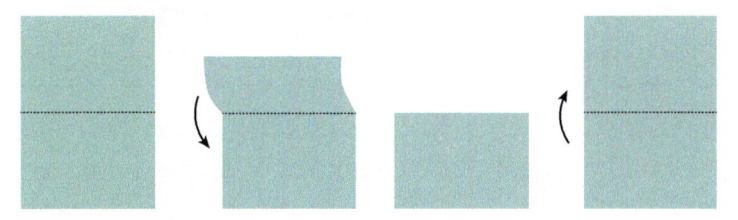

Turn the paper so that the folded end is at the top. Fold along the top corners into the centre, making sure to keep them even. Fold one bottom flap up.

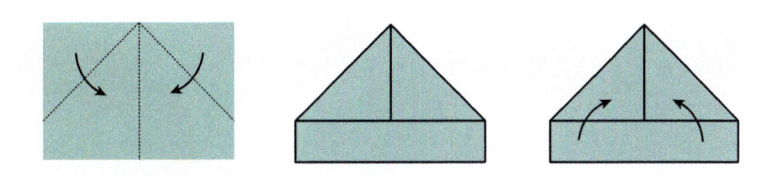

Turn the paper over and fold the other bottom flap up.

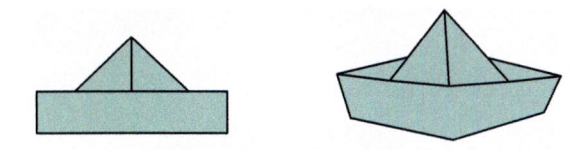

Sorting the birds

Which birds should nest at the bottom of the hat and which at the top?

Using bricks or blocks, build a tower to represent the birds. Investigate what happens when you put the small, light birds at the bottom and the heaviest birds at the top. What happens when you build a tower the other way up, with the biggest, heaviest birds at the bottom and the smallest and lightest at the top? Discuss with the children the best way for the birds to nest in Mr Brown's hat. Try not to give them the 'right' answer. Ask them to give you reasons for their thoughts and ideas. (There may be one you have not thought of.)

Using pictures of different birds printed from the internet or cut from magazines, or using plastic bird figurines, sort them into sets or groups according to attributes. For example, this bird is blue, this bird is yellow. Or this bird has spots, this bird does not have spots. Try to avoid always having positive attributes such as 'this has'; occasionally bring in negatives as well, such as 'this doesn't have'.

Use PE hoops to sort the birds.

Ask children to sort them in a different way, choosing their own rules. Use the results as discussion points with the group or the class.

Count the birds in each set. Older children can draw the circles with the birds in their right group and write the number in each set.

This is an easy introduction to data handling, using what the students will eventually come to recognise as Venn diagrams.

Measuring

A hat that fits

Pose the question, '*How can we make a hat that fits your friend's head? It can't be too big, or too small. How can we do that?*'

This is a problem you have presented to the children. It has become their problem, not yours. Do not give ideas or solutions too quickly. Take what the children suggest. Try out their ideas. Do they work? Children make the decision, not you! Some may try measuring around with cubes or blocks. Some may use string or wool. Some may just look at their friend's head. After a while, I usually say, '*I have an idea as well. Do you want to see my idea?*' This is the time to lead the children into thinking in a different way. But it is up to them if they take up your idea or not. Make sure that your idea is a good idea and not too complicated.

One resource that I love to use is learning links. They look a little like large paper clips. They are suitable for children aged 3 and older. You can use them for counting, making patterns and sorting.

This is how it works: '*I want you to look at your friend and see how big you think his/her head is. They may need to turn around so that you can see the back of their head as well as the front. Join links together until you think you have enough to fit around their head. Join the two end links so that you make a round shape. Try it on your friend's head. Is it too big? Is it too small, or just right? Add or take away links until the "hat" fits*'.

Use other vocabulary, such as '*compare, guess, enough, not enough, too many, too few, just over, just under*'.

Each child now has the *measurements* for both their own head and the head of their friend. Unclip two links and lay the chain flat. Cut a strip of paper the same length, plus a bit more which can be used as an overlap. Now you have a perfectly fitted hat, ready to be decorated.

Supply glue, scissors, paper, rulers, tape-measures and any resources that you have used or equipment the children need. It can include non-standard measures as well as standard measures.

Finish with a hat parade where all of the children wear the hat that has been made for them by their friend or which they have made themselves. Take photos to be used as discussion points or in a display later.

Representing and interpreting data

As an extension to this activity, you can make a pictogram of three columns or rows. Each child draws a picture of their own face ready to stick on the pictogram.

The results will show how many link hats were too big, too small or just right.

The more children use these links, the better they will become at estimating and measuring height, length and width.

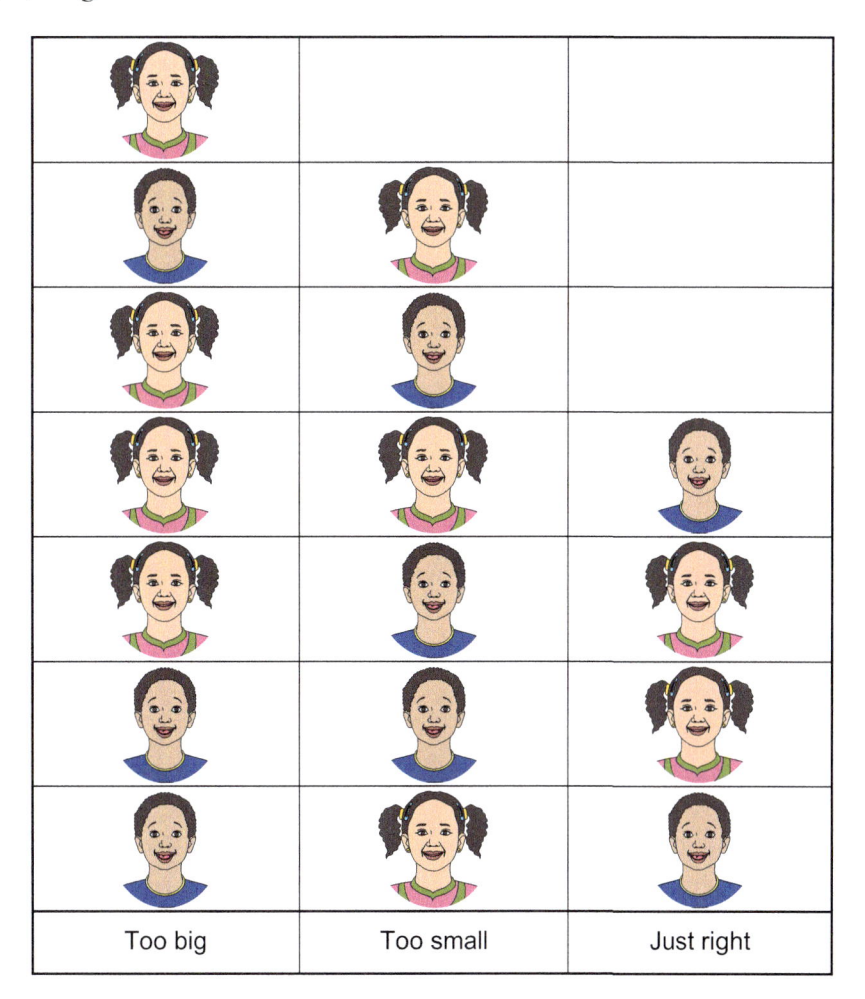

Too big	Too small	Just right

Designing and developing games

The quickest and easiest table-top game to make would be one that uses the idea of the hat supporting bird life. This simple game introduces picture matching.

Draw a large outline of Mr Brown's hat and draw squares on it to represent the bird homes. Inside each square draw a different type of bird, again using the story as a guide. Make a set of cards that duplicates the set drawn on the game board. Cut these cards and place them face down on the table.

One at a time, the children turn over a card and match it to its partner on the hat.

To extend this, make two sets of identical cards, cut them and place them face down on the table. Children turn over a card one by one as before and match it to a card on the hat. With two identical sets, there will be a time when a child turns over a card that matches one on the hat which is already covered. This introduces the 'miss a turn' experience, which children will encounter when playing games later in life. If a child has a card that cannot be used, that card is placed once again in the face-down pile.

If you like, you can make the child who covers the last picture the winner. But be careful about introducing winners and losers too soon. Once a child starts to lose a game, they will not want to play it again!

A second game could be made by following a trail though the park where Mr Brown walks.

A simple track game would involve counting forwards, maybe backwards as well, according to the rules.

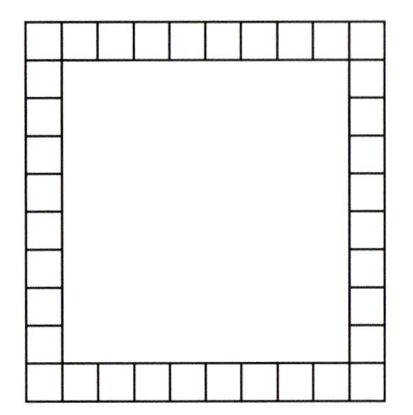

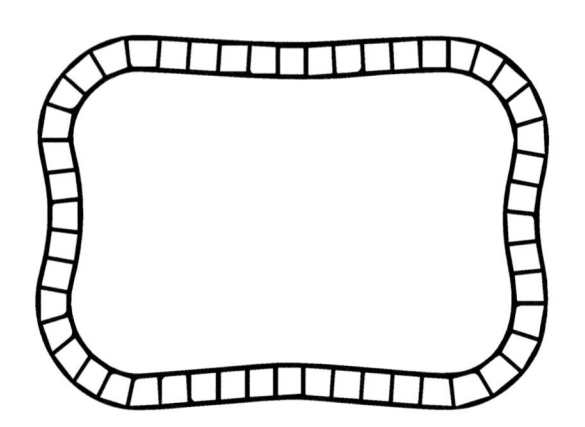

Liven the tracks up by putting trees, people, birds, seats and other park 'furniture', but make sure you have a definite start and finish point.

Use fewer rules for younger children and more complex rules for older children.

You can write numbers on the track or leave them blank. You can add rules to the track such as 'walk on two spaces', 'take a step backwards' or 'sit in the sun and miss a turn'. Draw some birds on the track. If you land on a bird, have another turn. You could make a track outside by drawing with chalk or use an outside play area to represent the park.

Developing trails

Developing a time trail that begins with Mr Brown living alone and having no friends and goes through the stages of the first woodpecker to the last page where the tree has grown will give children a sense of time passing by, sequencing the story. It will also show how changing seasons affect us as well as animals.

This can be done by producing a time line (similar to a number line but with no numbers). Work with pictures going from left to right (as in a number line) to show the addition of time. Children can paint, use a collage, make models, write parts of the story or contribute to a whole area of Mr Brown displayed on a wall.

Home/school links

If you have space, build a bird-friendly environment outside the classroom. Invite parents to come and help their children set this up.

Build a simple bird table

Choose the pieces of wood you want to use. This can be recycled or new wood. Make sure that they are not already painted with anything that might be toxic to both children and birds.

Decide on the size of the tabletop; this should not be too small as the birds might squabble to get the food.

Nail the edge pieces to the top of the tabletop piece. Leave small gaps at each end to make it easy to sweep out uneaten birdseed and to allow water to run out.

Attach a post to the tabletop, unless your table is going to hang from a tree with chains or rope.

You can add hooks to the side of the tabletop to hang feeders from.

Dig a small hole into the ground. If you have no ground, attach base pieces to the post piece, nailing four base pieces to the bottom of the post. Each one should be facing outwards to form a cross shape, creating a stand.

You could even use a cup and saucer.

Give each child a bag of suitable birdseed to take home and scatter on their grass, on their balcony, on their bird table, or anywhere else where they can see the birds as they come to eat their food.

If possible, parents can take pictures of the birds to help their child make a bird diary, which can be brought into school and shared.

We're Going on a Bear Hunt by Michael Rosen, illustrated by Helen Oxenbury
Published by Walker Books Ltd

A modern classic, the bear in Michael Rosen and Helen Oxenbury's story doesn't actually appear until three-quarters of the way in, and its eventual arrival – 'One shiny wet nose! Two big furry ears! Two big goggly eyes! IT'S A BEAR!!!!' – excites the children almost to fever pitch!

Getting to know the story

Before reading the story, ask the children to tell you about a bear that they have or know about. Ask them to bring a bear of their own into school. If there are children who don't have a bear, ask them to bring in another soft toy that they can share with the rest of the class.

Read the story. Start discussions with small groups or the whole class by asking questions such as '*How long do you think the search for the bear took? How did the bear feel when he was found? What do you think the bear will do next?*' Talk about different endings to the story. Children can write, paint, draw or build models of their story.

Find a large space and go through the story again, encouraging children to do the actions to '*over*', '*under*', '*through*'.

This can become a trail inside or outside where there are other opportunities for position words such as *on, off, below, above, inside, outside, next to*. Use any large play equipment that you may have.

Role play

Use the bears (or other soft toys) to make a display that is relevant to this story. You could set up a cave (a large cardboard box) or a pop-up tent so that the children can use it for their own story of the bear hunt. Use autumn leaves as a base. These can be real or cut outs. If you are short of space, make a tabletop area.

Set up a snack area where children can make their own bear-hunt–themed snacks. For example, using three cream crackers and soft cheese, build a triangular 'tent'. Use soft cheese to join the corners. If you can find bear-shaped mini biscuits (they are available in many supermarkets, or make your own), stand one at the *front of, beside, behind and on top of* the 'cave'.

Developing a prop box

Make a story prop box to hold the book and add puppets for each of the characters. These can be ready-made or come from the puppet-making sessions that the children will be offered.

Include maps, binoculars (these can be homemade using cardboard cylinders), magnifying glasses, hats, gloves and, if the box is big enough, several pairs of wellies.

Sorting and counting

Use the bears for simple counting. Sort them into *groups or sets* according to colour or height. Ask each child to draw their bear on a piece of paper and make a pictogram.

Chapter 1: Teddy bears 35

Which colour has the most/least bears? How can we find out? Count how many bears altogether. Find the number that is the same as the number of blue/brown/purple bears.

brown	🐻	🐻	🐻	🐻	4
blue	🐻	🐻			2
purple	🐻				1

Using weight and position

Using the balance scales, ask groups of children which they think is the heaviest or lightest bear. '*Do you think this bear is heavier or lighter than this one? How can we find out?*' Let the children discuss different ways of finding the weight of the bears. If they have already used the balance scales, they may well go to them again. However, there is always the element of surprise when working and playing with the young.

Use an empty shoe box as a cave. If you have a really huge bear in the collection, you may need to ask if anyone has had a microwave delivered or a fridge or a fridge-freezer, and if so, ask if you could have the box. Children can put their bear *behind, in front, beside, on top of, in, out* or *under* the cave. Some children can find the correct word that matches the position or make labels with the bear in position and the word written next to it.

Using height

Choose one of the bears and ask the children how we can measure the *height* of it. As you say the word, use your hands to show the meaning of height. Height must go from the toes to the top of the head. Think about the resources you may need so that the children can choose which to use. Cubes, string, rulers, ribbon, a metre stick – a trundle wheel!

Allow children to choose what they would like to use and if it does not work out too well, they can change their mind.

Once a height is recorded, put all of the bears back together again and ask children to find a bear that is the same height or shorter than the first bear. Use strips of ribbon or blocks to make a height chart and order the heights from shortest to tallest, and tallest to shortest. Sit the bears under their appropriate height.

Comparing length

Compare the lengths of children's and adults' footprints. You can always make a few paw prints with paper or card and scatter those around as well.

Being creative: making footprints

Children often enjoy making footprints in soft materials such as dough or wet/dry sand. Place a shallow tray on the floor with sand or dough in it and encourage children to make prints with bricks, blocks, their hands and their feet. Talk about footprints in the sand at the beach or in the snow in winter. Line a small, shallow tray with sponges or other absorbent material and get children to put their feet in and then walk across a large piece of paper. If this is a bit too adventurous, children can paint the bottom of their feet and then walk across the paper. This could also be done outside on the playground or a patio. 'Walk' a paint trail that can be followed by others.

Use the vocabulary of comparison such as *longer than, shorter than, wider than* when describing footprints. Use adult feet to add to the trails so a more definite difference is seen.

Puppets, trays and tabletops

Use a large tray to make a tabletop version of the story. Use small pictures of the story and stick them onto lolly sticks to make stick puppets of the family and the bear. Start with a house and end with the bear in his cave. The cave can be made of a cardboard box or large stones. The family can be moved along or around the tray, in order, whilst the children re-enact the story. Collect the materials needed from outside during a 'hunting' session. Make the snow from cotton wool balls, except in winter, when you may be able to use real snow. Shallow plastic trays are used to hold each material in a separate area. Otherwise they would all join together in one soggy mess.

With leftover materials (maybe not the water or mud), make sensory collages.

More ideas for puppets

Wooden spoons are ideal for making puppets. Making sensory storytelling spoons is always a welcome addition to enhance the story.

You will need seven spoons. They can be all the same length or different, whichever you choose.

You will also need paint, felt scraps, ribbon scraps, aluminium foil, cotton wool balls, real twigs, glue and scissors.

Let us go through the sequence of the places the family goes in the story in order:

Long, wavy grass: Cut thin triangles of green felt and glue their bottoms to the back of a spoon in between strips of green ribbon. Do not glue the top of your grass, otherwise it will not move. This makes a lovely, textured area of grass that can be moved by waving the spoon.

Deep, cold river: Cut a piece of blue felt the same shape and size as the back of the spoon. Glue it on so that it completely covers the back. Cut wide strips of a thin material or blue tissue paper and glue them so that they stick out to make a 3D rippled effect, like water. Once the glue is dry, they can be touched without coming loose.

Thick, oozy mud: Loosen some cotton wool balls and stick them to the back of the spoon so that the spoon is covered in an irregular pattern. Paint it over with brown paint and allow it to dry.

Big, dark forest: Use real twigs and leaf shapes cut from two or three different shades of green felt. Glue them in a random pattern on the back of a spoon. Check that there are no sharp edges or points on the twigs.

Swirling, whirling snowstorm: Use cotton wool balls again, but this time leave them in their original shape. Glue them to the back of the spoon and sprinkle on some white glitter. As the storm swirls and whirls, glitter will cover anyone and anything close to the snow, but this can easily be replaced.

Narrow, gloomy cave: This can be made from any empty yoghurt pot, or by moulding aluminium foil around an appropriate shape. Cover the aluminium foil with strips of paper glued securely down, both inside and outside. When the glue is dry, paint both the inside and the outside in dark grey or brown paint. Make it look as gloomy as you can!

It's a bear!: Paint the spoon with brown paint. Add some semicircles of felt for ears, a small black felt nose and white and black shapes for the eyes. Draw on a mouth.

Making maps

Assist the younger children in deciding where to put the six pictures or materials to represent the pictures. Older children may have a better idea of where to place their pictures. Divide a piece of paper into six equal parts by folding it vertically to give two spaces and then horizontally into three equal parts. When you unfold the paper, there are six spaces.

In the first space, create the 'long, wavy grass'. For example, cut a rectangle from green paper; A4 or crepe paper will do. Cut slits from one edge to about half way down and glue it onto the base sheet.

To make the 'deep, cold river', use a shiny piece of blue paper and glue it into the second space.

For the third space, 'thick, oozy mud', you will need some brown paint (use washable) in a small tub. Dip your fingers in and finger paint mud on the map. You could also sprinkle some sand over the wet paint to make it look more realistic.

The fourth space takes a little more planning. The 'big, dark forest' would look better if the trees were standing, so use small lolly sticks with a green paper top stuck on and stand them in dough.

To make the 'swirling, whirling snowstorm', use cotton wool balls. If they are too big, pull them apart and glue them in space five.

Space number six of the map is the 'narrow, gloomy cave'. Cut a cave shape from brown paper and cut a door that can open and close. Young children may need help with cutting. Let children decide whether they want to put a bear at the entrance to the cave or not.

As a finishing touch, draw a dotted line starting at the top left-hand corner of the paper going to the grass, onto the river, up to the mud and down to the forest. Continue from the forest through the snow and end at the bear cave.

If you have an outside area, act out the story there using the maps that have been made. For example, a tree could be the forest, a sand tray could be the mud; use a grassy area for the long grass, and make the cave under a slide. When you get to the end of the map, turn around and do the whole thing in reverse. Running and screaming makes a good ending!

Going on a Bear Hunt sensory bags

Bad news for children, but sensory play does not always have to be messy.

You will need resealable see-through bags, tape (highly recommended) and different materials to go in the bags.

We need to find suitable materials for each of these four areas:

1. For the snowstorm, use icing sugar.
2. For the forest, pick up broken twigs, some with leaves still on.
3. Use real mud and water for each of those areas, BUT my advice is to double-bag each of them. Trust me on this!
4. For the long, wavy grass, it's best to use ornamental grass as it lasts longer, but if that's not possible, use real grass but replace it quite often.

Even though you may be using sealable bags I also recommend that they are securely taped so that nothing can escape (or get in!).

The bags can be used when reading the story. The children will love exploring these no-mess sensory bags. Even though mess isn't involved, they can still see and feel the different materials. But, if mess is what you want, just lay all of these materials in a large, high-sided tray instead!

Sound effects for the story

This is a perfect book for making sound effects. As the family go to look for the bear, they travel through a field of grass, a river, mud, a snowstorm, a forest and finally end up in a cave where they actually find a bear!

Here are some ideas:

> Grass 'swishy swashy': A broom or a hand brush run along a floor
> River 'splash splosh': Shake a water bottle half full of water
> Mud 'squelch squerch': Slowly shake lidded containers filled with jelly
> Snowstorm 'hoooo wooooo!': Blow gently into the top of an empty bottle
> Cave 'tiptoe tiptoe': Bang softly on the table or floor with a wooden spoon

The nice thing about using sound effects is that they reinforce the order of the story and they are done twice, once on the way to the cave and again in reverse coming back home from the cave.

Trails

When developing an outside trail, make a health and safety obstacle course to represent the Bear Hunt so that children can go *'through'*, *'over'*, *'up'*, *'down'*, *'under'* and so on. This would be a good opportunity to use the outside area with a slide. Children can go *up* the steps, *down* the slide, *under* the slide. Or use a climbing frame, if you have one, in the same way. Use photographs to record the children working their way through their trail. You can annotate the pictures with the relevant words back in the classroom.

Prepare some paper trails for the children to complete by adding in the missing part of the story. These can be worked on in the classroom or on actual trails outside. The trail must have a beginning and an end and go through each of the obstacles mentioned in the book.

Ask children to design a trail. Again, this can be inside or outside. Talk to the children about different types of maps and show them examples. Compare their trails to maps. What is the same? What is different?

Home/school links

Make trails and treasure hunts for children to follow. Invite parents, carers, grandparents or friends for an afternoon of treasure hunting. Think about the age and stamina of all the participants and include a few rest stops. If the weather is warm, provide drink stops. Put drawing materials on tables through the route for recording what has been seen or done. These can be used back in the classroom for children to make their own books or as a display to show the route of the trail, with children's comments and drawings posted at relevant points.

Shapes

Bring together a collection of different shapes in different colours and sizes.

Pattern blocks are ideal for this activity. They allow children to see how shapes can be decomposed into other shapes and introduce children to ideas of tiling. They include multiple copies of six shapes: equilateral triangle (green); rhombus (blue); narrow rhombus (beige); trapezium (red); regular hexagon (yellow); square (orange).

Use a large amount (which can be used outside) or a small amount (for a tabletop). Ask children to make 'paths' that the bear can walk along. Try not to interfere when you can see something isn't going to work! Wait to see what happens and then ask questions such as '*Tell me about your path. What is happening? What did you do about it? Would you like some help? Where do you want your path to go? How do you know which shape to put next?*' This is a much more productive way to hear about children's thinking and understanding. I was observing a child trying to make a path that went down a slide; he didn't seem to understand why the shapes wouldn't stay still. After trying for a while, his friend came to help. Between them they worked out that if they started at the bottom of the slide and worked upwards, each new shape could be supported by the previous one. This worked until about half way up, and then the weight of all the shapes began to push down. But when you have a friend to help you, it doesn't seem to matter. They left the shapes where they were, chose a bike each, and rode off into the sunset!

But other questions to ask other children, pairs or groups could be '*Why did you put . . . next to the . . .? Have you used a pattern of shapes in your path? Tell me about your pattern.*'

Designing and developing games

Discuss the type of games that the children are used to playing. You may be surprised at how many/few games involve a board, where taking turns is a rule when playing.

Encourage children in pairs, groups or with adults to design and make a game. This could be a wonderful opportunity to involve adults from home. It could take place one afternoon in the classroom or at home and then be brought in to play with friends.

The games can be for outside or inside. They could involve their paths or not. Children can act out the characters in their game or they can use toys or dough models.

A simple starting point is a game that uses a track. This example can be used for many different stories.

Chapter 1: Teddy bears 41

Use something like this as a starting point adapting it to match the story. Add a cave and the five different areas that occur in the story. Make it a game for two players. Take turns to throw the dice and move than number of places. Make your way towards the cave, visiting each area in the order of the book. Once at the cave, turn around and go home again. The dice can be 1–6, 1, 2, 3, 1, 2, 3 or 0–5, or numbers above 6, depending on the children who are playing.

Winnie-the-Pooh by A.A. Milne, illustrated by E.H. Shepard

Pooh hears a buzzing noise and meets some bees.

Getting to know the story

Pooh hears a buzzing noise.
'That buzzing noise means something. You don't get a buzzing noise like that, just buzzing and buzzing without its meaning something. If there is a buzzing noise, somebody's making a buzzing noise, and the only reason for making a buzzing noise that I know of is because you're a bee'.[8]

The bear of very little brain is possibly my favourite character in any book, ever, and the Pooh stories in my opinion are some of the best comic writing of the last century.

Before reading the story to the children, ask them if they have ever heard of Winnie-the-Pooh.

Sophie age 5

He is a very famous bear who has lots of adventures in the Hundred Acre Wood where he lives. He has special friends called Christopher Robin, Piglet, Owl, Tigger, Roo and Kanga. If possible, have pictures of all of the characters, or you may be able to borrow actual soft toys that can become part of the Pooh Bear area.

Thinking very hard

This story is about Pooh thinking very hard about a problem that he has. What could be making that buzzing noise? '*Pooh Bear heard a loud buzzing noise. What do you think it could be?*' Accept lots of possible answers as children will have their own ideas. Don't stop when a child says 'bees', as that will stop other thoughts being offered. Although bees is the answer you're looking for, having asked the children such an open question as '*what do you think it can be?*', you owe them time to give their answers.

'*What do you think a bear likes to eat more than anything else in the world?*' After some ideas have been offered, and if no one has suggested honey, show a jar of honey to the class. Over the label, paste a new one that says **'Honey'**. '*Who knows what is in this jar?*' Some older children may be able to read the word, but others may need some clues. '*This is a jar with honey inside. It's Pooh Bear's very favourite food*'. '*And bees make honey*'. '*And bees buzz*'. '*It was some bees that Pooh Bear heard*'.

Collecting (or not!) the honey

Pooh looked up to the top of the tree and climbed, and climbed and climbed until he was at the top. And he sang a little song as he climbed.

Isn't it funny
How a bear likes honey?
Buzz! Buzz! Buzz
I wonder why he does.

Ask the children to crouch down on the floor and as you tell this part of the story, they should gradually stand up and grow as tall as they can. Then, when Pooh falls down, they collapse back onto the floor.

'*What could Pooh Bear do to get to the honey? What would you do? Talk to your friend and tell them what you would do*'. Give the children a minute or two to have that discussion and then gather feedback on some of the different ways they thought of.

A clever plan

Continue with the story. Pooh goes to find his friend Christopher Robin. He asks him for a blue balloon so that he can float up to the bees. '*Do you think that is a good plan? Do you think Pooh Bear will get the honey?*' Continue with the story. '*Did you like that story? What was the bit you liked the most? Did Pooh Bear ever get his honey?*'

Developing a Pooh Bear environment

Cover a cupboard or tabletop with leaves and twigs to be the floor of the Hundred Acre Wood. Paint a background of a tall tree with bees all around it. Supply paints for the children to paint the bees, but do not be too critical if you get a few blue, green or purple ones for your display. Paint blue balloons or blow up a balloon and attach the string to the display. Place a Pooh Bear and a Christopher Robin on the leaves and a small child's umbrella next to them. Children can use these props when playing and making up their own stories.

Rhyming words

Isn't it funny
How a bear likes honey?
Buzz! Buzz! Buzz
I wonder why he does.

This very short Pooh poem can lead to a host of activities using rhyming words. Rhyming words sound the same at the end, but do not necessarily use the same letters that make the rhyme. It is all about manipulating oral language. Rhyming helps children to improve their oral language skills. Children have more ownership over their language when they are encouraged to change it and play with how they speak. Be aware that some nonsense words may include words very similar to unacceptable words in the everyday language of a child.
You could also use:

How sweet to be a cloud
Floating in the blue!
Every little cloud
Always sings aloud

How sweet to be a cloud
Floating in the blue!
It makes him very proud
To be a little cloud.

And:

It's a very funny thought that, if Bears were Bees,
They'd build their nests at the bottom of trees.
And that being so (if the Bees were Bears),
We shouldn't have to climb up all these stairs.

Play a rhyming word game by giving clues such as:

You sleep in me. I rhyme with head
I am green and I can jump. I rhyme with log
You wear me on your head. I rhyme with cat
I'm big and round and very hot. I rhyme with fun.

Ask children for their ideas. Build a rhyming tree where pairs of words can be hung, perhaps written on leaves. This could be in or near the role play area. Do not forget a door in the trunk for Pooh or Piglet. How about Owl sitting on a high branch? This can bring in most, if not all, of the positional maths vocabulary, especially if the characters are able to move to new places.

Baking with honey

This activity uses everyday language to talk about size, weight, capacity and volume.

Children love to cook. It encourages their independence and awareness of healthy eating choices. Cooking can also be rich with mathematical language and thinking. You may want children to use simple recipe cards that have words and pictures to represent the sequence of the recipe, or you may want an adult to lead the session until children become more confident (and competent, especially with getting a broken egg into a bowl).

As they are blending, mixing and sorting ingredients, ask questions such as '*How many eggs do we need?*' '*What can we use to weigh the flour?*' '*How do we break the egg?*'

Eggs can be tricky!   *Maybe a smaller bowl next time.*

As the recipe progresses, ask '*What if the mixture is too wet/dry? What do you think we could do about that?*'

Honey cookies are very easy to make and are very popular with children. You will find a list of ingredients in the resource sheets section. Before starting, make sure that no children have food allergies or medical conditions that would stop them from making and enjoying the cookies.

You will need the following:

225 g self-raising flour
A pinch of salt
120 g butter or margarine
120 g soft brown sugar
1 egg
1 rounded tablespoon of honey

A few drops of vanilla essence
A greased baking tray. Or cover a baking tray with non-stick kitchen parchment
A bowl, a mixing spoon and a teaspoon per child

What to do:

1. Sift the flour and salt onto a plate and put to one side.
2. Measure the butter and sugar into a mixing bowl and beat well until soft. This can be done by hand or electric beater.
3. Crack the egg into a small bowl, add the vanilla essence and mix lightly. Gradually beat the eggs into the butter and sugar, a little at a time. Beat in the honey.
4. Add half the flour and mix to a soft dough. Add the remaining flour and mix to a firm dough.
5. Spoon out rounded teaspoons of the mixture and roll into balls. Place them on the baking tray and flatten slightly. This recipe will make about 30 small cookies. Space them apart from each other, as they spread whilst cooking.
6. Place the cookies in the centre of a pre-heated oven (350°F), gas mark (4) or fan oven (160°C) and bake for 12 minutes.
7. Lift each cookie onto a cooling tray. Wait 20 minutes for them to cool and crisp and then eat. Delicious!

Counting

The counting skills used in making simple cookies, or any baking, are, first, saying one number for each object (for example, when counting out ingredients), or spoonfuls or the number of cookies on the tray (Are there enough cookies for us each to have one?); second, remembering the pattern of the number sequence; third, when matching the number of cookies to the number of children, or understanding cardinality (the last number gives the total).

Measures

Throughout the activity, use the words of measure so that the children can hear and see what the words mean. For example, *half, a little, a lot, heavy, light, grams, more than, less than*. Use scales to weigh out the ingredients and point out the numbers on the dial, or the numbers on a digital display.

Developing a role play area: 1

Set up a role play area (a tabletop would do) where the children can set up a Cookie Shop. It is good to involve the children in the whole process of writing a shopping list, buying and then cooking with the ingredients, bought as independently as possible.

One way I have found to be really helpful for the very young children, or those who are currently working at a lower level, is to make cards for each ingredient and draw the number of bags needed. The contents of these bags have been previously weighed out so that the total equals the total on the recipe.

For example, there are seven bags of flour, each weighing 25g. Older children can weigh their own bags.

Space out the bags so that each of the filled bags can be placed on a picture. Therefore, when all of the pictures are covered, there will be the right amount of flour.

Do the same for butter and soft brown sugar, each package weighing 20g.

Older children can use balance scales for finding the weight of butter or sugar by weighing one and balancing the other.

Allow children to use real money rather than plastic money when they are doing their shopping. The coins that they use will be appropriate to the level they are at when using money. Plastic money cannot be used in a real shop for purchasing goods, so why not let the children get the feel of real money as early as they can? Use vocabulary such as '*How much, how many, buy, sell*'.

Encourage children to 'read' the recipe themselves, count ingredients and count how many spoonfuls. Spacing the dough on the baking tray is an achievement. They must not be too close together or you will get one giant cookie.

Packaging cookies

Once the cookies have been made, children can make a box to take their biscuits home in. How *long/wide* does the box need to be? How *high*, so that the cookies do not get broken? What are you going to make your box out of? Or maybe make a bag, similar to a party bag that children bring home from a party. How *big* does the bag need to be? How will you make handles?

Developing a role play area: 2

We all know that young children learn best when they are involved with self-chosen activities which can be both stimulating and challenging. Well-planned role play activities, such as den building, can be revisited and developed over time. The den in this story is Pooh Bear's house at the bottom of a tree in the Hundred Acre Wood.

But any bear story offers an opportunity to build a den.

All you need are long lengths of dark heavy material. Old blankets would do. Add torches, tree stumps, branches and leaves to build a den, pictures, plastic flowers, soft toys and story books, blankets and pillows and mugs, bowls and spoons to make it more homely.

If possible, develop the den in a corner of the classroom. Fix the long lengths of fabric to the ceiling or wall. Add a few of the extras mentioned in the paragraph above, but be careful not to provide too much, as the children will want to add their own ideas.

Encourage children to develop the den to support their own play themes. If possible, take pictures, or ask children to take pictures of the den and each other at play. Discuss the images and, where necessary, act as a scribe to write the children's comments in speech bubbles. These can be used as a display or combined to make a class book.

When the children have had lots of opportunities to explore and extend the inside den, offer them opportunities to take their den-making outside.

Chapter 1: Teddy bears   47

Enjoying a picnic

Have a teddy bear's picnic using real or fake food inside or outside the den. Use dough to make items for the picnic or bake cookies and make sandwiches.

Ask children what they think they will need for a picnic, apart from food.

Here is where the idea of having a big space comes into play.

Here we see a table and chairs set out ready for guests. This is set next to a river.

And here we have the addition of food and drink, with the teapot clearly marked.

Puppets: making bees

Staying with the theme of circles, these little bee puppets are very easy to make: circles for eyes, head and body, and parts of a circle for wings. The finger holes are made by placing dough beneath the bee and stabbing through the body with a pencil straight into the dough. This is much safer than trying to cut out small circles. Children can put their fingers through the holes, wiggle them about a bit and then you have a perfect bee puppet.

Another easy bee puppet also uses circles for the body and head, semicircles for the jersey and arms, legs and ears, and any additional parts as you like. To make it into a puppet, glue a handle on the back that four fingers can fit through, while the thumb grips the handle. Use the puppets to make a story or a show for others to watch.

Hint: If you have many bees buzzing around, clear some furniture out of the way or go outside. Use music, such as 'The Flight of the Bumblebee' by Rimsky Korsakov or, if you can get a copy, Arthur Askey singing 'The Bee Song', as part of the performance. (You can find a video on YouTube.)

Chapter 1: Teddy bears 49

Pattern and shape

Use pattern blocks to make hexagons. Allow free play with the blocks before asking children to do anything specific with them. But, as they are playing, you could point out that the yellow shape is the same shape as the honeycomb from the bees.

Investigate how many ways there are to make a hexagon.

Are these two ways the same or different? What is the same and what is different?

As a support for younger children, ask them to make hexagons on top of a yellow hexagon.

Developing the bee area

If possible, in the bee area, have pictures, posters, even photographs of beekeepers, their equipment and honeycombs. If there are local beekeepers nearby, ask one to come into school to talk to the children and show real honeycombs (though without bees, as lots of bees may be a problem).

As an alternative, buy a jar of honey that has honeycomb already in the jar. Children will be able to see the shape of it through the glass.

Making bee-themed games

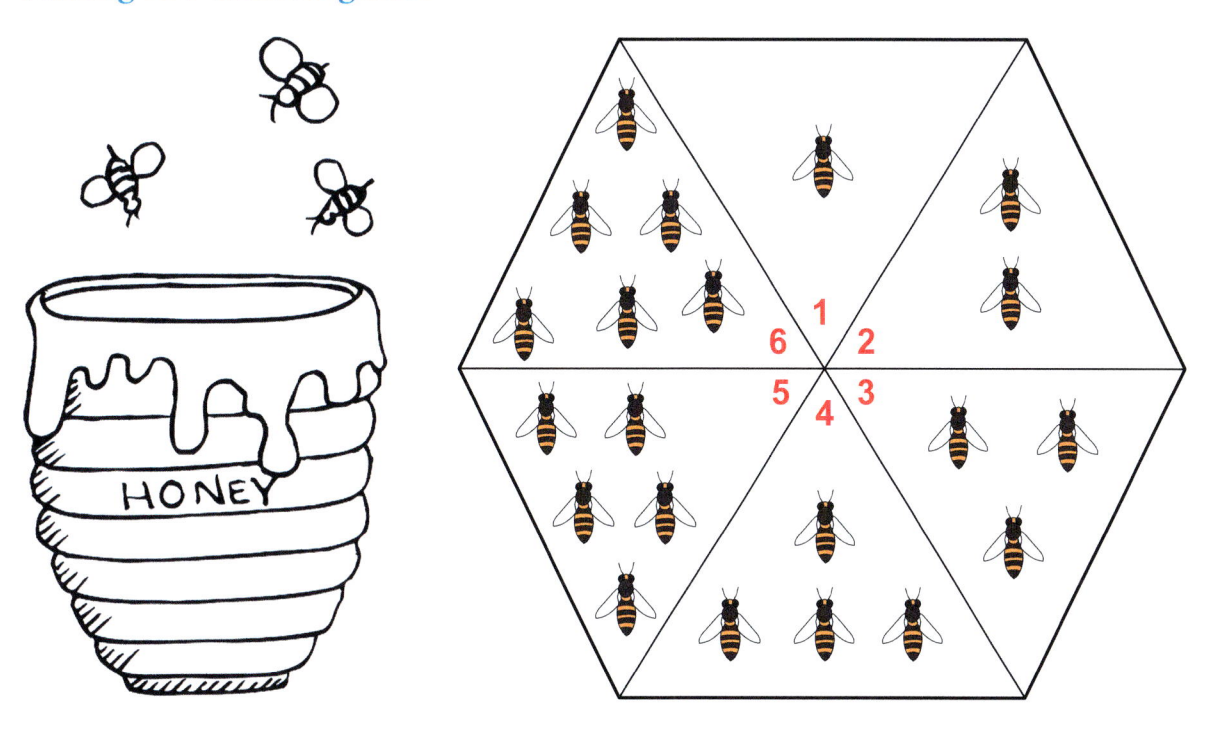

Honey pots

You will find photocopiable versions of this game in the resource sheets section.

Give each player a honey pot (picture or real) and dice or a spinner. These show numbers or sets of bees, or spots 1–6 or 0–5. Playing this game encourages taking turns as well as following rules.

Each child takes a turn at throwing the dice or spinning the spinner. To use the spinner, put a paper clip at the centre and hold it in place with a pencil point. Now just flick the paper clip, and round it goes. Collect the appropriate number of bee cards and put them in the pot. When all of the bees have been collected, each child counts their own bees. There is no winner. Therefore, there is no loser. This is a counting activity. Older children may want to compare the number of bees that they each got and so use vocabulary such as *'more than'* and *'less than'* or *'the same as'*. These are the types of games that encourage most children to play again and again. Just imagine playing a game that you can never lose.

'Did you enjoy playing that game? What did you like/not like?'

'Could you make a better game? What would you need to make your game? Who would you play with?'

Children can then design and make their own game. This can be at home or at school.

Being creative with circles and cylinders

Use what the children have learnt about circles to make Pooh Bear models. As before, check that all children are able to use scissors safely and effectively. If you want this activity to be about circles, some preparation may be needed. If you want it to be about children creating their own version of circles, then they can do their own cutting and sticking with help from you when/if they ask for it.

And, of course, we must not forget the bees: long bees, short bees, fat bees, thin bees, children's own imaginary bees. Talk about the cylinders that are being used. What do children notice about the shape at each end? You can discuss rolling, sliding and where they can see cylinders in the classroom, outside or at home.

How big does the piece of paper need to be so that the whole cylinder is covered? How can we find out? At the beginning, most children use a huge piece, much too big for the task. Or they use a small piece not big enough for the task. But these bees tend to be covered in patches of other small pieces of paper. The more children experience this type of activity, the better they will become estimating area.

Data handling: tasting honey

'Who has eaten honey? What did it taste like? Where were you when you had a honey sandwich? Tell me something you know about honey.'

Bring in some small pots of different types of honey. You will also need a small empty pot in front or behind each pot of honey. Check for dietary issues before you do this activity. Use lolly sticks (that can be bought at any craft shop) for tasting utensils. Give each child the same number of sticks as there are pots of honey.

Give each child a yellow counter or cube.

Children taste a small amount of honey from each jar, using a different stick each time.

Hint: Have a rubbish bin handy for the used sticks, as they can become quite sticky.

Children decide which honey they liked the most and put their counter or cube in the pot behind that honey jar.

When everyone has tasted from every jar of honey, put the lids on (small fingers have been known to explore the stickiness in the jars).

Build the cubes into towers. Or place counters next to each other. Compare the heights or lengths of each, using the correct mathematical vocabulary: *most, more than, least, less than, the same as, one, two, three. . . .*

Order the cube towers or the counter lines from shortest to tallest. Stand the relevant honey in front of each tower or line.

Counters can be put in rows so that they can be compared, using one-to-one correspondence.

Count the numbers of cubes or counters. Use sentences like '*There are two counters/cubes in this line and four in this line. Two is less than four. Four is more than two*'.

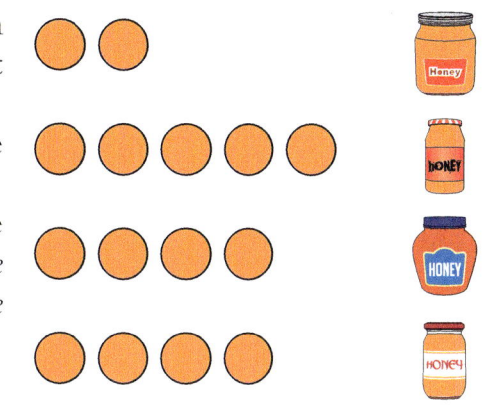

★★★

Moving away from bears, the next chapter will be all about houses and homes. Real homes, fictional homes, big homes, small homes.

Let us continue our journey into our next set of stories.

Chapter 2: Houses and homes

Why houses and homes?

Many aspects of the home environment can be used to stimulate mathematical investigation. Activities based around where we live can also help young children to relate to their home environment and their school environment and to draw the two closer together.

The aim of this chapter is to encourage close observation of houses and streets both in the local environment and through stories. It will also take the children through the mathematical processes of problem-solving, estimation, making connections, visualisation, communicating and reasoning.

Children will be working in pairs, small groups or individually. They will be discussing and solving problems whilst actively engaged in constructing mathematical meaning, learning problem-solving strategies, practicing a variety of concepts and skills and communicating mathematical ideas.

Problem-solving is at the heart of mathematics. Children have to:

> **Understand what they need to find out**. *How can Rapunzel escape from the tower?*
> **Find possible ways of solving the problem**. *Rapunzel could jump; the prince could build steps or a slide.*
> **Have a plan and carry it out**. *Children can choose their own way for Rapunzel to escape. Include pipe cleaners to make a ladder, cardboard cylinders cut in half lengthways to make a slide, blocks to make steps.*
> **Look back, think and discuss how the problem was solved**. *Encourage children to share what they did and why they chose that way.*

Children need to be able to talk to each other about what they are doing, any problems they encounter and ways to solve them.

Teachers and parents can encourage maths talk by being good listeners. In this way we can find out what a child is thinking. We can encourage children to explain their ideas clearly, organise their ideas by asking open-ended questions and not be too quick to ask questions ourselves.

All children have a home, whether it is small or big, a tent or a palace, a flat or a mansion. They can identify similarities and differences between their house and the ones in the story.

Mathematics

Sorting, ordering by height and weight

Ordinal and cardinal numbers

Sequencing

Ordering

Chapter 2: Houses and homes 53

Counting

Comparing

Number 3

Counting, understanding and using numbers

Discussing

Exploring capacity

Exploring volume

Calculating simple addition and subtraction problems

Describing shapes and measures

Problem-solving

Exploring time

Exploring position and movement

Mathematical processes

Choosing appropriate equipment

Being systematic

Making and testing predictions

Presenting results to others

Selecting materials and mathematics appropriate for the task

Drawing conclusions

Exploring and recording work

Classifying

Collecting, organising and recording information

Recording systematically

Communicating clearly

Talking about work

Planning strategies

Testing statements

Checking results

Explain how a procedure works

Ordering

Predicting

Discussing with others

Recognising patterns

Generalising

Completing a task

Looking for connections

Interpreting mathematical information

Looking for patterns

Asking questions such as 'what if'

Talking and asking questions

Estimating

Making sense of a task

Choosing a way to solve a problem

Vocabulary

Counting numbers

Count one, two, three . . . ten

1, 2, 3 . . . 10

Comparing and ordering numbers

First, second, third, compare, match, most, least, more than, less than, the same as, how many . . .?, enough, count, more, less, too many, too few

Adding and subtracting

More, altogether, make, take away, how many are left?

How many have gone?

Solving problems

Reasoning about numbers or shapes

Pattern, count, sort, group, sort, same, different, list

Problems involving 'real life' or money

How much, how many, buy, sell

Money, coin, penny, pence, cost, spend, how much?

Measures

Measure, size, compare, guess, enough, not enough, too many, too few, just over, just under, high, low

Length

Length, width, big, bigger, biggest. Tall, taller than, tallest. Small, smaller than, smallest. Short, shorter than, shortest. Middle size, long, too long, too short, taller, shorter, height

Mass

Lighter, lighter than, light, heavy, heavier than, weigh, balances, scales, weight, too much, not enough, gram

Capacity

Full, empty, holds

Time

Morning, evening, night, before, after, how long?, oldest

Exploring patterns, shape and space

Pattern, shape

2D shapes

Triangle, circle, hexagon, pattern, square, spiral, oblong

3D shapes

Cube, cuboid, cylinder

Position, direction and movement

In, out, under, behind, in front, beside, on top, inside, outside, next to, over, between, through, back, front, on, off, below, above, up, down

General

What do you think?

Why do you think that?

What comes next?

The Three Little Pigs

Getting to know the story

The Three Little Pigs is a fable about three pigs who build three houses of different materials. A big bad wolf blows down the first two pigs' houses, made of straw and sticks respectively, but is unable to destroy the third pig's house, made of bricks. He then tries to trick the pig out of the house by asking to meet him at various places, but he is outwitted each time. Finally, the wolf decides to come down the chimney. The pig catches the wolf in a cauldron of boiling water, slams the lid on, then cooks and eats him. In some versions, the first and second little pigs are not eaten by the wolf after he demolishes their homes, but instead run to their brother's house, and after the wolf goes down the chimney he either dies, as in the original, or runs away and never returns to eat the three little pigs, who all survive in either case.

Chapter 2: Houses and homes 55

Each exchange between wolf and pig features phrases such as:

'Little pig, little pig, let me come in'.
'No, no, not by the hair on my chinny chin chin. I will not let you in'.
'Then I'll huff, and I'll puff, and I'll blow your house in'.

Printed versions date back to the 1840s, but the story itself is thought to be much older. Many versions of the story have been recreated or have been modified over the years, sometimes making the wolf a kind character.

The story of The Three Little Pigs gives each child an opportunity to engage in mathematical ideas such as ordinal and cardinal numbers, reinforcing counting to three and beyond by adding mother pig and the wolf, sequencing, counting and ordering, the concept of time, size and an early understanding of money.

Tell the story and then use the pictures available in the resource sheets section for extension activities.

Extension activities

Make a split book as in the introduction.

Matching

Use the pigs, their building materials and the houses to find which pig met which man and who built which house. This can be an enlarged A3 book for class use or A4 for individual or pair work. Ask questions such as '*Do you think the first little pig in our book made his house of straw, sticks or bricks? Do you think he met this man, this man or this man?*' Turn the middle pages over as you ask the question. Choose more than one child to give their ideas and ask '*Why do you think that this man met the first pig in our book?*' There will be strong visual clues to help children decide. But they may have different ideas from yours. Accept all answers but always ask why that choice was made. Although we may think so, there is not necessarily only one answer. It depends on what each child thinks. If you answer a question that starts with 'What do you think?', the answer cannot be wrong. Some answers that I have received have been justified by statements like '*Cos I like this man*'. You cannot argue with that.

Attach hook-and-loop fastener or magnetic tape to the back of each picture to illustrate the story using a felt or magnetic board. The pigs can be matched to houses, to bundles or to tools. Emphasis should be placed on the mathematical language, in particular: *first, second, third*.

Sequencing

Sequence the events in the story. This can be done as a group using larger pictures or by individual children using smaller versions. The pictures and instructions for adults at home can also be used. This is a good, non-threatening introduction to 'doing' maths with your child. Do not forget to include vocabulary for adults to use, such as *before, after, first, second, third, in, up, in front, down*.

Counting

Simple counting to three and beyond using the pigs, bundles, houses, mother pig and the wolf can reinforce the work done in Chapter 1 with the Three Bears.

Making houses

Collect cardboard boxes, which can be made into the three houses. These do not need to be very big and can be put on a tabletop with an appropriate size pig.

Making spoon puppets

These can become the backdrop for a puppet show. Paint wooden spoons pink for pigs and brown for the wolf. Children can decorate the animals, draw on faces, cut triangles for ears and make a very angry looking wolf head. They can then take control of the story as they act out different versions of their own design. Maybe the wolf is nice, maybe the pigs all live together, and so on. Allow the children to be as creative as they like.

Measuring time

Time is a difficult concept for young children. If you like what you are doing, time seems to pass very quickly. If you do not like what you are doing, time appears to last forever. For me, sitting in a dentist chair seems likes five weeks. Ask questions such as *'How long do you think it will take to build each house?' 'Which do you think would take the longest time? Or the shortest time?' 'Tell me why you think that'*.

Have any children been to or seen a building site where houses were being built? Has anyone in the family built a wooden shed? Ask them.*'Tell us what you have seen'*.

Building materials

Discuss the materials used to build the houses. Gather other examples of straw, wood or bricks.

Investigate the building materials. Which is the *largest/heaviest/lightest?* Talk about the texture of each, such as hard, soft, rough and prickly. Be aware that for a young child, holding a real brick can be difficult. Hold it over a table or a rug on the floor.

Using the outside

Walk around the outside of your setting. What is your building made of? Do rubbings of the different materials and investigate the different patterns.

Collect materials from outside or ask children to bring them into the classroom from home so that they can make a collage of the three houses. Sandpaper is a good idea for cutting small bricks. It gives a very similar texture. Use what the children know about *triangles* to make a roof for each house.

Cover a sheet of paper with washable PVA glue, which spreads easily. Each child can choose which house they want to make by pressing straw, twigs or sand over the glue. Or even have them make all three and incorporate them into their own storytelling.

Investigating bundles

Investigate the bundles the pigs are carrying. Which is the largest bundle? What is in the bundle? *'What would you take with you if you were leaving home?' 'How would you carry it if it was very heavy?' 'What do you put your things in if you are going on holiday or going to visit someone?'*

Chapter 2: Houses and homes

Collecting, representing and interpreting data

'Do you think they have sandwiches in their bundles? If so, what is in them?' Choose three different fillings suggested by the children. Do a tally chart or pictogram to show their favourite filling. Discuss the results with the children. *'Which sandwich did most children like? Which sandwich did four children like? How many children didn't like cheese?'* This will involve simple addition.

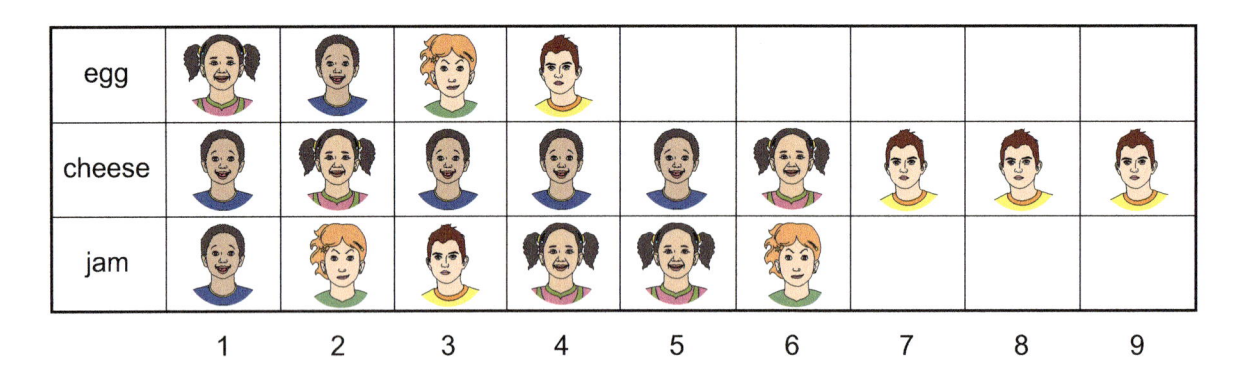

egg									
cheese									
jam									
	1	2	3	4	5	6	7	8	9

Being creative with sandwiches

Before involving the class in making the sandwich they liked best, ask caregivers about dietary issues and allergies. Each child can be responsible for their own sandwich. Cut them into halves and quarters. Use vertical, horizontal and diagonal lines when cutting. Ask the children if they have seen those shapes before. Introduce the new word 'square'.

Being creative with patterns

Creating patterns is a favourite activity for young children. Create a different design for each of the pigs' bundles. Provide paper or a plain material of any colour. These can be done by using sponges, potato prints, bricks, blocks, hands or even feet. This can include work on symmetry, shapes and colours. Discuss pattern on fabrics, around the classroom and at home as well as wallpaper, paper bags, book covers and pictures.

Investigating homes and houses

Investigate homes round the world from very cold to hot countries. Use picture books, atlases, internet research or visit a local library. *'What are they made of? Have you ever been in a house made of ice? How do you think it would feel?'* If you have families that come from a different country, ask if they will come in and talk about their houses and homes. Maybe they have photographs to illustrate their words. Or they may have been to a different country for a holiday and have photos they can share of where they stayed or what they saw.

Invite families to share photos of their home. Collect different pictures of homes. Estate agent brochures and home improvement magazines are a great source. Mount pictures on cardboard. Let children sort the pictures by house size, number of doors, windows, type of roof, single family, multi-family and so on.

Area? What's area?

Area is covered a lot in the early years; for example, finding a cloth the right size to put on a table; cutting a piece of paper to wrap round a cylinder to make a bee; finding out if there is enough surface to put things on (tabletop). But we do not refer to the word 'area' until much later on. Why not? Just say the word and some children will ask what it is. Be honest. It is not a state secret until they are eight years old. Some children may remember it, many probably will not. But use correct mathematical words whenever you can.

Show the children a piece of cloth which can be made into a bundle. Use different shapes and sizes for the clothes. Which shape makes the best bundle? How much can it hold? How will the bundle be held together? Can the children *predict* what it will hold? How many *small* things? How many *heavy things*? Do the pigs carry tools in their bundles? The first pig would need some string. The second pig can carry a hammer and nails. The third pig needs a trowel and a tape-measure. These questions can lead quite naturally into the role play area of a builder's yard. How *heavy* are the bundles? Use scales to find the *heaviest* and *lightest*. Find those that are *heavier than* or *lighter than* the others.

Role play: the builder's yard

Setting up a builder's yard inside the classroom can be quite messy. Wet and dry sand tend to drift away into the smallest corners of the room. Try putting a tarpaulin down and build an edge with large blocks or plastic bricks. If possible, an outside area would be best. Children need to be as independent as possible when choosing how and what they explore in the builder's yard.

Prop box

Start with your prop box. Involve the children in the discussion about what to put in it. These could be included:

>   Overalls, yellow jackets, boots, hard hats
>   Bricks – if using real bricks, make sure that there are gloves small enough for the children to wear, and be aware of health and safety issues. Or use plastic bricks (large and small)
>   Large cardboard boxes
>   Large sand tray filled with sand (wet and dry) and gravel
>   Planks of wood, heavily sanded to get rid of the possibility of splinters
>   Pipes, buckets, tape-measures, tools, rulers, spirit level and weighing scales

To use the idea of spending money and getting change you will also need a till, a calculator, pencils, notebooks or paper and a telephone.

Set up and display the items that are for sale. Put all the building materials together, with the tools on shelves and office equipment on a table. Decide where to put the weighing scales and measuring resources. Set up a check-out area with the till and plastic baskets.

Sort and count nails and screws according to size and colour. Make price labels for the goods in the yard.

Chapter 2: Houses and homes

Home/school links

If possible, ask a parent or adult who has building experience to come and show how brick walls are built so they stay strong and cannot be blown down. Build small walls with interlocking shapes or larger walls with wooden blocks. Go on a walk to see how different houses are built. Look for the *oldest* house, or the *tallest* house, or the *smallest* house. Ask children to draw pictures of their own house and write a few lines about it.

Send a three pigs game home to be played with adults and siblings. Send instructions, resources needed and mathematical vocabulary that can be used as well as extensions to the basic game. Ask for feedback on the game. Who played it? Did they enjoy it? Could they make a better game with their child that could be played back in school? Arrange a home/school afternoon for playing and sharing games.

Trails

Before starting to plan a trail, make early decisions about the involvement of adults and children. Who is going to be involved? Are the children going to be included in the decisions about the trail? The answer is yes! Are they to be consulted, with their interests and aptitudes taken into consideration? Again, yes. Are the adults going to prepare the trail for the children? Maybe. I suggest that children may benefit from following a well-prepared trail before being asked to make one of their own. But each group of children is different. Try it out and see what happens. If you have an outside area with play equipment, it could be used for the three pigs story. Ask the children what they think. Where could the three houses be? Where would the wolf live?

Trails can be an excellent opportunity for liaising between schools and classes and for creating home/school links. Within the trail, try to have some problems that can be solved on the spot. One example could be building a house of wood with blocks. '*Which blocks go at the bottom? Why did you choose that one?*' '*Would you put a cylinder at the bottom? Why not?*' Do not ask for too much writing from the younger children, but you can use visual clues to show the problem that needs to be solved or the activity at hand. Brick rubbings are always popular. Provide chunky wax crayons and plenty of paper.

Games

A photocopiable version of the game board can be found in the resource sheets section.

This is a simple game where children can choose which pig they want to be. It involves recognition of numbers and counting along a track in ones. Children can use a 1–6 spot die or 1–6 number die. Younger children can use 1, 2, 3, 1, 2, 3 dice. To make it more of a challenge, colour some of the sections in the relevant colour to match the house (i.e. yellow for straw, brown for sticks and red for bricks). If a player lands on a coloured section they can have another go or miss a turn or go back one space. The rules can be changed according to the players, how many times they have played the game and whether they can make a more interesting game.

Take the game home to play and have children use it to design and make their own game.

Chapter 2: Houses and homes   61

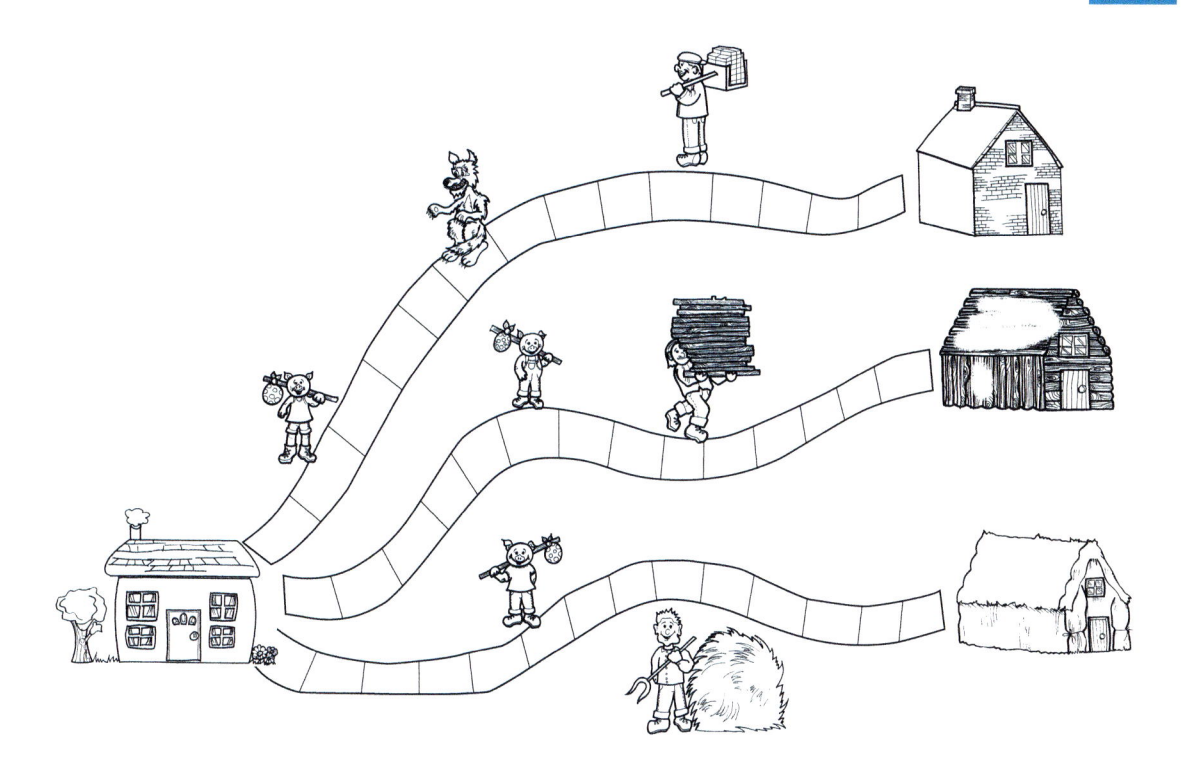

Using shapes and money

Which shapes can be used to make pigs? Use the shapes that children know already but be prepared to use shapes that they do not. The obvious ones are:

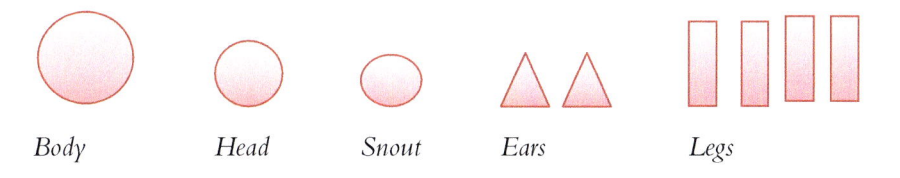

Body   *Head*   *Snout*   *Ears*   *Legs*

But what about showing children how to make a *spiral* for the tail?

Wind a piece of paper or a pipe cleaner around a pencil or a cylinder before carefully removing it.

The pigs will need *money* to buy the straw, sticks and bricks. If they need to fill their bundles with other materials, what else will they need to buy?

Learning about money is an important life skill. It can sometimes be hard to get young children to understand the concept of money, how much a coin is worth, what the different values are and how these can be spent. Giving change can be an even bigger worry.

I have found two ways that have really helped. First, make a money box.

Here the children can use what they already know about 3D shapes but introduce new words such as *cylinder, cubiod* or *cube*. Who knows which shape a child will use for the body of the pig?

Children can use a cardboard *cylinder*, two *circles* (one *larger than* the other), two *triangles* and a pipe cleaner. Paint everything except the pipe cleaner in an appropriate pig colour. You can give your pigs legs or not. An adult needs to cut a slit in the top so that it will take all denominations of coins. Leave the back of the bank open, otherwise there will be no way to empty it.

Using just pennies initially, play the game of Money, Money, Money. Have a plate with penny coins, a suitable die for the players and a piggy bank for each player. The aim is to collect the most money. Take turns rolling the dice and collecting a matching number of coins. Place the coins in the pig through the slit on the top. After five or ten throws each, each player totals their money by tipping it out of the open end of the pig. The player with the most money wins the game.

There are different ways to find out who has the most: simple counting, laying each penny along a number line and see which number is covered by the last coin or direct one-to-one correspondence with each player matching their coins. Use words such as *coin, coins, pennies, most, more than, less than* to begin to develop the concept of the value of money.

Second, use wooden sticks for those children who need to work with higher value coins. Paint some sticks, each a different colour, and glue a different coin at one end of each.

This is a fun way for children to look for and recognise the similarities and differences between the coins. As a start, use colour as well. '*Show me the white stick that has a penny*'. '*Show me the red stick that has five pence*'. Using 'show me' can be a good assessment tool. The teacher can see exactly what the child is thinking. Over time, drop the colours and just ask for the name of the coin.

Hint: Put the silver coins on the darker colours. They do not show up well on white.

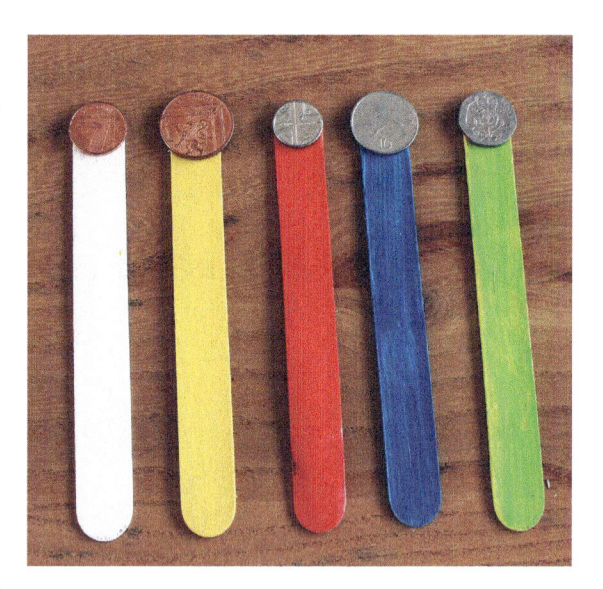

Using dough animals and making houses

Make dough with the children (see the dough recipe included in the resource sheets for Chapter 1). Use measure words such as *weight, balances, too much, not enough*.

Give each child enough dough to make an animal. Talk about what they have made and discuss the type of house that their animal would like to live in. You need to include size words such as *big, small, tall, short, wide, narrow*. Encourage discussion about different *shapes* and styles of house and different kinds of building materials. Talk about the animals' different needs. For example, the frog needs to be *low down* and *near* water; the bird needs to be *high up* in a tree. Provide materials for the children to use for their animal houses and make these as varied as possible. For example, modelling clay, card, straws, sticks, twigs, construction blocks, fabrics, leftover wallpaper and anything else you and the children can think of.

When the houses have been built, discussion should focus on the strengths of each, especially referring to shapes, the materials used and whether the houses are an appropriate size for the animals.

Designing and making houses

Each child designs and makes themselves a house that one of the little pigs would like to live in. Look at the *shapes* of houses, doors and windows. These could be changed as each child designs and makes their own house. Initiate a discussion about the *position* of the doors and windows.

How many straws, sticks and bricks would be needed to *cover* their model house? *How big* are the bricks? Area and estimation crop up all over the place. The good thing about estimation is that you do not have to be right. But the more you practice, the better you will become.

How many puffs will be needed to blow each house down? Investigate different ways of blowing – straws, balloons, bellows, hair dryers. Build a house or tower with light cardboard boxes. Test each of the blowing options. *Which was the best? How long did it take? Which was the worst? How long did that take?*

Sequencing

Sequence the building of a house. Do you know a builder who can come into school? Use words such as *first, second* and *third* which will give children the experience of working with *ordinal numbers*.

Provide bricks or wooden blocks for house building. '*What do you do first? Can you put the roof on first in case it rains while you're building? Why not? Tell me what you're doing*'.

Getting children to talk through their building has several advantages:

1 It forces them to use vocabulary of sequencing, for example, *first, then* and *after*.
2 It puts what they are thinking in to words. Being able to verbalise their thoughts is encouraging.
3 It allows children to clarify their thoughts.

Comparing

Look for differences in the pigs: clothes, bundles, shoes, ears. *Do they all look the same? What is the same and what is different?*

Compare the clothes the pigs are wearing. Talk about getting dressed in order. What do you put on *first*? What do you put on *last*?

Beginning to use 3D shapes

Use *3D shapes* such as *cylinders, cubes* and *cuboids* (or any other that is available) to make a set of pigs or a farmyard. This can be a tabletop farm or one set in a builder's tray. What is a set of pigs called? Well, that depends on the age of the pigs. They can be called a drift, drove or litter. Groups of older pigs are called a sounder of swine, a team or passel of hogs or a singular of boars. Or you can just call them a set of pigs. A male pig is called a boar. A female pig is called a gilt if she has not had piglets yet and a sow if she has. A baby pig is called a piglet.

Rhyming words

Make a 'wall' of rhyming words. Use *rectangular* and *square* shapes for the bricks of the wall and paste them onto a large sheet of backing paper. At the top, draw, write and put the appropriate materials under the words 'pig', 'stick', 'straw' and' brick'. Beneath these, write words that rhyme. This can be done on sticky notes and can always be added to as new words are discovered. Lead a discussion about words that sound like another word, such as *pig, big, twig, dig, stick, thick, trick, brick, straw, saw, paw*. Brick is an easy one because you will already have found words that rhyme with stick.

As we say goodbye to the three pigs, we embark on our next story.

Rapunzel

Rapunzel is a German fairy tale in the collection put together by the Brothers Grimm. It was first published in 1812.

Getting to know the story

Rapunzel tells the story of a young girl whose father was accused of theft when he took some vegetables for his wife from the garden of an evil witch. The witch made a bargain with the man and said that he could take as much as he wanted, but he had to give her the new baby when it was born.

The baby was called Rapunzel by the witch. She grew up to be a beautiful child with long golden hair. When she reached twelve years of age, the witch locked her inside a tower in the middle of the woods. Rapunzel was shut up inside this tall tower that had no doors or stairs. Most pictures of the story show a square or a circular tower. Challenge children to build towers of different shapes, with windows but no doors.

All about castles: developing a castle area

Talk about castles. '*Has anyone ever seen a castle? What was it like? Tell us something you liked about the castle.*' Show children pictures and photographs of castles and talk about different parts such as a drawbridge, a moat and turrets. Explain what each part was for. Put a basket with castle pictures and books in an area where children can build. Put a sign on the front that says '*Come and build a castle. Will your castle have a window? A door? A drawbridge? Turrets? A roof?*' Add baskets of bricks, blocks, plastic shapes, empty yoghurt pots and cardboard cylinders.

How would you feel?

After reading the story, lead a discussion about how it would feel to be locked in a tower. Keep a record of the words that children use to describe their feelings and use them as part of a display for the towers that the class will make later.

If you knew you were going to be locked in a tower like Rapunzel, what five (or ten) things would you bring in your suitcase? Encourage children to talk to a partner or friend. Do they want the same things or different things? Give templates of a suitcase so the objects can be drawn, or older children can draw their own suitcase and fill it.

A memory game: I Packed My Suitcase (sequencing)

I Packed My Suitcase is a classic memory game that is useful for all sorts of occasions, from a doctor's waiting room to a long car journey. You can adapt it to all ages of children, and adults enjoy playing as much as children. It is also good for older children who are beginning with phonics.

The first player thinks of a word beginning with the letter 'a' and then says, for example, 'I packed my suitcase with an apple'. The next player repeats the sentence and adds something beginning with 'b', for example, 'I packed my suitcase with an apple and a banana'. The next player adds a word beginning with 'c', for example, 'I packed my suitcase with an apple, a banana and a canary'. Play continues until someone cannot remember the list or makes a mistake. Depending on the players' ages, you can either prompt them or disqualify them. Keep going until all players but one are disqualified, or until you reach the end of the alphabet.

If playing with young children, it helps to make the words as silly and colourful as possible – they are more likely to remember them that way.

Mathematics talk

As the children are 'filling' their case, take the opportunity to talk about number bonds to numbers 5 or 10. '*You already have three things in your suitcase. How many more do you need to make five?*'

Have a set of old suitcases or open boxes for younger children to fill with actual objects. This can involve simple counting to 5 or 10. '*Let's count how many you have. One, two, three, four, five. Your suitcase is full' 'If you could take one more thing, what would it be? How many in your suitcase now?'* Use one more and one less in a practical way by putting in and taking out an object. *'If I take out your teddy and put back your car, do you still have five? How can we check?'* Start counting backwards until the case is *empty*.

Rhyming words

Every day the witch would call out to Rapunzel saying, *'Rapunzel, Rapunzel, let down your hair, so that I may climb the golden stair'*. One reason that the poem part of fairy tales persist in retellings is that it is often easier to remember things that rhyme.

What rhymes with Rapunzel? Not a lot!

Choose other words from the story such as *forest, tallest, shortest, fattest* and *highest* or *tree, me, see, bee, knee*. Post them on a 'brick' wall and refer to them whenever you can to reinforce the rhyming aspect of words.

Hair today, gone tomorrow!

Rapunzel's hair must have been incredibly strong. Cut strips of different materials such as paper, aluminium foil or tissue paper. All the strips must be the same length as each other. Hold one end of each strip in your hand and tie a small plastic bucket to the other end. Gradually fill the bucket with dry sand until the strip breaks. Measure the amount of sand in the bucket either with standard measures and grams or using the sand with balance scales and balancing the bucket with cubes. Make a graph of how much sand each strip could hold.

For example, using grams:

grams	grams	grams
paper	tinfoil	tissue paper

Build towers of cubes from the buckets

Being creative

Towers

Make a tower out of a large piece of cardboard or plywood, with a window opening where the children can peer out and pretend they are Rapunzel. If you have a long, strong cardboard box, use the open flaps to steady the tower and use the centre to be the tower itself.

If possible, leave a camera for children to use for taking pictures of their friends. These can then be shared with the rest of the class and generate discussion centred on the story.

Singing

One day a prince hears Rapunzel's beautiful singing voice and wants to meet her. He falls in love with Rapunzel when he hears her singing. Listen to recordings of various singers and ask children to decide which one sounds the way they imagine Rapunzel must have sounded.

Sing or say the rhyme 'There was a Princess long ago', which is a storytelling circle game. It involves actions and imaginative movement. Children hold hands to make a circle.

There was a Princess long-ago
Long-ago, long-ago
There was a Princess long-ago
Long-a-go!

One child plays the part of the princess and stands in the middle of the circle.

And she lived in a big high tower
A big high tower, a big high tower
And she lived in a big high tower
Long-a-go!

The children in the circle hold up their arms to show the meaning of tall.

One day a fairy waved her wand
Waved her wand, waved her wand
One day a fairy waved her wand
Long-a-go!

One child, pretending to be a fairy, leaves the circle and waves her wand (hand) over the princess.

The Princess slept for a hundred years
A hundred years, a hundred years
The Princess slept for a hundred years
Long-a-go!

The Princess lays on the floor, asleep. The fairy re-joins the circle.

A great big forest grew around
Grew around, grew around
A great big forest grew around
Long-a-go!

The children in the circle hold hands with each other and raise their hands high to make a forest.

A gallant Prince came riding by
Riding by, riding by

A gallant Prince came riding by
Long-a-go!

A child from the circle gallops around the outside of the forest.

He took his sword and cut it down
Cut it down, cut it down
He took his sword and cut it down
Long-a-go!

He uses his hand to 'cut down' 'the forest'. The children in the circle let go of each other and let their hands drop to their sides.

He woke the Princess with a kiss
With a kiss, with a kiss
He woke the Princess with a kiss
Long-a-go!

The Prince gently kisses the Princess.

So everybody's happy now
Happy now, happy now
So everybody's happy now
Happy now!

The Prince and Princess join hands and dance in the circle. The children in the circle clap their hands in a pattern set by the teacher.

Puppets

This is an activity that promotes creativity, environmental awareness and maths skills as well as imaginative play with a sprinkling of literacy.

You will need some wooden pegs and recycled materials from your junk box, tissue paper and wool for hair to create the characters from the Rapunzel story.

Use them to demonstrate a puppet show. Emphasise the maths vocabulary as you act out the story: *size, count, compare, nearly, just over, just under, about the same as, long, short, high, low, taller, higher, near, close, morning, evening, before, over, top, bottom, on, in, outside, inside, in front, behind, after, beside, next to, between, how many?* And this is just the short version of the story!

The peg puppets can be stored along the top of the castle, ready to be brought into action whenever the time is right. Leave them in your story corner with materials so that children can make their own puppets.

Whilst children are making their puppets, they are measuring (using standard, non-standard or guessing/estimating), problem-solving, practising fine motor skills such as cutting and colouring, as well as listening to and using mathematical vocabulary.

At the end of the time spent on Rapunzel and her story, why not have a celebration party for the prince and Rapunzel? The decorating possibilities are endless.

Party time!

Making lanterns is a very quick way to decorate a corner of the room or even a role play area outside, especially if you have trees and bushes to hang them from. Hang the lanterns around the classroom and even make some to take home.

As you are making them with the children, emphasise the vocabulary you use: *fold the paper in **half**; cut slits with your scissors. Only cut **up to** the line; open the paper **flat** and **turn it over**; put some glue along the **edge** and stick the other **edge** to it; push the **top** and **bottom** **towards** each other; cut a **narrow** piece of paper and glue both **ends** to the top of your lantern. This will make a handle.*

I have highlighted in bold the maths words. Whatever you are doing, it is difficult to get away from them.

1   Fold a piece of paper in half.

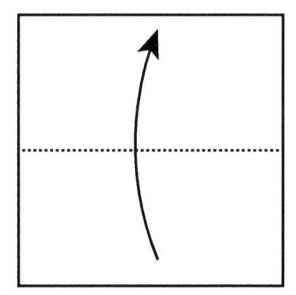

2   Keeping the paper folded, cut slits with a pair of scissors. Be careful not to cut too far. You could draw a pencil line 1 cm in from the open edges so children can see where to cut to.

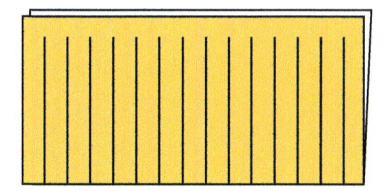

3   Open and turn over.

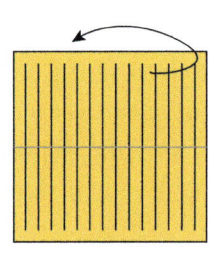

4   Overlap and glue the edges.

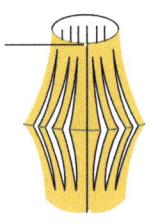

5   Gently push the top and bottom towards each other.
6   Cut a narrow strip of paper, attach both ends inside the top of the lantern, and you have a handle ready to hang.

These lanterns can be made with single-colour paper, wrapping paper of different colours and designs or seasonal papers. Children can decorate around the top and bottom to make them extra special.

As the children are making these, use precise mathematical language in your instructions. Use words such as 'half', demonstrating what half is as you make a lantern alongside the children. 'Open' and 'turn over' are direction and positional words. Say them as you demonstrate. 'Top' and 'bottom' are also positional vocabulary. Again, demonstrate as you say the words. 'Inside' joins the others as another positional word. Show and say the difference between *inside* and *outside*. Once they are made you can hang them somewhere *high* or *low*, again, using positional vocabulary.

Hang yellow streamers from the ceiling to resemble Rapunzel's hair. These can be cut from crepe or tissue paper which will blow gently in the breeze and will not pose a threat to the safety of the children. These strips can be *long, short, wide, narrow, far* or *near*. These are beautiful examples of *length* words within the area of measures.

If you have a party, you need party food. Find ways to incorporate the snacks into a party theme. Use heart-shaped biscuits and sandwiches, twisted cheese straws to represent Rapunzel's hair, gingerbread cut into small brick shapes and broccoli florets to represent the forest.

Encourage children to dress up for the party. This can be a full costume or just a halo, crown or witch's hat. There can be music, dancing and plenty to eat and drink.

How about making a cake? It could be shaped like the back of a person's head and then covered in long strands of yellow icing representing Rapunzel's long hair. Or shape the cake like a cylinder and ice it to look like a tower.

Maps

Show children examples of maps, including any that show information using pictures, such as a treasure map.

> *In our story we have a castle, a prince, a witch's house and a forest. Draw a map showing where each of these could be.*

For example:

Where shall we put the witch and the prince? What else do we need on our map?

Trails

Send the children on a treasure hunt where they must find hidden jewels. These can be small stones or beads which have been covered with coloured cellophane paper or coloured aluminium foil that is found around a popular brand of sweets, usually sold in big tubs at Christmas time. Or you can buy packets of self-adhesive jewels from craft and hobby shops. Each child collects one jewel after solving a clue. Provide rhyming clues that lead them to the final destination. For those children who have not yet mastered the art of reading, provide visual clues and use an adult for more support. Each destination should supply enough jewels for each child to have one as well as the next clue. At the last destination the children will be given a crown to decorate. They can then wear these to the party.

The following is a trail I have used, but write your own to suit where the children are. You may be able to use an outside area or you may be confined to a small room. Use the words from your rhyming wall to help you with ideas.

The handsome prince has been here today, he dropped some jewels along the way. Follow the clues – you need to be wise as they will lead you to your prize.

Clue 1. This clue is hiding in the dark in somewhere rather smelly. We put these on to jump in mud, it's hidden in a . . . (wellie).
Clue 2. This clue's snug and cosy go and take a peep. It's underneath a . . . where the dolls like to sleep (blanket).

Clue 3. This clue is on a table so go and take a look. It's hidden amongst words and pictures inside a favourite . . . (book).

Clue 4. In the morning we hear a rattle as letters fall to the ground. Go to something wooded where your next clue could be found (a wooden box under the letter box).

Clue 5. To hunt for this next clue pop some shoes on your legs. It's flapping in the wind held tightly on by pegs (somewhere outside on a washing line).

Clue 6. This clue is near a picture box we like to watch each day. It shows pictures of Peppa Pig and Postman Pat. Go find it right away! (television).

Clue 7. Your hunt is nearly ended; what a lot of jewels you've got. The last one is the biggest, you need to search for (add an adult name who works in your setting) sitting by the cot.

Making books for stories

Reading or telling stories can create a warm emotional bond between the reader/teller and the child. It helps children to develop basic language skills and expand their vocabulary. Books can help children to find out a lot about the world, different cultures and themselves.

Showing young children how to make picture books provides the opportunity to both record and share personal experiences. Two powerful ideas of thought and expression, the linguistic and the visual, are naturally integrated in the process of picture book making. Making picture books empowers young children who are struggling to master the reading and writing processes as they gain an understanding of how text and image work together to tell a story. But it increases their self-confidence when the finished book can be shared with their friends and family.

Adult-made picture books

These instructions show you how to make a six-page book with one sheet of paper.

Step 1. Take a sheet of A4 paper ☐ or A3 if you want a bigger book.

Step 2. Fold it in half lengthwise.

Step 3. Fold it in half again.

Step 4. Fold it in half again.

Step 5. Now you have a very small folded sheet of paper. But it is not a book yet.

Step 6. Unfold everything. Now it is a big piece of paper with lots of fold lines.

Step 7. Fold in half along the centre fold line. Make a mark with a pencil in the centre of the folded sheet. Cut from the **folded edge** to the centre dot. When you reach the dot, stop cutting.

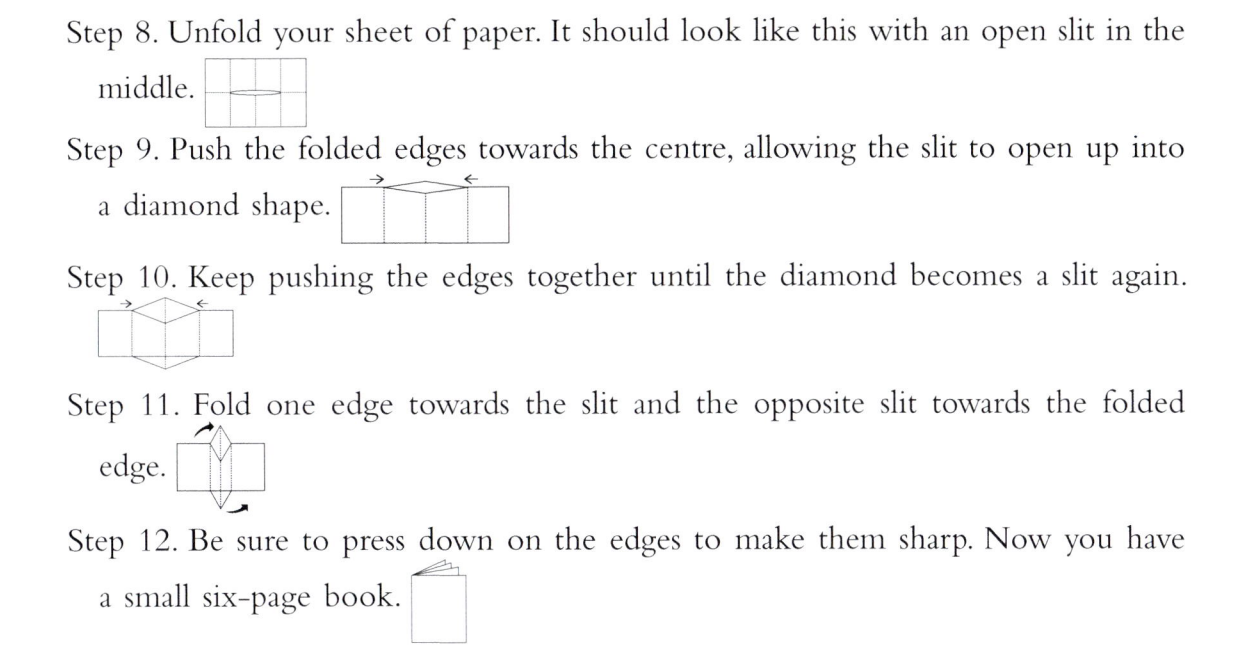

Step 8. Unfold your sheet of paper. It should look like this with an open slit in the middle.

Step 9. Push the folded edges towards the centre, allowing the slit to open up into a diamond shape.

Step 10. Keep pushing the edges together until the diamond becomes a slit again.

Step 11. Fold one edge towards the slit and the opposite slit towards the folded edge.

Step 12. Be sure to press down on the edges to make them sharp. Now you have a small six-page book.

Child-made picture books

You will need the following:

- Thick white paper or thin white card
- Scissors
- Glue

   Step 1. Cut the piece of paper or card in half lengthwise to make two *narrow rectangles*. It may be helpful for the child to fold along the line that is to be cut first. This makes cutting easier.
   Step 2. Fold the rectangle in half from top to bottom.
   Step 3. Fold the top flap in half again lining the bottom edge to the top crease.
   Step 4. Turn the paper/card over and do the same the other side.
   Step 5. Repeat these instructions for the left over rectangle.

You should now have two pieces that look like a capital **W**.

For younger children, let them have just one **W**. For older children, stick two together to make a longer book.

Children can decorate the front with a picture that is appropriate to the story and then draw pictures on each section that 'tells' the story.

More mathematical towers

Make a row of identical towers, each with an identical window. These can be made of kitchen roll middles. Paint them to look like brick or stone. Through each window, thread yellow cord of varying lengths. Tie a knot at one end so that it cannot come through the opening. Stand the towers in dry sand (not wet, or the cardboard will disintegrate) so that they can stand up. Show just the beginning of the cord at the window.

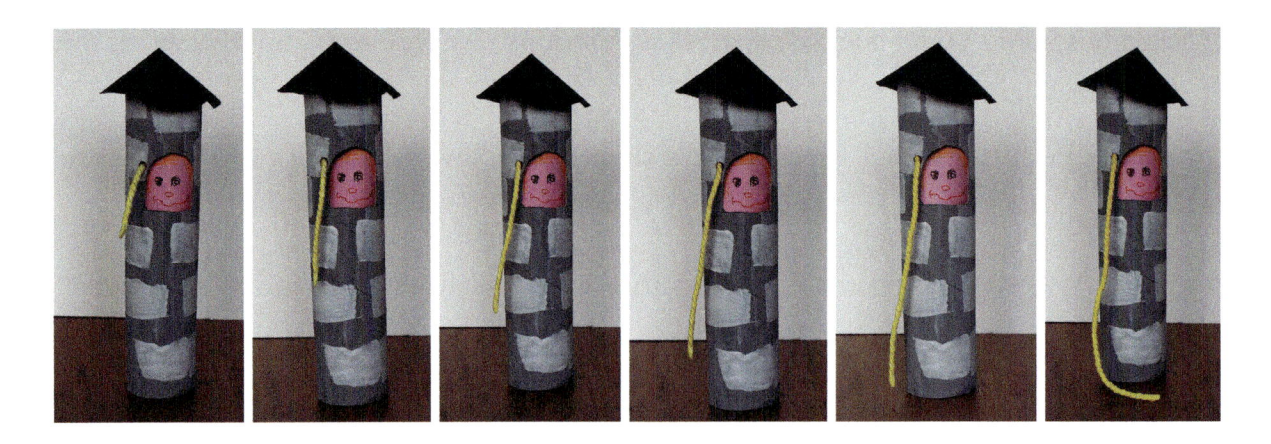

Challenge children to find the *longest* and *shortest* cords. Each is longer (or shorter) than all of the others. Pull them through one at a time. Move the towers to put them in order from shortest to longest to represent the passage of time while Rapunzel has been in the tower.

Using a rectangle stuck on to a larger piece of paper and a circle near the top of the rectangle, the children can make Rapunzel look out of her window. Cut lengths of yellow crepe paper for her hair. It should reach no further than the bottom of the tower. Children can measure the length of the hair using interlocking cubes. Make a series of these starting with short hair and moving on in a series of at least four more to the longest hair. Measure the 'growth' with interlocking cubes. Children can record their findings in any way they choose.

Children can make their own Rapunzel-in-the-tower pictures. Which Rapunzel has the *longest* hair? Which has the *shortest* hair? Use cut sponge to make the brick shapes and crepe or tissue paper for the hair.

I made a Rapunzel tower using different shapes.

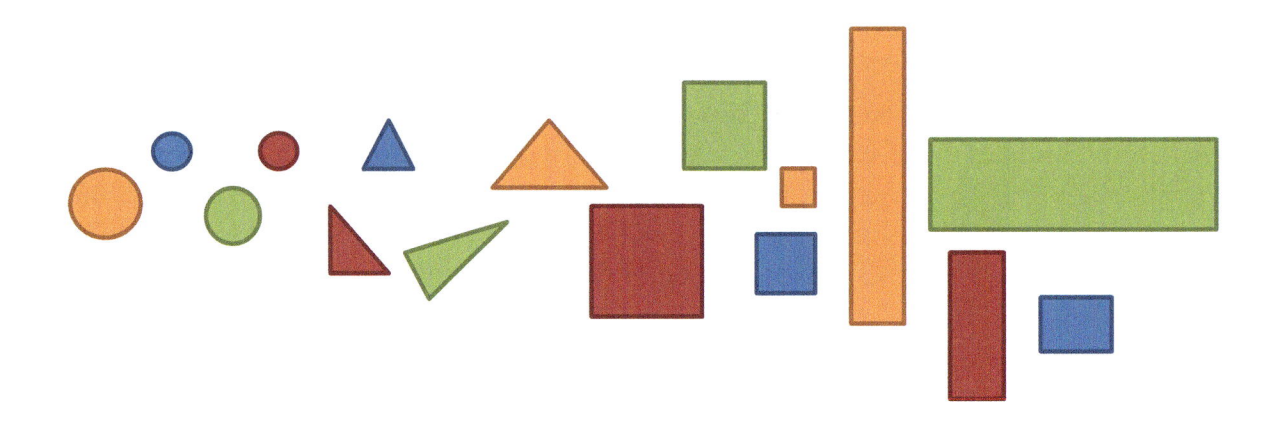

Chapter 2: Houses and homes   75

Older children can name and count the different shapes they used.

For example:

Be sure to offer different types of triangles.

Problem-solving

How can Rapunzel escape from the tower? Discuss various options with the children, and the safety aspects of each. For example, she could jump, but what would happen when she landed? The prince could build steps. The prince could build a slide. Let children choose one to create.

First, construct the tower. Cardboard cylinders are perfect for this. Provide a selection of materials so that children can choose their own way of escaping. Include pipe cleaners to make a ladder, cardboard cylinders cut in half lengthways to make a slide, or blocks to make steps.

Encourage children to share what they did and why they chose that way.

Short activity

When the children are in the outside area, rather than just climbing a ladder to get to the top of the slide, why not pretend to be the witch or prince and climb up Rapunzel's hair? This should help to stimulate children's imaginations so that they can lead the story themselves.

Or, in a different situation, climb up to a rocket ready for launching. Count down from five or ten when getting ready to launch. On zero, slide down the slide.

Or link it with the forest and climb up to the top of a very tall tree and describe what you can see in the forest or park below. Where else would you need to climb a ladder and be higher than everyone else? Ask children for their ideas.

Now that the prince and Rapunzel are happily married, let us move on to the next story.

Come Over to My House by Dr Seuss
Published by Random House

Getting to know the story

First written in 1966, this multicultural beginner book about home and friendship features typical Dr Seuss rhymes as well as artwork of the various styles of homes that children from around the world live in. It also covers what children eat, how they sleep (Japanese wooden pillows), play (sledding on pine needles) and even how they clean up afterwards (Polynesian hot spring). It is a book that is suitable both for beginners and for being read out loud to a group of children. The message of the book – that children are the same all over the world – is as true today as it was 50 years ago. It is perfect for expanding a child's world view.

Gather items from other countries to start an interest area. Add to them or change them when you can.

Many of the items in this photo were donated by parents who were on holiday and collected souvenirs, but some were bought at charity shops (the bunting is from Oxfam and is made from old saris), auctions and jumble sales. Also be sure to include anything the children have made (clay divas) during other themes or projects.

Mathematical activities

After reading the story, gather different building materials such as bricks, sticks, straw and tin. Be aware that strips or pieces of tin can have sharp edges. You can replace a sheet of tin with washed out tins from beans, tomatoes or soup and wrap tape around the top. Make dough and colour it to represent mud. Place all the materials on the interest table. Ask questions such as '*What does this feel like? Is it heavy or light? Is it warm or cold? Is it waterproof or not? How can we find out?*'

Discuss what houses in this country are made of. Make a set of houses from junk modelling resources. Take a picture of each child and put their minimised photo standing at the doorway of their house. Talk about similarities and differences between the houses. Use words such as '*tall, taller than, wide, wider than*'. Count the windows and doors. Look at brick patterns and find similar ones around the school. Discuss the different shapes that can be seen inside and outside of the classroom, both man-made and natural. Look for leaves, pine cones, bark textures, shells and snails.

Make round houses, square houses and any-other-shape-you-like houses. Share ideas about the different shapes involved. *A circle, a square, a round, a box*. Remember if you are talking about 3D shapes rather than the shape of the faces you need to use '*cube*', '*cylinder*' or '*cuboid*' as well.

Make houses and paint them different colours. Put out primary and white paint colours and let children mix their own paints if they want to. '*What colours did you use to make this colour? What colour is this? How did you make it?*'

Using shapes to make kites

Making kites can be as simple or as difficult as you like. But for children to have an active part, start with something simple. Look for sticks around your setting. Go on a stick hunt, but only for sticks that have already fallen from the tree. If that is not possible, ask caregivers at home to send some sticks into school. Make it clear that you are not really looking for logs, just sticks.

> Step 1. Use string to tie the sticks into a cross. You need the horizontal stick to be slightly shorter than the vertical stick.

Step 2. Tie your string firmly around the ends of the sticks. You may have to cut small notches in the sticks to help the string stay in place.

Step 3. Unfold a newspaper and cut a pattern to match the shape of your kite frame. Make it 3 or 4 cm larger than your frame all the way around so you can fold the edges over.

Step 4. Spread the newspaper over your stick frame; fold the edges over your string and glue in place.

Step 5. Tie a long string to the kite where the sticks cross. Add a tail if you want to.

Step 6. Hold the long string, start running and fly your kite.

Design and make boats that float

On a table next to a water tray put out a range of materials such as tubs, cardboard boxes, cotton wool, pieces of aluminium foil, pieces of different fabrics, plastic interlocking cubes, slices of apple, a sponge and small blocks of wood.

Demonstrate the meaning of 'float'. **Hint:** It is more likely to be successful if the material being used is not thrown with some force into the water to make a big splash.

Demonstrate the meaning of 'sink'.

Ask the children to guess which objects they think will float and sink. You may want to have two small hoops or boxes which have the labels 'float' and 'sink' and sort the objects into two *sets*.

After experimenting with each type of material, children can change their minds about what they think will happen.

As an extension, older children can put weights in some of the 'floating' set and see how heavy it needs to be to eventually sink.

Making a paper boat can be a bit tricky. Some children I have worked with have taken a piece of paper that originally sank, screwed it into a ball which was put on top of the water and watched it float. Explain that to a three-year-old! Talk about the hidden pockets of air that are trapped inside the ball and that once the paper is really wet and the air has escaped, it will sink.

Step 1. Fold a piece of A4 paper in half vertically. Open the paper out flat.

Step 2. Fold in half again, but this time horizontally.

Step 3. Fold in the corners to the fold line made in Step 1.

Step 4. Fold up the edges on both sides.

Step 5. Pull out the sides and flatten.

Step 6. Fold back and front layers up.

Step 7. Pull the sides apart and flatten.

Step 8. Pull top flaps outwards.

Step 9. Squish the bottom and pull the sides up.

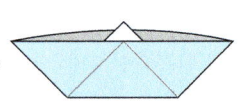

Well done! Now see if it floats.

Boats, like cars, trains and aeroplanes, take you away from your everyday life and can lead to an exciting adventure.

All you need is some paper or thin cardboard. As you are making the boats, talk to the children about where they would like to go if they had a real boat. It can be a real or made-up place. What would their boat look like? Do they want to sail around the world? Where is the first place they would like to stay? Keep a record of their ideas and use a **W** book (shown in the Rapunzel ideas) for them to show their story.

Using measures: recipes from around the world

These recipes have been written for you, the adult, to follow and cook with. You might like to make child-friendly recipes so that the children can follow what you are saying and doing in order to make their own chapattis. Laminate recipe cards and include pictures that children can follow.

Check for special diets and allergies before involving children in baking.

From India

Chapattis

This recipe makes about 16 chapattis.

You will need the following:

250 g wholemeal or chapatti flour
Spices such as ground cumin, coriander or paprika
175 ml water
Flour for use in rolling the dough
A large bowl, a damp cloth, a rolling pin, a frying pan and some oil

What to do: (children can do all of this except frying the chapattis)

1. Put the flour into a large bowl and add the spices. Slowly add the water and mix together using your hands.
2. Continue to mix with your hands until the dough is smooth.
3. Cover the bowl with a damp cloth and leave for 30 minutes.
4. Mix the dough again. Spread a little flour on your hands and divide the mixture to make 16 balls.
5. Sprinkle some flour on a flat surface.
6. Roll each ball into the flour and flatten it with a rolling pin until it is about 15 cm wide.
7. Fry the chapattis for about one minute on each side.

Chapter 2: Houses and homes

From the United States

Chocolate brownies

You will need the following:

120 g melted margarine
250 g caster sugar
2 eggs
1 teaspoon vanilla flavouring
50 g cocoa powder
75 g self-rising flour
Pinch of salt (optional)
Icing sugar (optional)
Baking parchment, 20 cm-square cake tin, fork or whisk for beating

What to do:

1. Put the oven on at 180 °C to get hot.
2. Put baking parchment in the cake tin.
3. Take the melted butter and add the sugar, eggs and vanilla. Blend together.
4. Stir in the cocoa powder, flour and salt.
5. Beat the mixture.
6. Pour the mixture into the tin. Put the tin in the oven for 25 minutes. When cool, tip the cake out onto a cooling tray.
7. Sprinkle with icing sugar.

Hint: Brownies are very tasty. Try adding chocolate chips or fresh strawberries or use white drinking chocolate.

From Mexico

Avocado dip (guacamole)

You will need the following:

Spoon
Fork
Medium bowl
2 ripe avocados
Juice from 1 lemon

You could also add one chopped spring onion and a half teaspoon of ground chili powder. However, I have found that it is best for most children to leave out the onion and chili.

What to do:

1. Slice the avocados in half. Remove the skin and the kernel. **Warning**: the flesh of the avocados can be very slippery. Take out the kernel using a spoon, not a knife.
2. Put the avocados in a bowl and mash them with a fork or a potato masher.
3. Add lemon juice (small amount).
4. Eat the guacamole with crisp nachos or as a sandwich filling.

Chapter 2: Houses and homes

This is a good activity for involving the home. Ask adults to come into the school and make their recipe. If this is not possible, ask them to send in their favourite recipe, saying why they like it so much. Make them into a book. Perhaps sell the book to raise funds for school.

Early fractions: using festivals

These activities help children to appreciate the food that they eat. For example, Divali (or Diwali) is the Hindu and Sikh festival of light. It takes place in October or November and lasts up to five days. At Divali people light small lamps called divas.

To make divas, use clay or dough.

Roll it *Flatten it Squash it* *Decorate it Dry it* *Paint it*

Using food

Start with a selection of fruit (check for any food allergies and dietary requirements); a knife; plates; information books; and pictures about different festivals.

Start by talking about the importance of food during festival times. During a Muslim festival called Ramadan, people stop eating for a short time. This helps them to understand what it is like to be poor and hungry. Show some fruit that you have bought for snack time. Cut one piece of fruit into four pieces and give four children one piece each. How do the children who have not been given a piece of fruit feel? Involving the children, divide up the rest of the fruit so that everyone has a piece. Invite one child to hand the plate of food around. Explain that it is important to take just one piece because otherwise there will not be enough for everyone. Make sure you have enough for everyone else.

Use different ways of eating food such as with a knife and fork, a spoon and chopsticks.

Prop box

Start small. There is so much that could go in, that you would need an enormous box. Start with stamps, coins, postcards and gift cards from different countries. Talk about them; compare them to what you have in your country. Look for similarities and differences. Include plain white paper plates to make clocks, story books from around the world in different languages and clothes or material samples from different cultures.

Role play

Decorate a corner with flags from other countries. Design and make a flag for an imaginary country.

Use fabrics from other countries to put over the tables and hang on the walls. Inspired by posters showing children from around the world, make papier-mâché globes.

Blow up a round(ish) balloon. Cover it with blue paper. This can be done with one sheet of blue tissue paper pasted over with wallpaper paste or diluted PVA glue or by small torn pieces of blue paper soaked in wallpaper paste. There are lots of types and makes of paste so make sure that the one you use is child friendly. Mix the paste in a bowl and allow the children to dip their paper right in so that it gets very wet. You may want to ask the children to wear rubber gloves in case they (a) put their fingers in their mouth or (b) develop an allergy to whatever is in the paste. When the paper has dried, pop the balloon and carefully pull it out so the world does not collapse. Children can cut or tear green pieces of paper for the land and white for the north and south poles. These can then hang in the role play area.

Make paper plate clocks set to different times around the world. Write the name of the country and a picture of a child from there. There are many pictures on the internet that can help you.

Display a world map with sticky dots of where the children have been or where they want to go.

Gather postcards from around the world. Add to those in your prop box over time. Collect different stamps and coins. Look at similarities and differences between your stamps and coins and those of other cultures.

Collect stories from around the world and put them in a box or basket so that children can choose which to read.

Clothes from around the world are always interesting. Look for pictures, photos and actual clothes that children can try on.

Trails

Tell a story about an explorer who loves to travel to different countries all over the world. *Who can tell me what an explorer is? What does an explorer do?*

'*The explorer in our story is off to travel the world. What do you think he or she will need to take with him or her?*' Plan a survival kit that he or she can take with him or her which will help him or her cope with the different types of weather. You need to think about keeping warm or keeping cool. '*What do you wear when the weather is hot? What do you wear when the weather is cold? Tell your friend what you wear when it is raining very hard. What helps to keep you dry?*'

Discuss the answers with the group. Are all of the answers the same? If you have a flip chart you can use, draw outlines of children and then add, or ask the children to add, the different items they have suggested for each type of weather. Use the pictures as a display in your role play area.

You can discuss the different types of weather. List things for protection: different hats, warm clothing, food and water. The children can try to create a small personal survival kit to help the explorer. Limit the size of the kit; a lunch box or small shoe box would be good to use.

Draw a class map for the explorer to use.

'*Where will the explorer start from? Where does he or she want to go?*' Those two things can be put on the map to get children thinking about where else he could visit. '*Does he or she want to go somewhere hot or somewhere cold? Will there be animals there? What sort of animals? Will there be people to help him or her?*' Gradually build up the map and then display it. You could build up different types of maps for different areas and use them to show the different journeys an explorer could make.

Games

Put together a selection of games from around the world. These are easily found on internet sites.

For example, Mancala is a game from East Africa. The word 'mancal' is Arabic for 'to move'.

Chapter 2: Houses and homes

This is a game for two players. You will need a Mancala game board. This can be a six- or 12-place egg box. Use the box of six for the younger children and for older children to start with. Each player will also need 24 counters for a 12-egg carton, and 12 counters for a six-egg carton as well as a small tub each. Place the small tubs at each end of the egg box.

Use an empty 12-egg carton.

Cut the lid off. Put a small tub at each end of the carton. You may want to tape them in place.

Now you are ready to play.

Place the board (egg carton) horizontally between you and your opponent.

Put four of your counters in each pocket on your side of the box. Leave the end tubs empty until play starts.

The first player takes all the counters from one of the six cups on their side of the egg carton.

Moving to their right, drop one counter into each cup you come to, including the end tub. Continue to drop a counter into each cup on your opponent's side. However, do *not* put any counters in your opponent's end tub. If the last counter in your hand lands in your end tub (called the Kalaha), you have another turn. Otherwise it is your partner's turn.

If the last counter that you drop goes into an *empty* cup on your side, you take all of the counters in the cup directly across from yours. When you capture these counters, you take all of them, including the single counter that did the capturing, and put them into your Kalaha. It is then your opponent's turn.

The game is over when all six cups on either your side or your opponent's side are empty. When this happens, the player who still has counters in their cups moves all of them into the Kalaha. The winner, the one with the most counters in her Kalaha, can say 'shinda', which means 'I've won!' in Swahili.

Another game comes from Korea and is called Five Field Kono. This game develops logical thinking (but younger players will just play regardless of any thinking). This develops over time. But the game can be simplified by using a smaller board and fewer counters.

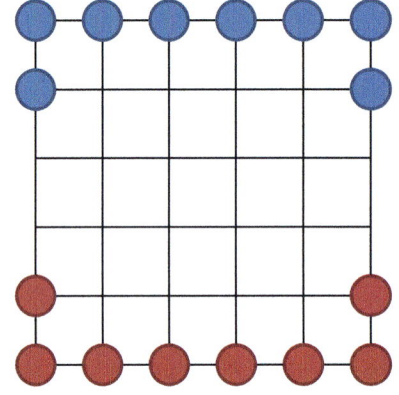

Players place their counters as shown. In turn they move their pieces one at a time diagonally across a square to the next point, either forwards or backwards. No jumping over pieces is allowed. The object of the game is to move pieces across the board onto the points occupied by their opponent at the beginning of the game. The first player to do this is the winner.

Outdoors

Put a pile of sand outside in an open space (desert). Draw the shape of it or put it on a piece of paper and draw round it. Visit your sand pile every day. *What happens to your pile? What kind of weather changes it most?* Draw the changes that happen.

Make a collection of metal objects – nails, nuts and bolts, coins. Leave them outside. *What sort of weather damages them the most? What happens?*

Short activities

Making an African necklace

Gather some ideas about artefacts that come from other cultures. For example, African women in national dress wear bright, colourful clothes and usually some sort of jewellery. How about

Chapter 2: Houses and homes   83

designing and making an African necklace? Use a circular paper plate, cut out a wedge so that it fits around a child's neck, and cut out the central circle. These necklaces can now be decorated using bright colours and maybe some jewels. I used just primary colours for one set with four-year-olds. I had hoped that the colours would merge into each other to produce new colours and a few surprises for the children. But this did not always happen, as the children tended to drift off to other activities before returning. By then, alas, the paint had already dried.

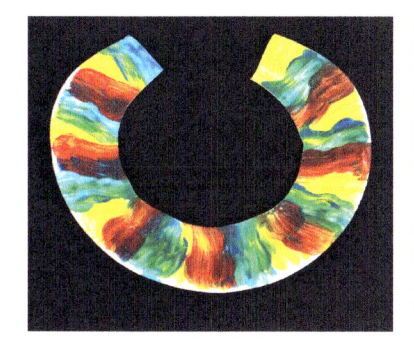

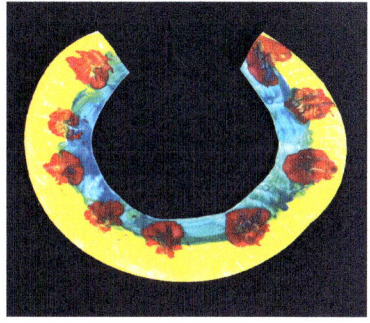

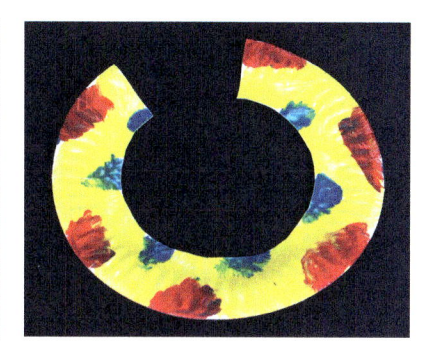

Making an Aboriginal rainstick

In my experience with early years children, Aboriginal rainsticks are quite popular. A rainstick is a long, hollow tube partially filled with small pebbles or beans and has small pins or thorns arranged on its inside surface. When the stick is upended, the pebbles fall to the other end of the tube, making a sound reminiscent of rain falling. Rainsticks can be made from any of several species of cactus. The cacti, which are hollow, are dried in the sun. The spines are removed and then driven into the cactus like nails. Pebbles or other small objects are placed inside the rainstick, and the ends are sealed. A sound like falling water is made when the rainstick has its direction changed from horizontal to a vertical position and back again. Rainsticks may also be made with other common materials like kitchen towel rolls instead of a cactus, and nails or toothpicks instead of thorns.

A simple rainstick for children can be made from a cardboard cylinder, some paint and two circles of paper to fit over the ends with two elastic bands to keep the circles in place. You will also need small pebbles or dried beans. **Hint:** Be aware of the safety rules when using any type of raw bean. Do not give children uncooked dried beans. These can be very toxic.

Paint the outside of the cylinder. Allow the paint to dry. Cover one end, put in the pebbles or beans and seal the open end. Shake gently to hear the rain.

Try using different sizes of cylinders or adjust the number of beans or pebbles and you will get slightly different sounds.

A more sophisticated stick can be made by painting a kitchen roll tube with acrylic paint. Leave it to dry and then apply another coat of paint.

Make up a palette of differently coloured acrylic paints. Use a cotton bud for each of the different colours. Paint and decorate the outside of the tube with different dot patterns.

Cut the necks off two balloons and stretch one of the balloons over the end of the tube. Secure with masking tape. Cut a long piece of foil and crinkle it up to make a long, thin sausage. Fold it in half and twist to create loops for dry rice to fall though. Put this into the tube.

Add about half a cup of rice. Seal the other end of the rainstick with the other balloon as before. Paint over the masking tape and leave to dry.

When it is finished, slowly turn the cylinder up and down and listen to the sound of rain.

Singing songs

Listen to music and songs from other cultures. There is a huge variety on YouTube. Give musical instruments to the children for them to make their own special music. Add dance to this and you almost have a concert.

Making flags

Make a 'flag of me'. Ask the children to design their own flag – something that suggests what their interests are, where they come from, what they believe in, and so forth.

The flag might include representations of:

- Their favourite colours, animals or sport.
- Their families or pets.
- An outline of their country of origin, or that of their parents.
- Languages they speak.
- Places they have visited or want to visit.

What would yours look like?

Home/school links

Ask parents to send in photos of places they have visited. This could be at home or abroad, seaside or forest, urban or rural. Make a photo album. Watch a travel programme that visits different continents. Talk about the similarities and differences. Draw on any personal experiences of the children.

Same, Same but Different by Jenny Sue Kostecki-Shaw Published by Henry Holt and Co.

Getting to know the story

Elliot lives in America and Kailash lives in India. They are pen pals. By exchanging letters and pictures they learn that they both love to climb trees, have pets and take the bus to school. Their worlds might look different but they are actually similar. Same, same but different.

Setting up a holiday area

Ask children if they have ever been to any other country. Where have they been? Who did they go with? Why did they go there? It may have been for a holiday or because a family member moved for work. It may have been to visit family. Talk about overseas visits. Many of the children may have gone on holiday. Setting up a holiday area can make connections to real life experiences.

Discuss holidays and where the children go. Make tickets and posters. Paint pictures of holidays. Send postcards to children, share stories about journeys and discuss excitement and fears, visit travel agents to get information and posters. Write letters.

Children can make postcards, with a picture on one side and a message on the other, and actually post them. This could involve a trip to a post office if there is one nearby. Look at, discuss and then design stamps. Talk about 'how much' and 'how many'.

Making and using games

Look at maps, globes and atlases and talk about the weather. Use weather symbols. Make a board game from weather symbols. You will find a full-size version in the resource sheets section.

Use a cardboard cube to make a die. An empty tissue box is good for this. On separate paper, draw each of the weather symbols. Paste them on the six faces of the box. Using only the top part of the board to start with, take turns to throw the die and cover a matching picture on the board with a cube or a counter. Each player has their own colour counter. Keep playing until all of the pictures have been covered. If a picture already has a cube or counter on it, it cannot be removed and that player misses a turn. For younger children you could use a 3 × 3 or a 4 × 4 grid.

If you wish to determine a winner, ask each player to take their own colour counter or cube and make lines of counters or towers of cubes. Compare the lines or towers. The longest line or the tallest tower wins the game. If you do not wish your young players to compete, just build towers or lines of counters and use them for counting and comparing.

Ask questions such as '*How many counters/cubes do you have? Do you have more than five? Do you have less than ten? Do you have more than your friend? Do you have less than your friend? Who has most? Who has least?*'.

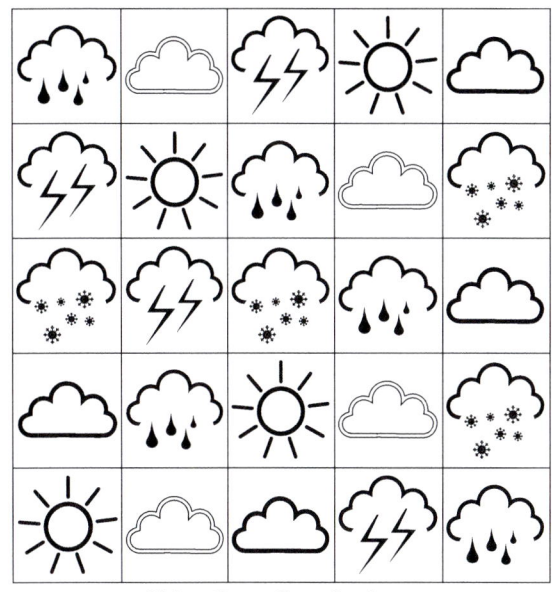

An extension to this game is to use both the top and bottom parts shown. This time, add numbers to the pictures in the lower grid. These need to be appropriate to the level at which the children are working. If recognising numbers is still not an option, draw spots to represent the numbers in a regular dice pattern.

This time children take turns to throw the die, look for that number/spot pattern and match it to the weather symbol. They then find that weather symbol on the main board and cover it with a counter. Play continues until all the symbols are covered. Then find who has the most counters as in the previous game.

Weather Symbols

Become a weather forecaster

> Be a weather forecaster.
> Add a weather area to your holiday area.
> Hang weather symbols to twigs.
> Make daily weather charts using the conventional symbols.

Apply magnetic tape or hook-and-loop fastener to the back of pictures of the weather symbols. Draw a large map of where you live (the county or country). Use the weather symbols to describe the weather.

Investigating weather

Compare weather in India with weather in your own country. Use your existing knowledge of the children and their families if possible. Invite parents or other visitors into the classroom to talk about the weather where they have lived.

Shadows: you need a sunny day and a warning not to look directly at the sun, items with interesting shapes, black sugar paper and chalk.

> Let the children experiment.
> Try having pairs chase each other's shadow.
> Try having pairs copy each other's shadows.
> Can you make your shadow disappear?
> How do you get long/short/fat/thin shadows?

The best shadows can be caught on white paper (use coloured chalk), cut and displayed indoors.

Rainbows: can you make a rainbow? Use a tray of water. Put some cooking oil on top of the water. Shine a torch onto it. What do you see?

Fill a clear plastic jar or bottle with water. Hold a piece of white paper behind it and shine a torch through the water onto the piece of paper. What do you see? Try some ideas of your own.

Keeping dry: make a collection of different kinds of cloth and paper. Can you find which things are waterproof? You could try putting a piece of each cloth and paper on a table and sprinkling water on them. Which ones let the water through?

Cover a parcel to keep it dry. Make a bag to hold your swimming things. Make umbrellas. Use art straws or garden canes to make a frame. Cover your frame and test it.

Recording weather: use weather symbols to keep a record of your daily weather and the weather in India.

Designing

Design a pair of wellie boots. Give the children an outline of a pair of boots and ask them to decorate them in any way they like, using what materials they would like. A good book to read would be 'What if Rain Boots were Made of Paper?' by Kevin Beals and P. David Pearson, published by Amplify. It links beautifully with science ideas and allows children to think, talk and compare their thoughts with others.

Developing a prop box

Put together a prop box to include a large poster or map of where you live, a pointer, laminated pictures of weather conditions, weather symbols, weather words, a camera (for outside pictures to show different weather types), a rain gauge, thermometer, compass and photographs of different clouds. If there is room, add weather clothing accessories such as an umbrella, sun hat, coat, winter hat and scarf.

Collect examples of different currencies that have been left over from previous holidays. Adults from home may be able to help with this.

Allow time for the children to explore the map. If it is of the local area ask them to find where they live, or find a shop or the school.

Chapter 2: Houses and homes   87

Role play

The travel agency

Find a space to set up a travel agency. You will need holiday booking forms, homemade or gathered from an actual travel agent. Otherwise, use the form available in the resource sheets section.

Include some luggage labels. The prop box could be an actual suitcase. Ask for some posters from travel agents that can become the display on the back wall. You will also need an open and closed sign. Collect some brochures that show holidays in warm and cold climates. Look at the pictures in the brochures and use them as discussion pictures when talking to the children. Include on the 'counter' some books made by children who have cut pictures from various brochures to show seaside hotels, city hotels or hotels in the countryside. Give 'customers' a questionnaire to complete.

WELCOME TO THE TRAVEL AGENCY

1. What country do you want to go to? _____

2. Where do you want to stay?

   A town   ☐

   The seaside   ☐

   Country   ☐

3. Do you want to stay in a

   Tent   ☐   Caravan   ☐

   Cottage   ☐   Hotel   ☐

   How long do you want to stay? _____

   How many adults?
   How many children?

The main thing in the travel agency is to make the customer comfortable. Provide two or three chairs for customers as well as a table and chair for the travel agent. And do not forget a globe to show where the holiday locations are.

An extra detail if there is somewhere to hang it is the papier-mâché globe that was used earlier in the role play section. To make a new one, you will need a round balloon, PVA glue and blue, green and white tissue paper. Cover the whole balloon with blue tissue to represent the sea, either as a whole piece or smaller pieces torn from a larger piece. Once the 'sea' is dry, tear some green pieces of tissue to represent the land and some white to represent the north and south poles.

Once all of this is dry you will be able to carefully deflate the balloon and remove it. Thread some cotton or thin string through the top of the globe and hang it. This will be quite delicate so young children may squash or scrunch it quite easily. My advice is to make more than one.

The post office

This links nicely with the travel agency, as many letters, parcels and cards are sent from and to different countries. A post office and postman/woman offer so many experiences in so many areas.

Resources: uniforms and bags; post boxes through the school of different 3D shapes (they can also be different heights); posters and pictures showing the history of post boxes; letters and parcels to sort; sacks for letters, stamps, scales, pens, paper, till and real money; franking stamps and pads. Do not forget forms. The post office is awash with forms.

Visit a local post office. 'Borrow' a few different forms, including passport application forms. Children can draw pictures of themselves for their passport.

Develop children's vocabulary with words such as 'send/deliver', 'collect', 'time', 'sort', 'stamp', stick' and 'wrap'.

Make parcels of different weights and shapes. Wrap them and see how much paper it takes to completely cover them. Can it be done with just one piece of paper? How much more do we need? How much is left over? Using newspapers is a cheap way of doing this.

There are many links that can be made with other stories about postal carriers and letters.

Children can write letters and post them in the boxes around the school. Be sure to put collection times on the post boxes.

Make a class address book. Draw your own house on a large, hand-drawn map of the area. Explore other mathematical links, such as money, time and weight.

Money

Display a price list for envelopes: small, medium and large. Display stamps and the price options. Talk about first class and second class, explaining the difference between them. Have a selection of (real) coins for children to sort through.

Sorting

Use shoe boxes for sorting envelopes and letters. Each child has their own box, which can be cut down to save on space, and decorates it with a photo of themselves and their names to make sorting the letters easy for the postal carrier. Encourage adults at home to write a letter to their child. This can be dropped off at the school at the beginning or end of each day, ready for sorting and posting the following day.

Shapes

Design a stamp. This activity uses the notion of area but without mentioning the word itself.
   Use different 2D shapes. Show examples from around the world.

Time

   Write the opening and closing times of the post office.
   Write the collection and delivery times.

Weight

Have a set of scales either to measure the weight of parcels and letters using standard measures of grams but also balance scales to find 'heavier than' and 'lighter than'. Fill empty boxes with everyday materials such as wooden blocks, interlocking cubes, a pair of gloves, some stones and some sticks.

Trails

Everyone involved must be aware of the 'why' of trails. There needs to be a clear understanding about the benefits for the children, the staff and the wider community. As well as these, what are the objectives as far as maths is concerned? Be clear about whether the trail will cover one part of maths (in which case, do not get side-tracked) or as many parts of the maths curriculum as possible.
   One aim is to give children the experience of feeling like a mathematician and therefore being mathematical. Being mathematical has many different interpretations, but some descriptions of what it means might include the following:

- Thinking about and communicating ideas.
- Engaging in problem-solving activities. Too much of mathematics is about learning facts and practising skills. We need to think about how we can support learners in being mathematical. They need opportunities to explore problems and to pose problems of their own.
- Creating and identifying mathematical problems within given contexts.

The emphasis of a trail should be in the journey through a problem rather than the answer. This will produce active learners – the learning is in the doing and will allow children to take responsibility for their progress.

A senses trail

The words 'seeing', 'hearing', 'touch', 'taste' and 'smell' describe our senses, and they are five words with huge importance. They sum up the key ways in which we learn throughout our lives about the world around us. As St. Thomas Aquinas said, 'The senses are a kind of reason. Taste, touch and smell, hearing and seeing, are not merely a means to sensation, enjoyable or otherwise, but they are also a means to knowledge – and are, indeed, your only actual means to knowledge'. St. Thomas was an Italian Dominican friar, Catholic priest and Doctor of the Church and is thought by many to be an influential philosopher of his time. His influence on Western thought is considerable, and much of modern philosophy developed or opposed his ideas.

The concept of sensory play is now recognised as one of the most important methods of educating all children from a very early age, playing a crucial part in their development.

Sensory play includes any activity that will stimulate any or all of a child's five senses so as to help them develop and refine the use of those senses. All children need help learning how to use their senses.

Sensory play can be easily incorporated into a trail.

Sense of sight. Creating simple paper plate frames by cutting out the centre, children are able to concentrate on smaller details in the environment. Along the trail, look at flora and fauna before, after and even during a rain shower. Compare this with what you know (or can find out) such as the rains in India before, after and during a monsoon. What would be the same? What would be different? Or compare the heat of a desert and the snow at the polar regions.

Concentrate on looking for and at minibeasts. Some can be taken back into the classroom to examine and draw before being released back outside. As before, compare with minibeasts in India using what you know or can find out.

Sense of sound. There is always so much to listen to outside, whether from natural or man-made objects, depending on where you live. You could listen to birds or buses. When comparing your environment's sounds with Indian sounds, add bells or wind chimes to your trail. Use a table along the trail to display different musical instruments from India and from your country. Oxfam has a large range of props from India, including musical instruments.

Sense of touch. Gather together different materials of different textures from traditional clothes that would be worn in your country and in India. For example, silk, cotton, wool, denim or corduroy. Put each piece into a small bag or box. If using a box, cut a hole in the side so that a child can put their hand in to feel what is inside without seeing it. It may be helpful for some children to have pictures of adults and children from both countries wearing traditional clothes. Add a small piece of the fabric to the picture so that children can feel what they can see as well as what they cannot see. This will make a match easier to begin with. Ask children what they can feel. Is it rough? Is it smooth? What else can they tell you?

Sense of taste. Check allergies and religious beliefs before asking children to taste food. Set up a food trail around the classroom. Each table can have a different selection of food from your country and India. These can be both sweet and savoury, but probably not too spicy. Most supermarkets sell a variety of Indian food, including snacks. But if parents can cook and provide some examples, that would be a good way of introducing them into the school. Involve children in preparing the food. Making chapattis is fairly easy. They may not look perfect, but they will smell and taste delicious.

Buy or make naan bread. Cook some brown rice with a small amount of curry powder and chickpeas so children can taste a little spiciness. Show children how to tear off a piece of naan and use it to scoop up some rice.

Sense of smell. Smell will be a major part of food preparation. But in addition to that, add some incense sticks. Compare them with the reed diffusers that are available to buy in most candle shops. They are very similar to each other in that they bring perfume into a room. But what are the differences?

Festivals

Learn about Indian dance and how to put on a sari.
Listen to Indian music.

As mentioned, Divali (or Diwali) is the Hindu and Sikh festival of light. At Divali, people light small lamps called divas and they send special cards to each other.

Divali prop box

Divali greeting cards.
Child-made clay or dough divas.
Tea lights or battery tea lights to put in the divas.
Posters and pictures of Indian celebrations.
Jewellery.
Chalk or coloured sand to make rangoli pictures.
Pictures and story books with dual languages if possible. Ask at your local library where you could get these.
Indian clothes for men and women, including sari lengths.
Indian and English cooking utensils.
Photos of Indian and English food.
Recordings of Indian music.
Fairy lights to decorate the play area.

Clay rangoli

How about creating an extra-colourful rangoli pattern this Divali? Use clay or dough to roll up a welcome rangoli and place it outside your classroom door. This is easily made by using coloured clay or dough rolled into snakes and then curled to make a pattern. Older children can produce quite complex patterns whilst younger children start with the basic shape of a circle and build on it. It can also be made out of coloured sand, coloured rice or dry flour but you may want to put that into a tray so that the sand/rice/flour does not end up all over the place.

Games

During Divali, children have a holiday from school. Presents are given and delicious holiday food is prepared and exchanged. New clothes and jewellery are worn. Parties are held, and dice and card games are played.

Dice games are largely believed to have originated in India. A simple one is called Passa. To make it easier for children to play, use a pair of blank dice with only four numbers written on them: 1, 3, 4 and 6. Leave two faces blank. The adult game is based on rules of gambling, but for children I leave that bit out.

Children take turns rolling both dice together. If the outcome shows no matching pair of numbers, the dice are passed to the other player and are rolled again. As soon as a pair is rolled, the outcome is decided. A pair of fours or sixes is a winning pair. A pair of ones or threes is not a winning pair. It is a rather simple game, similar to heads or tails, but more fun because dice are used.

Chapter 3: Big and little

Why big and little?

Children are often interested in size differences of everyday objects. They see them in the home and when out shopping such as a variety pack of cereal and a full-size pack, a single pack of biscuits and a double pack of biscuits, a small jar of jam and a large jar of jam.

When learning about measuring they need to move on with their development of mathematical vocabulary and refine their understanding of 'big' and 'little'. Words such as 'long', 'short', 'tall', 'thick', 'thin', 'wide' and 'narrow' can be introduced through practical activities related to stories. As we have seen in previous stories, 'big' and 'little' are comparative terms so that the same object can be 'big' in some contexts and 'little' in others.

Using open questions such as *'What's the biggest thing you've seen today?'* gives children the opportunity to show their understanding of big. Using closed questions such as *'Who is the smallest person in our class?'* can have only one right answer. In the same way, *'Who is bigger/smaller than you?'* can have many different answers.

Mathematics

Counting

Understanding numbers

Comparing

Ordering

Addition and subtraction

Using money

Using measures: length, weight, money, time, capacity

Discussing

Exploring patterns and shapes

Describing shapes and measures

Problem solving

Mathematical processes

Being systematic

Making and testing predictions

Selecting materials and mathematics appropriate for the task

Exploring and planning

Making and testing hypotheses

Classifying

Collecting, organising and recording information

Recording systematically

Communicating clearly

Talking about work

Using trial and improvement methods

Making and testing statements

Explaining how or why a procedure works

Explaining and reporting results

Ordering

Predicting

Discussing with others

Recognising patterns

Generalising

Completing a task

Looking for connections

Looking for patterns

Asking questions such as 'what if?'

Talking about work in progress and asking questions

Estimating

Making sense of a task

Interpreting mathematical and other information

Vocabulary

Counting numbers

Count number one more

How many? One less, amount,

1, 2, 3 . . . 10, one, two, three, four, five . . . ten

Pairs, pair, most, least

Comparing and ordering numbers

Compare, order, odd, even, sets, more, least, match, sort, how many?

Adding and subtracting

Difference between

Add altogether

Solving problems

Problems involving 'real life' or money

Coin, penny

Measures

Length

Taller, short, shorter, shorter than, shortest, tall, longest, long, short, height, high, tall, as tall as, too long, too short, compare, taller than, high, biggest, large, smaller than, size, big, little, thick, thin, wide, narrow, large, the same as, fat, small, too big, too small

Mass

Heavy, light, heaviest, lightest

Capacity

Hold, holds most, holds the same as, holds less

Time

Autumn   Monday   Tuesday
Winter   Wednesday   Thursday
Friday   Saturday   Sunday
Before   After   Spring   Summer

Money

Coins, pence

Exploring patterns, shape and space

Triangle, circle, square, star, pattern

Position, direction and movement

Above   Below   Next to   On
Behind   Inside   Outside   Left
Up   Down   Bottom   Right
Onto   Middle

General

Matching, number line, 100 square

Jack and the Beanstalk

Getting to know the story

Jack is a young, poor boy living with his widowed mother and a dairy cow in a farm cottage. The cow's milk is their only source of income. When the cow stops giving milk, Jack's mother tells him to take her to the market to be sold. On the way, Jack meets a bean dealer who offers magic beans in exchange for the cow, and Jack makes the trade. When he arrives home without any money, his mother becomes angry, throws the beans on the ground and sends Jack to bed without dinner.

During the night, the magic beans cause a gigantic beanstalk to grow outside Jack's window. The next morning, Jack climbs the beanstalk to a land high in the sky. He finds an enormous castle and sneaks in. He climbs up several times, and each time he takes items from the castle. He takes gold coins, a goose that lays golden eggs and a magic harp. Soon, the castle's owner, a giant, returns home. He smells that Jack is nearby, and recites a rhyme:

Fee-fi-fo-fum!
I smell the blood of an English man:

*Be he alive, or be he dead,
I'll grind his bones to make my bread.*

Jack then must make a daring escape.

Building an interest table

To introduce the story, begin with an interest table collection of *big* and *little* objects. This collection can include both natural and man-made objects, but include *long, short, fat* and *thin* as well as *small-heavy, small-light, large-heavy* and *large-light* objects.

Find some *big* things and some *small* things. Ask children to go on a *big* and *little* treasure hunt around the classroom or outside. Add what they find to the interest table. Using two hoops or some boxes, ask groups of children to sort the objects into two *sets*. Encourage the children to talk about what they are doing and their reasons for doing it. For example, '*Tell me why you put that cube in the "little" hoop/box*'. '*Why is the pencil in the "big" hoop/box? Is it the biggest thing there?*' Ask them to *compare* the sizes of the various items with other items or objects from around the classroom or outside. This will extend their use of size vocabulary and deepen their understanding. It will also beg the question '*When does something stop being small and become big?*'

Trail

If possible, go outside the classroom and use the opportunity to go on a 'size' walk. Walk around your school, setting or garden and look for things that are 'big in an upwards direction' (trees mainly). But it can include sunflowers, bird tables and washing lines – anything that is taller than the child. When you are back inside, introduce the word '*taller*' for those things that you saw. In this context it means *taller than* the children themselves. On another day take the children outside again (or this can be when walking home, to the shops or visiting grandmother) and ask them to stand next to something that is *taller than* themselves or *shorter than* themselves. After each turn ask children to explain how they knew if something was *taller* or *shorter*. Give an example of you standing next to something *shorter*. '*This wall is shorter than me because I can see over the top of it*'. '*This tree is taller than me because I can't see over the top of it*'.

Building towers

Back inside, ask the children to build the *biggest* tower that they can. This will show children's understanding of 'biggest'. The tower may be *tall* or *wide*. Use the finished towers as discussion pieces before they are dismantled. Bring in the more refined language of *tall* and *wide* instead of *biggest*. This can be with boxes, blocks, cubes or any other suitable materials. My youngest grandson was recently found stacking the blocks from my kitchen parquet floor. When I asked why he was doing that, his reply was 'I'm building a tower'. Obvious, really! Children can be very inventive. Compare the *height* of the tower to a chair, table, friend or adult. Encourage use of the words *taller than, shorter* than to describe their measurements.

Find the biggest

What is the *biggest* thing you have ever seen? Ask the children to tell you something that they think is really *big*. This gives an opportunity to practice mathematical language relating to size. Ask '*Why do you think it is big?*'

Ask '*Have you ever seen a giant?*'

Encourage a discussion between pairs, groups or with the whole class. Gather ideas from the children about what a giant is. Where do giants live? What will a giant's house look like? What does a giant eat? Do giant children go to school? How *long* are their tables and how *high* are their chairs? Do they eat really long fat chips?

Draw pictures of what the children think a giant looks like. Use them as a display with appropriate words around and in between the pictures that the children have chosen and written. This can become the start of the giant role play area.

Mathematical ideas

Tell or read the story and then enlarge, colour and, if possible, laminate the pictures provided in the resource sheets section.

Once you have the pictures you can use them to introduce these extension activities.

Sequence the story using words such as '*size*', '*tall*', '*taller*', '*short*', '*shorter*', '*up*' and '*down*'. This can be done as a group, in pairs or with individual children. As the teacher, without interrupting the story too much, add a few questions: '*What do you think happens next?*' '*What happened before this?*' '*What do you think the giant will do/say?*' '*Will Jack be scared?*' '*How would you feel if you met a giant?*'

As a class or working with small groups, build beanstalks out of stacking bricks, draw and cut leaves and stick them onto the beanstalks. Start at the *bottom* with *large* leaves moving to the top with *smaller* leaves. Draw and cut a house or castle to stick at the top of the beanstalk. Make flags to put *on* the buildings. These can be any shape but try to include shapes such as *triangles* and *circles* that have already been encountered. This would be a good time to introduce new shapes such as *square* or *star*.

Number lines

    1 2 3 4 5 6 7 8 9 10

Create a number line with leaves around the interest table. *Count* the leaves as you point to the *number*. Change the *order* of two numbers and ask the children if they can spot where the numbers are in the wrong places. Some children may be able to sort the numbers into *odd* and *even*. Make a *number line* with only *even* numbers *in order*, or only *odd numbers in order*.

Make a vertical number line starting with zero at the bottom and climbing to ten. Although some children may still be working to three or five, I feel they should be given opportunities to see higher numbers and where the numbers they do know fit into the whole consecutive numbers concept. A length of plastic pipe or a polystyrene swimming aid can act as the beanstalk. Equally space and divide the numbers into sections with coloured tape. If the numbers are placed in the spaces, the children will be using a number track. If the numbers are attached to the coloured tape, the children will be working with a number line. Attach the numbers with double-sided tape or sticky tabs so that they can be moved to different places. Start counting from the bottom and back again from the top. Glue a giant's castle to the top. Add pictures from the resource sheet of the giant and Jack, who can climb up and down the beanstalk. Make it into a game. Who can get to the bottom first? Two players, one the giant, the other Jack, take turns throwing the dice and move the character according to the number shown.

Addition

Introduce simple *addition* by *counting* how many different things Jack takes from the giant.

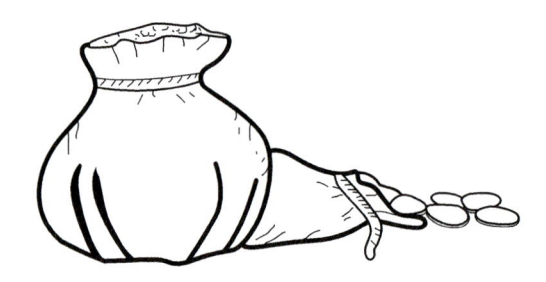

How many times does Jack need to go up the beanstalk to get all of the items?

Simple number bond activities can be introduced. Use white butter beans which have been coloured on one side using nail varnish. **Safety tip:** Do not give children uncooked dried beans. These can be very toxic. Make sure that there is an adult nearby to ensure that the beans do not go into any mouths. If there is any chance of that happening, cut the beans from card, colouring one side. Start by throwing five beans and increase to ten for those children who can work with higher numbers.

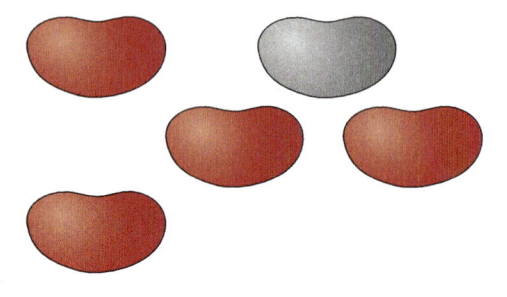

4 red and 1 white = 5 altogether

Each child has a set of coloured beans. They drop them onto a small piece of material. This lessens the noise and also stops the beans from sliding. Some will land white-side-up and some coloured-side-up. This can be repeated many times. Investigate how many different ways there are to make five.

You can paint beans golden and use them for counting. Leave a pile of golden beans and a range of leaves with numbers or spots in a dice pattern for children to explore. As they are playing, sometimes say things like '*Tell me about your beans*' or '*Tell me about the cards you've used*'. This will encourage the describing and communication strand of thinking and reasoning. Ask, '*Why did you choose that leaf? What would you need to do to have the same number of beans as the number on your leaf?'* or *'I have some beans, and you have some beans. How many do we have altogether?'*

The maths in this activity could equally come from groups of objects collected by the children themselves, rather than the beans connected with this story. Children could create patterns with their beans and record the patterns they have made.

Making games

Create a game based on the story. Let the children decide on the style and content of the game, the rules and the illustrations. Encourage the children to play it with their parents or other caregivers. This can be inside or outside, made of paper, painted or using chalk.

Send the Jack and the Beanstalk track game home for the children to play. Include rules, equipment and vocabulary to use. See the resource sheets section for a full-size version. Ask adults to play the game and ask for suggestions to make it better. You could add colours to the tracks which each have a rule. Use children's suggestions and start a games library in your classroom. Parents and children can borrow the games to take home and then return. Or plan a games afternoon for everyone to design, make and play games.

Using money

Use the *coins* that Jack steals to provide opportunities to talk about money. You will find two photocopiable outlines in the resource sheets section.

Take up to ten *penny coins*, put them in a paper cup and tip them out onto the floor or table. *Sort* the *coins* into heads and tails and cover one sack with heads and one sack with tails. *Compare the amounts* in each. Which has *most*? Which has *least*? Find different ways of answering the question. First, the coins could be laid one row *above* the other, *matching* coin for coin. The *longest* line has most, the *shortest* line has least. You may get 'the same as' if the lines are the same *length*. Second, the coins could be put *above* and *below* a number line so that the most will have the higher number while the least will have the lower number. Third, you just count each set and make a decision. *'If we did this again, do you think you will get the same thing happen or do you think it may be different? Why? Let's try it and see'*. This is an activity that can easily be done at home.

Children can dig to find coins that are buried in a sand table and *sort* them on a sorting tray. Or hide some coins around the classroom giving clues such as '*It's above . . .*', '*Its next to. . .*', '*Its behind . . .*' and so on, using positional vocabulary. How many coins can *pairs* of children find before a time limit runs out?

Finding height

Ask a group of no more than five children to measure themselves back to back and line up one behind the other, in order of height. Choose a child from the middle of the line and show that all the children in front are *shorter*, and all the children behind are *taller* than this child. Change some of the children with others in the class. Is a *shorter* child from before still *shorter*? Is a *taller* child from before still *taller*? Discuss how shorter and taller can be different for some children.

Use a computer or photocopier to enlarge or reduce pictures. Make a family of giants in this way so that children can order the heights *shortest to tallest* or *tallest to shortest*.

Make big cups, saucers, plates, spoon, knife and fork for a giant. Cover the cutlery in aluminium foil.

A giant trail

Make a trail of a giant's footprints. These can be to and from specific points *inside* or *outside*. Change them from day to day so that children have different trails to follow. Maybe put a task, a treat or a new toy related to the story at the end of the trail.

Problem-solving

Ask questions such as '*Do you think a giant could come to our school? Do you think a giant could fit through our door? How can we find out?*'

Take some time to listen to what the children offer as a solution. Try a few of the ideas. Discuss the results. '*I wonder if we could use the giant's footprints to help us to find the height of the giant?*' '*How could we do that?*'

Again, try some of the ideas suggested. Do they work?

Discuss the *length* of the footprint. Is it *longer* or *shorter* than their footprint? How many of their foot lengths would be the same as the giant footprint? '*Draw around your foot. Ask your friend to help you*'. If you have a photocopier, copy each child's footprint five or six times. Rather than cutting out each print, just cut along the end of the big toe and the heel. Use them to find how many child's feet fit along the length of the giant foot.

As an estimate, children could say that the giant is about six times taller than them because his foot is the same as six of their feet. This is a thought, an opinion, and therefore, at this stage perfectly acceptable. Mathematically, of course, it may not be accurate, but children will learn about ratio and proportion later in their school life.

Growing tall using measures

Grow or make some very large, tall flowers for the giant's house. Plan in advance if you want to grow sunflowers or beanstalks.

Chapter 3: Big and little

Use the concept of capacity (how much something holds) and volume (how much space something takes up) when filling pots with soil. Use different size pots to see the difference in capacity. Make a display which can be added to through the day or week with the label '*How much does this hold?*' Put the display near to the water or sand tray. You can add *holds most*, *holds the same as* and *holds least* for older children.

Use standard or non-standard measures to find the height of the plants. This picture is of my grandson Jack standing in front of his beanstalk.

Look, see and say

Use pictures or photographs for 'look, see and say' activities. Look at the picture, see what you can see and then share it with your friend. This activity encourages dialogue between children, developing and enhancing their language skills. An adult may need to be involved to model the activity until children understand what to do.

Which is taller, the beanstalk or boy? How do you know?

James age 4

Use any pictures or posters or cut outs from magazines that show comparisons of height, weight, (elephant and mouse, for example), length (snake and worm) or capacity (cup and bucket). Ask children to look, see and tell their friend what they have seen. Take some of the children's thoughts and make them into a display by using pictures and speech bubbles of what the children have said.

Prop box

For the role play area, prepare a prop box of items. Discuss with the children what they think a giant's castle would need or would already have. Use their ideas to make a list of the contents of the box.

This could include:

- Very large salad bowls or mixing bowls.
- Large cardboard cutlery covered in foil.
- A large cereal box made from a large box. Children can decorate it with their own pictures of their favourite cereals.
- Very large plates.
- Big table napkins or small paper table cloths which can be made into napkins.
- Big teapot, cups and saucers.
- Big slippers, giant's beard and giant glasses.
- Big hats.
- A HUGE newspaper.

Hint: Do not try to put all of these things in at the same time. Introduce new items slowly or the box will just become one giant muddle.

Find a corner in the room for a castle. This can be just the entrance, a table behind and some items from the prop box. Or it can be a full castle with a front, sides and a possible drawbridge. It all comes down to space. Use brick pattern wallpaper on top of thick card to represent the walls. Or paint the walls grey and sponge print the individual blocks. The drawbridge can be a strip of painted card, which could be brown for wood or grey for stone. Place it as a doormat to enter the castle. Inside there should be a table with huge plates, bowls and cutlery. If you have space, hang big white clouds from the ceiling to make it seem as though the castle is very high. Make windows of different shapes. Add or change props regularly so the area does not become boring. Add a bag of money, a magic harp and a chicken with at least one golden egg.

Short activities

Draw giant pictures to put around the giant's house. These can be other giants, giant minibeasts (can you have such a thing?), giant toys or giant animals.

Make a miniature village and put in large farm animals or people or a train going around the outside of the village. Or you could use photos from a visit to a model village and use them as look, see and say pictures.

Make *big* footprints and make a trail through your classroom.

Make a 'giant' book or a story map. Make up stories and act them out.

Look at different types of beans that can be planted outside. Use pots or raised beds. Have canes ready to support them as they grow and keep them well watered.

Record singing in loud and quiet voices. What do you think a giant sounds like? Show or read *The BFG* by Roald Dahl.

Walk with long strides and short strides. What is the *longest* stride you can do? How can we measure that? What is the *shortest* step you can do? How can we measure *that*? Ask the children the questions. Do not always be the one with the answer.

What would it be like to have a friend who was a giant? Through discussion, encourage children to talk about similarities and differences between themselves and their friends.

What do they like about their friends? Why do you think your friends like you? Encourage the idea that we are all different but we can still be friends.

Another concept that children can explore is area. Draw a large hand on a piece of paper and give every child a copy. Ask each child to put their hand on it and draw round it. Do this in a different colour. Give children counters or cubes to represent beans. Do not give children uncooked dried beans. These can be very toxic. Ask them to fill their hand with 'beans' and *count* how many there are. Join the cubes together or make a line of counters. Next, cover the giant hand in the same way. Compare the two amounts. *Which hand holds the most? What's the difference between the number they each hold?* Use simple one-to-one correspondence for this, or build two towers of cubes and place them next to each other.

Make a giant-size shoe print. Ask children to draw round their own shoe and cut around the outside edge. This is easier if they take their shoe off first. Compare the giant's shoe length with their own. *'Tell me what you notice about your shoe print. Is it longer or shorter than the giant's shoe print? Tell us something about the giant shoe print. How many giant shoe prints are the same length as your table? How many giant shoe prints does it take to get to the door/window?'*

Let the children *measure* things in the classroom using both sets of shoe prints, and then *compare* the lengths. Let the children take the prints home and measure things there.

You can make a mini greenhouse for each child. Cut the shape of a greenhouse out of card leaving a square hole in the middle and give one to each child to decorate. Put some kitchen roll or cotton wool in a sealable food bag with a little water and one or two beans. Seal the food bag and tape it to the underside of the greenhouse so that it shows through the hole. Tape the whole thing to a window, preferably one that the sun shines through. The sun will cause condensation inside the bag which will keep the beans watered. Then wait for the bean to grow. This is a fun and an easy way to watch the beans as they grow.

Use green pipe cleaners or strips of paper to chart the growth of a beanstalk. Keep a record to show what happens as time passes.

Billy's Sunflower by Nicola Moon
Published by Scholastic

Billy had a beautiful sunflower that he had grown from a seed. It was taller than Billy. It was taller than Billy's dad.

This story has very short and simple text, with bright supporting illustrations, helping the beginner reader to follow the story. It is part of a series created especially for children who are just beginning to read. It goes through the life cycle of a sunflower which can lead to discussion in the classroom about how seeds grow and what happens when a flower dies.

Getting to know the story

Read the story and talk about why plants die. Introduce the words '*autumn*' and '*spring*' and talk about what happens at each time of year.

'Has anyone ever seen sunflowers growing? Where did you see them? Tell me something about the sunflowers that you saw'. As the children give you mathematical words, keep a record of what they say. These words can be used later when discussing height.

Growing sunflowers

Growing sunflowers is an easy beginning gardening project for children. Sunflowers are one of the easiest flowers to plant from seed directly into the earth. They quickly grow into large, magical flowers that children love to admire and enjoy.

Invite your children to help plant, grow and care for sunflowers for an outside activity this year.

Sunflowers should be planted early in the spring so they have enough time to grow to full height during the summer. They grow best when you plant them directly into the ground after your last expected frost. But you can use large pots inside or outside of the classroom if you have little space to plant outside. Sunflowers love to grow in a sunny spot with lots of direct light.

First, look for a sunny spot. Next, use a cultivator (a fork or spade) of some kind to prepare the soil for planting. This can be started by an adult and finished off by children using hand forks. Be sure to supply gardening gloves. If your soil has a lot of clay or sand in it, your sunflowers will do a lot better if you mix in some organic compost or organic soil before planting. You also need to make sure that the ground is moist where you will be planting sunflowers. Water the area first.

Sunflower trail

Go for a walk around your setting with the children and ask them to find nice sunny spaces where the sunflowers can grow. Think about a planting plan. Do you want a formal walkway with sunflowers on either side? Or do you want random planting that can include different varieties of sunflowers? Or do you want seeds that have been planted in pots to lead the way?

Children can measure the height of the sunflowers as they grow. They can take pictures of the growing process over time. Encourage mathematical language by talking about *small, short, growing taller, shorter than me, taller than me*.

How to plant sunflower seeds

1. Place the sunflower seed in the ground.
2. Gently push the sunflower seed into the soil.
3. Cover the sunflower seed with dirt.
4. Press down firmly.

5   Give them plenty of room to grow.
6   Water sunflower seeds.

Growing and caring for sunflowers

Sunflowers grow best when they are allowed to establish deep roots. Give them lots of water infrequently for best results.

If you are growing a tall variety you may need to stake them once they reach a certain height so they do not fall down.

Role play

Develop a gardening role play area. Include pots, compost, gloves, packets of seeds (cress is good because it grows so quickly), aprons, sun hats, trowel, fork, jugs ready for watering and any other things you and the children can think of. You may want some bulbs that are in pots and already flowering. Be aware that some bulbs are poisonous, so some children may need close observation. Add more stories about sunflowers so children can choose a book for themselves.

If you want more of a garden centre area, then add a cash till, money and bags. Have a selection of real and artificial plants and flowers and shelves for displaying goods. If outside, include sand and gravel. And do not forget a wheelbarrow. You may need more than one of these as they are very popular. Include gardening books or magazines.

Decide with the children on different areas for the garden centre. Which will you set up first? Put plants in seed trays ready for watering.

Price plants and any other items using real money up to ten pence or beyond for older children. Put the price and some coin pictures on each label. Younger children can then match the pictures of the coins to the real coins.

Count plants, flowers and pots. *'How many plants can we fit in this seed tray? Is there room for one more?'*

Have a selection of pots that children can sort according to size, colour or position. *'How can we find out which pot holds the most/least?'*

Fill buckets with wet or dry sand or compost and ask children to lift them. Which is the *heaviest/lightest*?

Hint: Take care with equipment especially when handling real tools. Show children how to handle plants carefully. Instruct them not to open seed packets unless there is an adult present.

Would it be possible to visit a garden centre? Take clip boards along and ask children to draw what they see and like there. Use these drawings back in the classroom as starting points for discussion. Children can make their own books about the visit.

Outside, create a mini pond using a water tray or paddling pool. Emphasise the safety aspect of water. Display water plants or float paper and flowers. Put plastic goldfish in the water and frogs on the edge.

Home/school links

Develop home/school links by planting seeds in a pot, sending it home with instructions for its care and ideas of how to keep a diary of its growth. This can be children's drawings or photos, preferably ones they have taken themselves.

Short ideas using pattern, measures sequencing and designing

Join cubes together to make the stem of a sunflower. Ask the children to work with a friend. Each pair in the class has the same two colours, six of one colour and six of a different colour. For example, green and red.

Children join the cubes together, making a pattern of no more than twelve cubes. When the flower stem has been made, discuss how many different patterns there are. *What colour would the next cube be?* Children in the early stages of understanding a repeating pattern will probably make a very random one.

Draw and cut a sunflower to stick at the top of the stem. *Can you make the stem taller? How many more cubes does your taller stem have? What's the tallest stem you can make before it falls over? As tall as you? As tall as your chair? As tall as your teacher?*

Use the characters from the story: *How tall do you think Billy is? How tall is Billy's dad? Is Billy as tall as your teacher or as tall as the door? Who is shorter than dad but taller than Billy?*

Make a set of sequence cards using pictures from the story. For example: Billy next to his sunflower; the sunflower dying; the birds eating seeds from the bird table; the seeds dropping to the ground; Billy's mum wiping his tears; Billy amongst the petals and leaves as the flower is growing.

Design and make a bird table ready for when the seeds fall out.

Making predictions

'*How tall do you think your sunflower will grow?*' This question allows children to make predictions based on what they already know or think about. This is an important part of problem-solving. If possible, mark the children's estimates on an outside wall. Write their name at the top. This will need to last until the flowers have grown, so do not use a wall that is going to be pelted with rain. Follow up in the summer/autumn when the plants have grown as tall as they are going to but before the flower dies.

Ask children to draw the head of their sunflower. Discuss any drawings that the children have done. '*I see that you have drawn a middle to the flower. What else is in the middle that you can see? I can see you have drawn shapes in the middle of the flower. What do you think they are? I like the way you have drawn the big leaves. I wonder why the plant needs them. What do you think the plant looks like under the ground?*'

Help children dissect a sunflower and learn about its different parts. Make sure that children wear gloves or wash their hands after handling different parts of the plant.

Height and length

Make a 'How *tall* am I?' wall. Measure the *height* or *length* of each child with green crepe paper. Height and length being one and the same thing, just in a different orientation, is difficult for some children to understand. You may have to do both height and length and *compare* the strips of paper. This will be a very visual way for young children to make the connection.

Ask them to paint or draw a huge sunflower head that can be attached to the top of their height strip. Write their name on or next to the flower.

Add a label: 'I am as tall as my sunflower'.

Making sunflower stick puppets

Cut triangular shapes out of a small paper plate. This will create the sunflower look. Paint the plate yellow. Paint different lengths of sticks green. This allows for *taller/shorter/the same as* vocabulary to be used. Glue or tape the sticks to the back of the sunflowers.

You can either glue sunflower seeds in the middle or ask the children to paint faces, one on each plate. These can be all happy and smiling or make a set of emotions. For example:

☺ ☹ 😐 😕

Games

Play musical sunflowers.

This is actually a version of musical chairs but can include simple subtraction by one each turn. When playing with younger children I have found that using only five or six players while the others play elsewhere is a good idea. This is so that when the children are out, they can go off and play with their friends rather than sit on the floor and wait for the game to end.

Make a set of sunflower pictures. It is best to use a non-slip paper such as sugar paper. Also make a picture of a slug or snail, both of which like to eat the plants, or a ladybird or bees, which help the plant, and stick them on the sunflowers. Or you could have both.

Just as in musical chairs, place the pictures in a circle. Have the same number of pictures as there are children. At the beginning, each child stands on a picture. When the music starts, the children move round the circle onto the next picture. Whilst the music plays the children keep moving. When the music stops, the child standing on the slug flower is out. As each child is out, remove a sunflower from the circle (not the one with the slug). Keep playing until only one child is left. To make it easier for the children who are 'out', have three or four slug pictures. Not only does this help self-esteem, it also makes the game a lot shorter.

As play continues, ask questions such as '*We started with five flowers, but one has been taken away. How many are left?*' Increase the number of flowers as children become more confident with numbers.

The Elves and the Shoemaker

Getting to know the story

There are different versions of this story depending on the telling.

- A poor shoemaker and his wife need money to pay the rent. He gives away the last pair of shoes he has to a needy lady. He has leather to make one more pair of shoes. He cuts out the pieces of leather before going to bed so that he can sew them into a pair of shoes on the morrow. Elves come in the night and make the pair of shoes, which he sells for more than his asking price the next day. He uses that money to pay the rent and buy food and more shoe leather.

- He has just enough money to buy enough leather for two pairs of shoes. He cuts the pieces of leather for two pairs and retires for the night. The elves come again that night and make two pairs of shoes with the additional leather. He gives away one pair to a needy person and sells the other pair to a customer who is very satisfied and pays more than the shoemaker asked for.
- He buys leather for three pairs of shoes and stays up to find the elves making the shoes. The shoemaker and wife make clothes for the elves the next day, but the elves are freed when given clothes, so they leave, and the shoemaker and his wife never see them again.

This story is perfect to hear, learn and use the vocabulary of time. It includes sequencing the days of the week, developing understanding of 'day', 'tomorrow', 'night' and 'morning'.

Once upon a time there was a shoemaker and his wife.
They were very poor.

It was *Sunday* night. The shoemaker only had *enough* leather to make *one pair* of shoes.
'I will make them *tomorrow*', he said to his wife, and they went to bed.
On *Monday* morning the shoes were ready. The shoemaker didn't know that a *little* elf had been there in the *night* and made the shoes.
They were very well-made shoes with laces.
And the shoemaker sold them that very *day*.

He bought enough leather to make *two pairs* of shoes.

'I will make them *tomorrow*', he said to his wife, and they went to bed.

On *Tuesday morning* the shoes were ready. The shoemaker didn't know that *two* elves had been there in the *night* and made the shoes. There was a *pair* of clogs and a *pair* of men's boots with laces.

They were well made and the shoemaker *sold* them that very *day*.

He *bought enough* leather for *three pairs* of shoes.

'I will make them *tomorrow*', he said to his wife, and they went to bed.

And so the story continues. This is a perfect story for looking at the aspect of time with days of the week as well as morning and night. Not only that, there are opportunities for *counting in ones* (elves), *counting in twos* (shoes), and *sequencing*. Measures can be included, both standard and non-standard, as well as early concepts of money. All you need now is a role play area of a shoe shop and a selection of shoes.

Prop box

Use the idea of a prop box when setting up the role play area. Link it with ideas from the children, especially at the beginning of a new term when they may recently have visited a shoe shop to have their feet measured.

Include labels in your prop box. Ask a local shoe shop if they have any spare empty shoe boxes. Try and get as many different sizes as you can. You need a till and money. If possible, use real money rather than plastic. Children need to get the feel and sight of real money to make it more of a real-world experience. (Although, to be honest, there are no shoes that can be bought for two pence.)

Include measuring resources such as rulers and shoe sizers. These can be homemade or, if you are lucky, borrowed from a shoe shop.

Pop in a few laces, paper carrier bags, mirrors, and notices and adverts (made by the children) and anything else the children suggest.

Role play: the shoe shop

Children can design and make shoes for the shop. These can be sewn, glued or made with any junk materials lying around. Encourage the use of the word '*pair*' and back it up by showing identical shoes put together to make a pair. You can also introduce the words '*left*' and '*right*'.

You will need shoes of different *sizes* as well as different fastenings: hook-and-loop fastener, laces and zippers. Keeping their socks on, ask children to try on shoes and make sets of *too big*, *too small* and *just right*. Include samples of shoes from other cultures. Charity shops are a good source of these. Perhaps ask parents to donate some shoes, but be aware of shoes with very high heels, which do pose a safety risk.

Sorting and testing in the shop

Sort the shoes by the types of material used to make them. How many different materials are there in our shoe shop? Are they all suitable to wear in the rain? What would happen if you jumped in a puddle while wearing sandals? Fill a water tray with water and test the shoes. Which shoes get wet inside? Which stay dry? Test everyday materials to see which are waterproof, such as paper, aluminium foil, cotton and plastic.

Over time, additional activities can be introduced such as writing matching descriptive labels for shoes on display or shoes for the shoemaker's shop. Discover a letter written by the elves asking the children to make them some clothes. This will lead to '*How tall is an elf? As tall as six blocks put together? As tall as a pencil? As tall as a book? What do you think?*'

The children can reply to the elves by sending them a drawing of the clothes they will make.

Short activities

Organise pairs of shoes by size. These can be children's shoes, children's and adult's shoes or a collection brought from home.

Work out the cost of the shoes. Use money values that the children are familiar with.

Match shoes. Discuss how you know that these are a pair.

Make patterns using the bottom of children's shoes. This can be done by covering them with paint and then walking on paper, by putting a piece of paper over the bottom of the shoe and rubbing with a wax crayon or pressing the shoes into dough or wet sand.

Children can design their own pattern for the bottom of their shoes. Give each child a set of shoe bases that have no pattern. What patterns can they make?

Design and make your own pair of shoes. Cheap slippers like those in a hotel room are perfect for this. Usually this involves lots of glitter and glue. They may match as a pair, or they may not. But one thing is for sure: if glitter is used it will shed across the floor for at least six months.

Thanks to James, Oliver, Stephen, Jack and Thomas

Chapter 3: Big and little

Snow White and the Seven Dwarves

If the word 'dwarf' is a problem in your setting, change it the Snow White and the Seven Short Men.

This is the last story in this chapter so, by now, children should have a good idea about the vocabulary and meaning of measure words. However, more reinforcement is not a bad thing.

Getting to know the story

Snow White is a lonely princess living with her stepmother, a vain queen. The Queen worries that Snow White will look better than her, so she forces Snow White to work as a scullery maid and asks her Magic Mirror daily 'who is the fairest one of all?'. For years the mirror always answers that the Queen is, which pleases her.

One day, the Magic Mirror tells the Queen that Snow White is now 'the fairest' in the land. The jealous Queen orders her Huntsman to take Snow White into the forest and kill her, which he does not do. Lost and frightened, the princess is looked after by woodland creatures who lead her to a cottage deep in the woods. Finding seven small chairs in the cottage's dining room, Snow White assumes the cottage is the untidy home of seven children.

In reality, the cottage belongs to seven adult dwarves who work in a nearby mine. Returning home, they are alarmed to find their cottage clean and suspect that an intruder has invaded their home. The dwarves find Snow White upstairs, asleep across three of their beds. Snow White awakens to find the dwarves at her bedside and introduces herself, and all of the dwarves eventually welcome her into their home after she offers to clean and cook for them. Snow White keeps house for the dwarves while they mine for jewels during the day, and at night they all sing, play music and dance.

Meanwhile, the Queen discovers that Snow White is still alive when the mirror again answers that Snow White is the fairest in the land. The Queen creates a poisoned apple that will put whoever eats it into the 'Sleeping Death', a curse she learns can only be broken by 'love's first kiss', though she is certain Snow White will be buried alive. The Queen fools Snow White into biting into the poisoned apple under the pretence that it is a magic apple that grants wishes. As Snow White falls asleep, the Queen proclaims that she is now the fairest in the land. The dwarves return to their cottage and find Snow White seemingly dead. They place her in a glass coffin trimmed with gold in a clearing in the forest. A year later, a prince visits her coffin. He kisses her, which breaks the spell and she wakes up.

Ordering and measuring

This is a well-known story; so many children will probably already be familiar with it. Using the pictures provided in the resources, discuss and order the story. Ask questions such as '*What happened next?*' '*How do you think Snow White felt when she went into the house? What would you do if you were on your own in a house?*' '*Why did she go upstairs? What is upstairs in your own house?*' '*Can you remember the beds? What happened when Snow White laid on a bed? Was it too long or too short for her?*' Reinforce the idea of length by saying things like

'*Yes, the bed was too short for Snow White*' or '*Yes, Snow White was too long for the bed*'. Using whole sentences gives children a model for when they pose their own questions or answer questions from someone else.

'*How do you think the dwarves felt when they found Snow White?*'

Using models or dough figures, make a bed for each dwarf. '*How will you know how long to make the beds? Are all the dwarves the same height? Make a bed for Snow White. Will her bed be longer or shorter than the dwarf beds?*'

Use a shoe box to make the dwarves' house. This needs to be filled with appropriately sized furniture. Children will need to talk about ratio and proportion but, of course, using sentences such as '*This won't fit, it's too big/high/long*'. There will be a great deal of problem-solving going on when making and filling the houses. Children will be discussing the problem using the communication strand, reasoning about possible solutions: '*I think this because . . .*', using logic and proof as they fit their pieces into the house, as well as making and monitoring decisions throughout. Remember, the decisions are the child's, not yours.

Games

As with the other stories, encourage children to make and play their own games. These can be played on a tabletop, floor or outside using the resources that are available there. The model dwarves that they used for making beds can be used as playing pieces for the game.

Encourage children and parents to take their games home where they can be played with adults or siblings. Have a game playing afternoon in school. Invite parents/carers/other members of the family into the classroom or hall to play games with the children. Supply resources such as paper, colouring pencils or pens and dice so that new games can be designed and played.

Examples

A couple of easy games that need very little equipment.

1   Using two dice, spot or number, and a strip of seven squares for each player, take turns rolling the dice and adding the spots/numbers of the two top faces. Some children will count the spots, others will use the numbers. Have a small number line on the table in front of where they are playing. Every time a player rolls a total of seven, they can draw a dwarf's face in one of their squares. The first to draw seven dwarves is the winner.

The next illustration is just a visual clue of the description of the game. The children will do much better!

You can ask questions such as '*You have drawn four faces. How many more do you need to make seven?*' Early stages will be counting, but older more confident children may know their number bonds and answer without counting.

2   Use a pack of cards with the picture cards and number cards 7–10 removed. Place all the cards face down. The first player turns over two cards. If they total seven,

that player keeps the cards. If not, they are placed face down again and the second player tries to find two cards totalling seven. The winner is the player with most cards at the end. You may want to start with just one suit and build up to four. The suit does not matter; the children need to concentrate on the numbers. They can use the symbols on the cards to help when counting.

The possibilities are 1 + 6; 2 + 5; 3 + 4. But, of course, these can also be read as 6 + 1; 5 + 2; and 4 + 3.

Making books

Sequence the events in the story. This can be done as a group using big pictures or by pairs using the smaller pictures. Encourage the use of correct vocabulary such as '*before*' and '*after*'. Children can create their own story book and present it to the rest of the class.

Using two sets of dwarf pictures provided in the resource sheets section, a counting book can be made. It will look better if the dwarves are coloured in but it is your choice whether to ask the children to do that.

> Step 1. Cut four pieces of A4 card in half lengthways.
> Step 2. Using the card positioned lengthways and one set of dwarves, stick a dwarf at the right-hand side, placing it as close to the edge as possible. Do this for each of the dwarves and you will have seven pieces of card, each with a picture at one end and the rest of the strip blank.
> Step 3. Stick the second set of dwarves as a complete piece onto the remaining piece of card. This will be the top page of the book. Keep the dwarves in the same order as the set of complete dwarves when building page on page.
> Step 4. Place the card with the seventh dwarf face upwards on to the table.
> Step 5. Place the next piece of card on top so that it shows the seventh dwarf underneath and to the right.

> Step 6. Cut the top piece of card so that the left-hand side matches the bottom piece.
> Step 7. Place the next picture on top so that the previous pictures show and then cut to size. Repeat this until all seven dwarves are in a line.
> Step 8. Take the poem provided in the resource sheets and cut this into separate verses.
> Step 9. Attach the first verse to the back of the front cover (the full line of dwarves). Stick the second verse to the back of the first dwarf (the smallest piece of card), the third verse onto the next page, and so on.
> Step 10. If possible, laminate the pages and bind them together.
> Step 11. You now have a book which, when you turn the pages, will have one less dwarf each time to fit the poem.

Chapter 3: Big and little 115

Count and order the dwarves and beds: one, two, three, four . . . seven; first, second, third, fourth . . . seventh.

Make a split book as before with the Three Bears and the Three Little Pigs, only this time there will be seven dwarves.

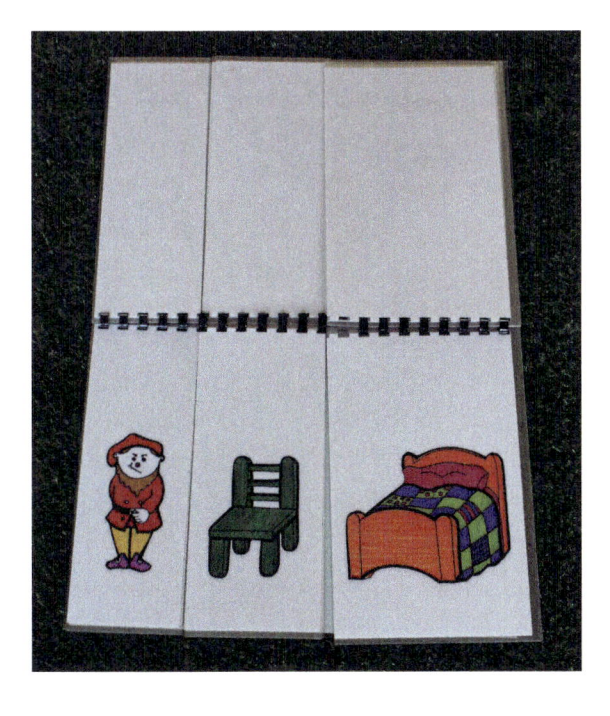

As you are putting it together, have a rule that can be found when linking the dwarves, beds and chairs. In my example I used colour, but there are many other rules within it, especially when you ask '*Why did you choose that dwarf to go with that chair?*' or '*Why do you think the red chair goes with the blue bed?*' If you ask children what they think, they will tell you. It may not agree with what you think, but that is unimportant here.

Problem-solving

What does each dwarf wear? Use black and white outlines of dwarves. Provide different sets of buttons, hats or shoes. These can be by colour or shape.

Prepare a template of seven dwarves. Use the picture provided in the resource sheets section. Using only three different colours, how many different ways can the dwarves be dressed?

Both of these activities can be recorded by a photo with the child's face included. Build this up into a display that can be used for discussion with the class.

Make a washing line of clothes; look at '*pairs of*' so that children can match socks, hats and coats where there is a colour or pattern to find.

Cut out some sock shapes using different patterns. Wallpaper is good for this. To strengthen the paper, mount it onto card, or laminate the individual socks. Using a washing line strung between two chairs, children can hang the matching pairs on the line. This involves sorting, recognising patterns and fine motor skills. For example:

Maybe have an odd sock and some blank sock templates. Ask children to draw the same pattern from the spare sock onto a sock template.

Whilst looking at pattern, create a different design for the quilts on the dwarves' beds. This could involve symmetry, shapes and colours. Some children may need a quilt printed for them; some may be able to draw their own. Or use the one that is already on the bed in the resources section.

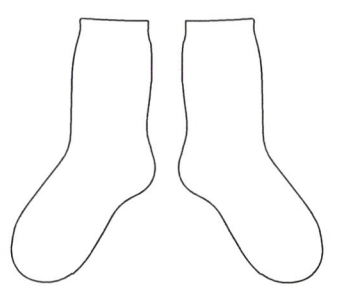

Pairing the dwarves

Explain what 'a pair' means. Relate it to something the children already know, such as a pair of shoes or a pair of socks. Put the dwarves in pairs. This can be done with pictures or models.

One dwarf will be left on his own. This can either be an introduction to odd numbers or a reinforcement of work previously done.

'*There is one dwarf left out. Why does this happen? Let's pair them in a different way. Is there still one left over? What could we do to make that dwarf not be on his own? Let's take a dwarf from here (another pair). But now that dwarf is on his own. We need to solve this problem. Who can we put with this dwarf?'* (Snow White may be the answer, but it may well be something else that has nothing to do with the story!)

Number activities

Make a number line of dwarves. By adding or removing one dwarf from the line, work on *one more* or *one less* can be reinforced. Progress to two more or two less as children become more confident with addition and subtraction.

Reinforce the concept of addition by having the seven dwarves entering the house one at a time after a day at the mine. As they enter eyes, noses, legs and buttons can be used for counting. For example, one dwarf has two legs; two dwarves have four legs and so on. If you have a large hundred square in your room or a number line, look at the pattern that these numbers produce. After the seven dwarves have all arrived home, can children predict the next number in the pattern? And the *next* number? Can they reach 20 with the *pattern* still intact?

Apples

Remind the children that the Queen gave Snow White an apple to eat and that apple was not very nice. *'Do you like apples? Where do apples come from?'*

The dwarves liked apples. They liked raw apples and cooked apples. Explain that you are going to cook some apples for the dwarves.

In a safe environment, make sure the children have washed their hands and put on an apron each. Peel and core the apples. Give children safety knives and a plate with apple slices on. Ask them to cut the apple slices into *smaller* pieces so that they will cook quicker. This needs to be done in small groups unless you have many adults around. Once the apples start to cook, show the children the changes that are happening to the fruit. Be careful of the hot pan. Once the apples are ready, put them in a dish or on a plate and pop them into a nearby fridge (if you have one).

When the apples are cold, offer a small spoon to each child so that they can taste the cooked apple. *'Which apple do you like the most? Raw apple or cooked apple?'*

If there is time, make some pastry (or buy it ready-made) and make an apple pie. Serve it with ice cream or warm custard as a treat instead of other snacks. Have some raw apples cut ready in case the pie is not very popular.

Role play

The role play area will become the dwarves' cottage in the forest. If possible, cover an area of wall or screen with plain paper and ask the children to cover it in patterns of seven for the wallpaper. This can be handprints, block prints, drawings of their choosing or coloured paper strips. How many different patterns of seven can be made?

Provide dwarf costumes, which can be made very easily with adult t-shirts and belts or ties. Hats can be made by sewing two triangles to make a cone.

If possible, find a table and seven small chairs.

You will also need to provide at least seven cups, knives, forks, spoons and plates. IKEA has a lovely selection of colours, which could match the colours of the hats.

Find seven small blankets, to be made into beds (again, IKEA).

To decorate other walls, collect and display posters of forests, woods and trees.

When developing the role play area, set out the table and seven chairs for the dwarves. Ask children to put out the correct number of plates and spoons so that each dwarf will have his own set. For older children, investigate how many different ways the dwarves could be sat around the table. They can find two, three or four, but finding all the possibilities (5,040) will take a very long time. (Maybe a challenge for the adults at home?)

Make laminated name cards for the dwarves, Snow White, the prince and the Queen. Punch holes in them and thread them with cord to make name labels. Children should wear the appropriate pendant when entering the role play area.

Exploring feelings

Remind the children that the story is made up and not about real people. The story is sad at the beginning but has a very happy ending.

How do you think Snow White felt when she was left alone in the forest?

Ask who loves you/who do you love? Talk about families and how they look after each other. Ask children to make models of someone who loves them or paint a picture.

'I made my mummy. She broke. I love her. She has curly hair. Mummy loves me'. Henry age 4

- **Friendship**: talk about how Snow White found some friends. They looked after her. Who are your friends? Why do you like them?
- **Keeping safe**: the dwarves in the story told Snow White not to open the door. They wanted to keep her safe. Did she do as she was told? What happened? Discuss why it is important for children to do as they are told.

Exploring language

Encourage the children to talk about the story. *'Did you like the story? Which part did you like best? Was it a happy or sad story? Which parts were happy? Which parts were sad?'*

Draw a line across an A3 piece of paper. Ask children which part of the story they liked best. They draw that part of the story above the line. The bottom part of the paper is for children to 'write' what they liked the best. This can be emergent writing, copying or completely the child's own independent writing. Look at the pictures and discuss the sequence of the story, using such words as '*before*' and '*after*'. Display them in the right order or make a class book.

Developing an understanding of pattern

Print some wallpaper patterns. Use hands, feet, sponges, blocks, cut carrots or potatoes, anything really, that will transfer paint from a plate to a piece of paper. Use it to decorate the role play area.

Show children pictures of fairy tale castles and ask them to design one of their own. Leave a lot of pictures or photos around so that children have some visual references of castles.

Suggest that they may like to build a castle. Use what they know about making strong brick patterns. They can use blocks or interlocking shapes. Or, start a collection of same shape and size cereal boxes. These can be small, medium or large.

A not so good wall

A good wall

Any books made by the class or by individuals can have the covers formed into the shape of a castle. Use sponges to decorate the covers by printing large blocks or bricks.

Make a crown for the Queen and prince by decorating strips of gold or silver card. Decorate them before stapling their edges together to make headbands. Ask children what pattern they made or used when they are wearing their crown.

Counting and matching

Have pictures of the seven dwarves and their hats. Spread the dwarf pictures and the seven hat cards face up. Can you give each dwarf a hat? How many dwarves and how many hats are there? If we take one hat away will there be enough hats for each dwarf? **Challenge:** Here are four hats. How many dwarves will not get a hat?

Count in sevens on a number square. Put a counter on every multiple of seven. Can you see the diagonal pattern? What would happen if you started counting sevens from another number?

Chapter 3: Big and little

What do you know about forests? Who or what else may live in a forest?

If possible, take the children for a walk in a wood or a local country park. If this is not possible, see if you have a Forestry Commission near to you. The Forestry Commission is a non-ministerial government department responsible for forestry in England and Scotland. It was set up in 1919 to expand Britain's forests and woodland after depletion during the First World War. To do this, the Commission bought large amounts of former agricultural land, eventually becoming the largest land owner in Britain. Over time the purpose of the Commission broadened to include many other activities beyond timber production. One major activity is scientific research, some of which is carried out in research forests across Britain. Recreation is also important, with several outdoor activities being actively promoted.

Or get in touch with Forest Schools. Forest Schools offer learners regular opportunities to achieve and develop confidence and self-esteem through hands on learning experience in woodland or in natural environments with trees.

Short activities

'If you could name the seven dwarves, what would you call them? Does one dwarf look angry? Does one dwarf look sad or mischievous? Which dwarf would you like to be?'

Draw the seven dwarves and write about them. Make your drawings and writing into a book. Take the book home and share it with someone there.

'The seven dwarves have four cousins. The cousins come to visit them. What could their names be? What do you think they look like?'

Building

Challenge the children to build a castle with a construction kit and a small cottage with small bricks or blocks. Talk about the similarities and differences of both.

Singing: heigh-ho, heigh-ho!

Put the children into groups of seven as closely as possible. Add adults if necessary. Each group of seven makes a line. The leader of the line chooses a way of walking: small steps, big steps, marching, hopping. The others behind the leader have to copy, weaving in and out of the spaces and paths of other groups. This is best done outside. Do it to the soundtrack of 'Heigh-ho, heigh-ho'. For the full version of the song, see www.stylyrics.com or search on YouTube.

Mathematics

Counting

When the dwarves get to work, they dig and sieve the earth looking for gold. Supply sieves in the sand tray and bury some golden treasure. Prepare some golden nuggets – these could be wooden beads painted with gold paint. Hide the gold nuggets in a sand tray. Count how many nuggets have been found.

Repeat the activity but use a one-minute timer. When one minute has passed, stop digging and count the number of golden nuggets.

Make patterns of seven with the nuggets. Use a ten-frame if you can. Ten-frames are two-by-five rectangular frames into which counters are placed to illustrate numbers less than or equal to ten and are therefore very useful for developing number sense within the context of ten. Various arrangements of counters on the ten frames can be used to prompt different mental images of numbers and different mental strategies for manipulating these numbers, all in association with the numbers' relationship to ten. For example:

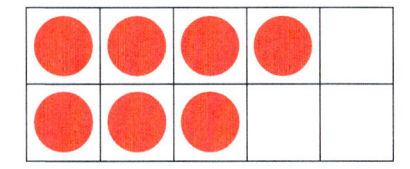

Plenty of activities with ten frames will enable children to automatically think of numbers less than ten in terms of their relationship to ten and build a sound knowledge of the basic addition/subtraction facts for ten, which are an integral part of mental calculation in later years.

Find one more or one less than a number under ten

Count the groups of seven you can see on the walls.
Set the table for the seven dwarves. Count out loud as you set each place.
Snow White is joining the dwarves for tea. How many more of each item will you need to put on the table? Will there be enough chairs?

Chapter 4: Dinosaurs and dragons

Why dinosaurs and dragons?

Dragons are one of the world's most popular mythological creatures. They are represented in cultures all over the world. They are popular in books, films and TV. In the past, when giant bones were uncovered around the world (dinosaur fossils, as we know them now), people assumed they were dragons.

Some dragons can fly, some cannot. Some dragons are small and others are huge. Some dragons live in deep places under the sea, others hide in deep caves and some perch on high mountain tops.

Dragons can be frightening or, as in China and Japan, symbols of good fortune.

Dinosaurs have held children's imagination for many years. Many people still believe that they are a close cousin of the dragon or are, in fact, dragons. But both can lead to many exciting adventures.

This chapter explores stories that include a wealth of mathematical ideas such as calculating, simple addition and subtraction problems, comparing, counting, understanding and using numbers, discussing and problem-solving, matching, measures including length, weight and time as well as investigating shape and pattern.

Sit back, relax and enjoy!

Mathematics

Ordinal and cardinal numbers

Sequencing

Reasoning

Adding and subtracting

Problem-solving

Measures including length, weight, mass, time

Exploring patterns and shape

Exploring 2D and 3D shapes

Choosing appropriate equipment

Being systematic

Making and testing predictions

Presenting results

Selecting materials for a task

Exploring and recording work

Making and testing hypotheses

Recording systematically

Communicating clearly

Talking about the work in hand

Planning strategies

Making and testing statements

Explain how or why something works

Explain and representing results to others

Thinking logically

Ordering

Predicting

Recognising patterns and relationships

Generalising

Completing a task

Interpreting mathematical information

Looking for connections

Looking for patterns

Asking questions

Estimating

Making sense of a task

Choosing ways of modelling a problem

Trying alternative strategies

Vocabulary

Counting numbers

1, 2, 3 . . . 10, count, 1st, 2nd, 3rd . . . 10th

Comparing and ordering numbers

More, less

Adding and subtracting

How many more? Take away

Take away, left

Solving problems

Why? How? What? When?

Reasoning about numbers or shapes

I think this because . . .

Measures

Length small, big, taller, shorter, bigger, smaller, huge, tiny

Tall, long, enormous

Mass

Heaviest, grams, weigh, measure, heavy, heavier than, lighter than

Time

Telling time, clock, hours, minutes, seconds, watch, year, day, month, Christmas, Easter, birthday, before, after

Exploring patterns, shape and space

Pattern

2D shapes

Triangles, squares, circles

3D shape

Cylinder

Position, direction and movement

On top, beside, next to, behind, between, in front

General

What do you think?

Why do you think that?

What comes next?

What is the same?

What is different?

Elvira, the Dragon Princess by Margaret Shannon
Published by Scholastic

Getting to know the story

This story is about a little dragon that does not enjoy fighting and would rather make daisy chains than eat princesses. One day, Elvira decides that she has had enough of other dragons teasing her and sets off to live her life as she pleases.

Familiarity with the story is central to the successful development of these activities. It can be introduced to children through class story time, small groups sharing the story, sharing the book with an adult helper or sharing the book with an older child.

Mathematics

Finding and making a pattern involving simple counting to and from 10

Use a set of cut out daisies to make a pattern. These can be printed on paper then cut and pasted onto cards. This is much quicker than cutting each one individually. You can use two or three different sizes.

Show a pattern of daisies. Begin with simple counting such as one small, one big.

Ask children if they can see any difference between the daisies. Can they tell you what the difference is? Encourage words like *taller, shorter* as well as *bigger* and *smaller*. 'Can you make a pattern using ten daisies? Tell me about the pattern you have made. Take four daisies away for Elvira so that she can make a pattern. How many are left? Elvira has four daisies, how many more does she need to make seven?' Ask simple addition and subtraction questions for those children who are working with numbers up to ten. For younger children, go as far as five and gradually increase as they become more confident. If you have no daisies, use white cubes. Put a small yellow sticker in the middle of one face and you have daisies! '*Make two different patterns that Elvira might like to make. Tell your friend about your pattern*'. For children who are not very confident about pattern making, start a pattern for them and ask them to carry on the pattern to make the chain *longer*. As an extension label a different set of daisies with 1st, 2nd, 3rd, 4th and so on. This will give opportunities to talk about ordinal numbers as well as cardinal numbers. As a further extension, colour the daisies in three hues and ask the children to make a pattern using size and colour.

Share two sets of cards with two children and set them a problem such as '*What is the longest chain you can make that has the same pattern all the way from the beginning to the end?*'

Weight

'*How can we weigh Elvira? How can we measure how tall she is? How long is her tail? How much water will Elvira need to put in her bath?*' As there are no really definitive answers possible, gather ideas to put with an Elvira display. Link the questions to the experiences of the children. Encourage the children to talk about their reasons for choosing the non-standard measures they will be using during this activity.

Do you think Elvira is very *heavy*? What would happen if she accidently sat on a princess? *How big* would a chair for Elvira need to be?

Can you find something *heavier than* you? Can you find something *heavier than* your favourite toy? This activity will develop the language of weight and encourages children to use the words 'heavier' and 'lighter'.

Can you find a way of *weighing* your favourite toy? This is an open-ended investigation allowing the children to think about what they are going to use to weigh an object. Encourage them to use non-standard measures such as beads, cubes and blocks.

Which is the *heaviest*? Find three toys in the classroom. Ask the children to discuss how they will weigh these objects. This activity is an interesting project for a pair of children to work on together and will give you the opportunity to assess their problem-solving strategies. The children can give verbal or pictorial feedback.

Capacity

'*Elvira loves bath time. She likes looking after herself by keeping clean*'. These activities develop problem-solving skills using capacity. Find a large bowl or a baby bath that can be used in or out of the classroom. Talk to the children about Elvira taking a bath. Do they think this bath would be *large enough* for a dragon? If not, why not? Find out how many jugs of water it would take to fill the bath, then estimate how many Elvira might need for her bath. Would she need *more or less*? How many jugs of water would you need to make the bath overflow? What happens to the water level when you put something in it?

Find several large containers the dragons might like to drink from. Which container holds the most? How can we find out?

Being different

'Elvira is different from the other dragons because she does not want to fight. Look at your friend. Does your friend look like you? What is the same and what is different?' Encourage children to talk to their friend about the similarities and differences between them. Ask some of the pairs to tell the rest of the class what they found out.

For example, *'We both have hair. Mine is short and hers is long'*.

Present the class or a small group with the three dragons shown below. *'These dragons all look the same, so can you find a way to make them all different using different shapes? This dragon will have triangles. This dragon will have squares and this dragon will have circles.'* See the templates provided in the resource sheets section.

'Show me what you have done. How did you make the dragons different? Tell me about your dragons.'

For younger children, use just one dragon each but use all of the shapes. Use their pictures as a display showing similarities and differences.

Role play

Children love developing caves and dens. If you have an outside space, use the environment that you have in different ways. Can you import logs to make a den?

> *Children find something thrilling in creating their own special place, somewhere on their scale where the grownups can't go. Making dens usually involves taking the sofa apart, or draping old blankets over upturned chairs, but children also love to build outdoor dens.*
> *(Fiona Danks in Nature's Playground)*[9]

Writing in *Nursery World*,[10] Helen Bilton says that den building 'is a pastime that generation after generation has enjoyed. . . . But a den can only be a den if it is allowed to be an open ended process that enables children to dictate the direction of the play. . . . All the great designs of this world came about through a process, through trial and error, involving the making and rectifying of mistakes, involving standing back, pondering and considering'.

Do you have a slide that can be used as a cave by draping a blanket or large piece of material over the top of the slide? Make sure it reaches the ground so the children can use the space below as a cave.

Do you have a folding clothes dryer that can be covered, thereby producing a cave? This has the advantage that it can easily be taken down when necessary so that you can use the space for something else.

Or maybe you could attach an old blanket to the wall and pull it out when it reaches the floor to produce a cave. The lower part can be attached to the back of two chairs.

If none of these is possible, make a dragon area on top of a cupboard or a table where the children can get involved in small play. Use a suitably sized box and fold the edges into the box for added strength. Paint both the inside and outside a suitable cave colour. After discussion with the children about what they would like to include in the cave, you can start to develop a prop box.

Children can work together to build and maintain the cave which will then become an imaginative play area for groups or pairs to use.

Talk about feeling afraid of the dark. Emphasise that we should be sensitive to any children who express this fear. What else are children afraid of? How can they help each other? Develop self-esteem through discussion and group activities. Use circle time to explore how it feels to be teased.

Prop box

You will need:

- Other dragons for the tabletop cave.
- Some treasure. Old costume jewellery is good for this. You can also use strings of silver and gold beads sold at Christmas designed to decorate your tree.
- A CD player or iPod dock to listen to other dragon stories and music. The soundtracks for the films *Pete's Dragon* or *How to Train your Dragon* are available online.
- Some smooth rocks, some sand or gravel or autumn leaves to make a floor.
- Some bones; you can make them from papier-mâché, and then paint them. To make them extra strong, put a wash of diluted PVA glue over them.
- Dragon puppets.
- Other dragon story books. Listen to these stories in the dark cave.
- *A Dragon in a Wagon* by Lynley Dodd is about a girl who wishes for a more exciting pet. When Susie Fogg takes her dog for a walk, she dreams of having a more exciting pet. Something huge, fierce or odd, like a dragon in a wagon. She soon gets carried away by her imagination.
- Dragon faces, hats and masks.

Making a book

Make a group book about 'a day in the life of Elvira'. Talk about the activities that children think Elvira might do. Put them in order (*sequencing*) from early morning until bed time. Illustrate the book, using one page for each activity. Older children who have been investigating time could add a clock face to each page with hands showing the time.

Invite older children to dress as a dragon, using just a mask and a hat, or with a whole cloak and gloves with claws attached, and read or tell a not-too-scary dragon story.

Use the dragon outline provided in the resource sheets section to make a dragon display or an illustration in a book. Children can choose words to describe different dragons. Write them on and around an enlarged picture. Include words such as *'quiet'*, *'kind'*, *'helpful'* as well as *'fierce'*, *'scary'* and *'loud'*. Reinforce the fact that not all dragons are bad. Elvira was a good, kind dragon.

Trails

Before designing the trail, talk generally about travelling and journeys. Why do we travel? What journey do the children make when they come to school? What do they see? What other journeys do they take? Has anyone been on a long journey that took a long time? Or a short journey which did not last very long? Ask children to draw a picture of a journey that they have been on. It does not have to be anywhere very far; it could be a journey around their bedroom or going from downstairs to upstairs. Draw a large picture map of Elvira's journey from dragon land to princess land. Talk about the different areas shown on the map.

Games

20	19	18	17	16
11	12	13	14	15
10	9	8	7	6
1	2	3	4	5

Dodge the dragon: a board game

Rules

The game board here is one suitable for children who are working with numbers up to 20. But you can reduce it to ten or increase it to 50.

You will need one die per pair of players. This can be a 1, 2, 3, 1, 2, 3 or 1–6 die, whichever is more appropriate. You can include zero, which would act as a 'miss a turn' throw.

The dragons could stand for anything you want them to mean. They could mean go back one space, or keep very quiet and miss a turn, or your partner has two throws before you can throw again. Or, for the very young, they can just be decorations for the board.

Matching games

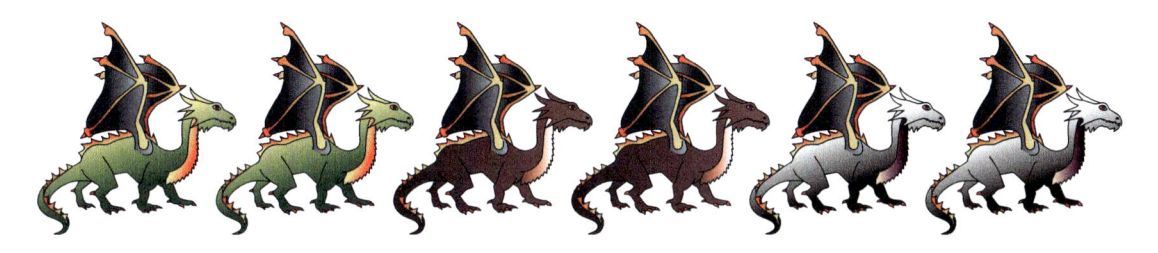

Pairs: a matching game

Make a set of cards each with a standard picture of the same dragon. Using the idea of pairs, colour each pair of dragons in a different way. This can be a colour match, a pattern match, a number match or a colour and pattern, or a colour, pattern and number. Numerals could be represented by spots on the body that the children need to count. It can be as easy or as difficult as the child needs it to be. It is all about observation, discussion, finding similarities and differences and reasoning. *'I think these two go together because. . . .'*

Both of these games can be sent home to be played with adults and siblings or a friend next door. Be aware that in some circumstances you will also need to send home the resources needed to play the games.

Being creative with mathematics

Being creative is not usually associated with mathematics. But maths is one of the most creative areas of learning that I know.

Numbered dragon footprints around the classroom are always popular. They can go across the floor, up a wall, across the ceiling, out of a door into the outside area. Make the footprints *huge*, otherwise young children will have difficulty seeing the number. Stomp over the ones on the floor as you call out the number. This will not work if you try to get a class of 30 on the same print.

How many children, from a very young age, do paint splash or splosh pictures? You will recognise it. Fold the paper in half. Open it flat. Splash or splosh some paint on one side. Fold the paper over along the original fold. Press down gently all over the paper. Open it and be amazed by the symmetrical picture that has been created. Almost magic! Then wipe up all the paint that has be squeezed out of the edges.

This is a very early introduction to mirror-image symmetry. And the resulting pictures look stunning on a display wall. But take it a bit further and make the pictures into dragon heads. Bits and pieces can be added such as glitter, ribbons, googly eyes and red paper for flames. Leave a lot of possible resources for the children to choose from and be wowed by what they create! You may need to wait a while before the glue dries before you can add them to a display but be patient. It is worth the wait.

Use just shades of green with a little yellow for a symmetrical Elvira head. Eyes can be added later.

Another craft that is very easy and very popular is to make paper chains as we have at Christmas time.

Take strips of different coloured paper and stick the two ends together to make a circle(ish!), linking one circle to the previous one. When the dragon is long enough (having different lengths would be useful for discussion afterwards), think about attaching a head. Use a circle folded in half for the dragon head. Add eyes on the upper part and teeth and a tongue inside the fold and you have your dragon. Add feathers if the dragon needs to fly. Add a garden stick to both ends and you have a dragon puppet.

Use different shades of green for Elvira.

Puppets

There is already one idea for a puppet mentioned in the previous section. But making a puppet ready for a dragon parade is quite another thing.

You will need a head and a tail ready for colouring. You can use the sheet provided in the resource sheets section.

Colour and cut out the head and the tail. Using a strip of strong paper such as sugar paper, and making sure that it fits the width of the dragon's head and tail, fold it in a fan or zigzag pattern.

Tape or glue the head of the dragon to one end of the sugar paper and attach the tails to the other end.

Tape or glue craft sticks to the back of the dragon puppet. Hold the puppet by the sticks and make the dragon's body dance. Or, as you can see in the picture, go outside on a sunny day and make the dragons into shadow puppets.

Play some appropriate dancing dragon music and have a dancing dragon parade.

Explore a range of materials when making puppets. Just talking about them can open a whole new set of ideas, thoughts and vocabulary.

Using socks

Any socks will work for a sock dragon. You can use plain or patterned, long or short socks.

Chapter 4: Dinosaurs and dragons   131

You will need a sock, matching colour craft foam or felt, scraps of yellow and orange craft foam or felt, glitter glue, googly eyes or eyes made from felt.

Cut two wings and a tail from the craft foam/felt. Decorate with the glitter glue.

Put the sock over your hand and mark where you want the eyes, wings and tail to go. Lay the sock flat and glue on the tail, wings and eyes.

While this is drying make your flames by cutting a yellow flame shape and a slightly smaller one from orange. Glue them together.

Put on the sock puppet and, using your thumb as the lower part of the mouth, mark where the flames will go.

Take the puppet off and glue on the flames. These will need to face the back of the sock so that they turn the right way around when you put your thumb in.

Using spoons

Elvira is the green one!

How about a two-handed dancing dragon? Start with a painted spoon, decorate the face and then stick tape or thin string onto the back of the head. This can be long or short according to children's preferences. Attach the other end to an upside-down spoon (also painted). Decorate with ribbons: *wide, narrow, short, long, smooth, bumpy* and any colour that you fancy. Have a dancing dragon festival.

Using equipment already in your setting

Bricks and blocks that fit together are ideal for making models. Oliver has made a very fierce dragon. But how about Elvira? Put only green blocks on a table to get different models of Elvira. Light green, dark green and maybe some yellow. Do not give too many instructions beyond '*make a model of Elvira*'. Each child will interpret and display their own ideas. Some will be big, some may be small.

Put them in order of size from smallest to tallest to represent Elvira getting older.

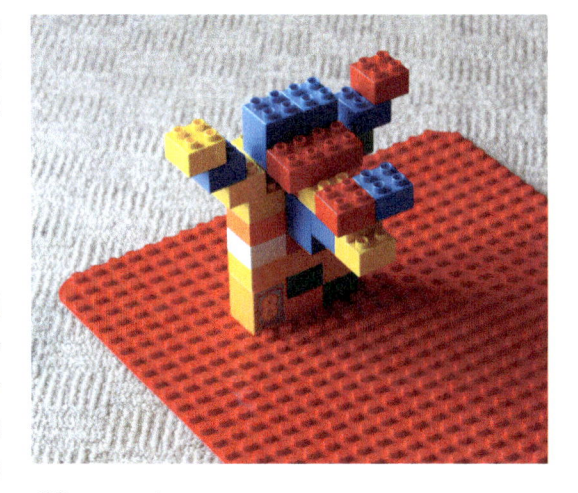

Oliver age 4

'The dragon is a he. He's a lava breathing dragon with big balls of lava. And he has a tiny mouth. And he also likes to eat, he's a meat-eating dragon and he's a carnivore. His favourite food of all is people! And he used the lava balls to kill the people and then eat them. His name is Joggyjoggydodo. He likes to run around and fly.'

Chapter 4: Dinosaurs and dragons

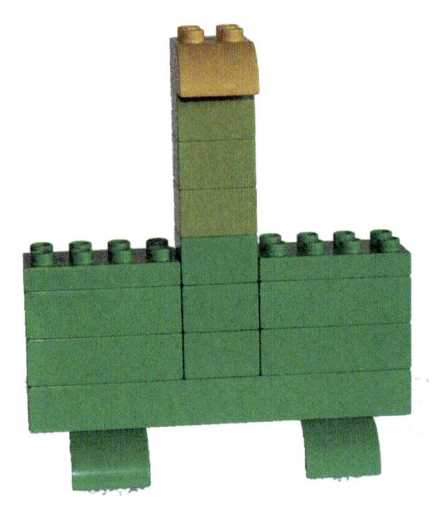

Elvira with her wings out

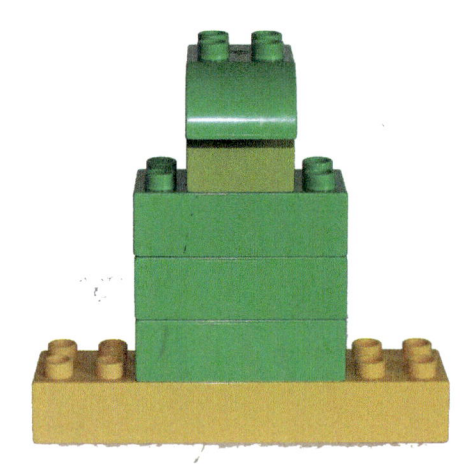

Elvira playing in the sand

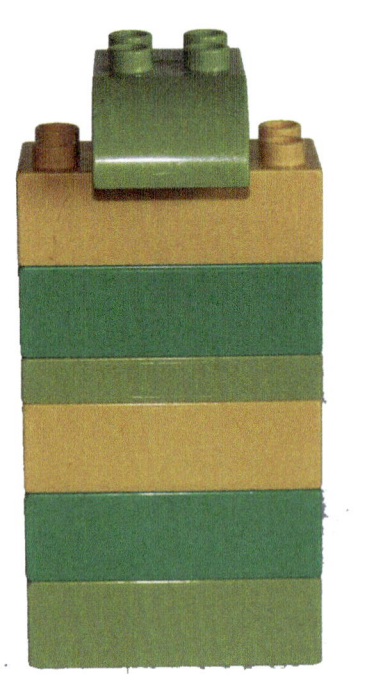

Elvira made by using a colour pattern

Elvira growing taller

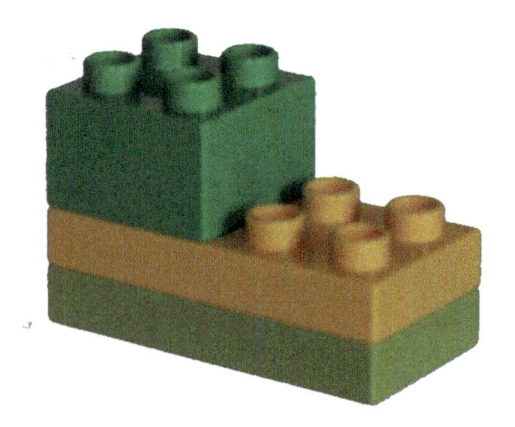

Baby Elvira

Chapter 4: Dinosaurs and dragons

Wake Up Charlie Dragon by Brenda Smith
Published by Scholastic

Getting to know the story

Charlie Dragon has been asleep for ages. He slept through Christmas. He slept through Easter. He even slept through his birthday. But today his friends need him to wake up and help them.

This story is perfect for looking at friendship, caring and special events through the year, including special days that people have.

Role play

Children love exploring and making dens. A dragon cave made from boxes, screens, long pieces of material and smaller boxes to make into rocks gives children the opportunities to change the cave every day, keeping it as a semi-permanent fixture. It also affords many places for hiding, sleeping or eating.

Include such props as masks, green shiny material to be used as a cape, gloves and hats.

An outdoor climbing frame would be ideal to change into a cave, or the underneath of a slide. Cover the climbing frame/slide with dark material (old curtains are ideal). Make the entrance quite small so that the inside remains as dark as possible. Make sure that children with mobility problems can still use the cave.

Safety: emphasise that it would be rather dangerous to climb the walls of the climbing frame or use the steps on the slide while they are disguised as a cave.

You might want to check with parents if children have any particular fear of the dark.

Another alternative is to use a black out pop up tent.

If there is room, and it is not too dark, place discovery boxes for the children to explore. If the cave is too small, place these boxes by the entrance. The discovery boxes will contain different things for children to look at and integrate into their play such as bones made from clay, flour and salt dough or papier-mâché. Baskets of books about dragons, and perhaps logs, bark, driftwood, pine cones and autumn leaves, which give a lovely scrunchy sound, can also be in a box. The cave can be finished off to simulate night time with animals such as bats and spiders.

Include cobwebs and torches. Cobwebs are easy to make. You can either buy materials that simulate cobwebs (usually from a stationery shop) or make your own by drizzling PVA glue onto round margarine lids in a cobweb pattern.

Sprinkle them with glitter. Leave them to dry, peel them off the lid and hang them up in the cave. **Hint:** Give children small plastic bottles with a limited amount of glue and a very small opening in the nozzle. And a small opening on the glitter bottle!

Paint the outside of the cave and cover it with paper leaves and creepers. Draw and paint dragon footprints going into or leaving the cave.

Crawling in and out of the cave through the tunnel or small entrance will require care and coordination.

Be aware of the limited space inside the cave. Move carefully so no one is hurt or the structure damaged.

Finding the mathematics

Dragon shapes

This activity uses the same four shapes to create new shapes with the same area. The first activity is a simple one working with four equilateral triangles.

You will need crayons and glue.

Set up the activity for individuals or pairs. Provide each child/pair with a copy of the activity sheet and the four triangular tiles. You will find these in the resource sheets section.

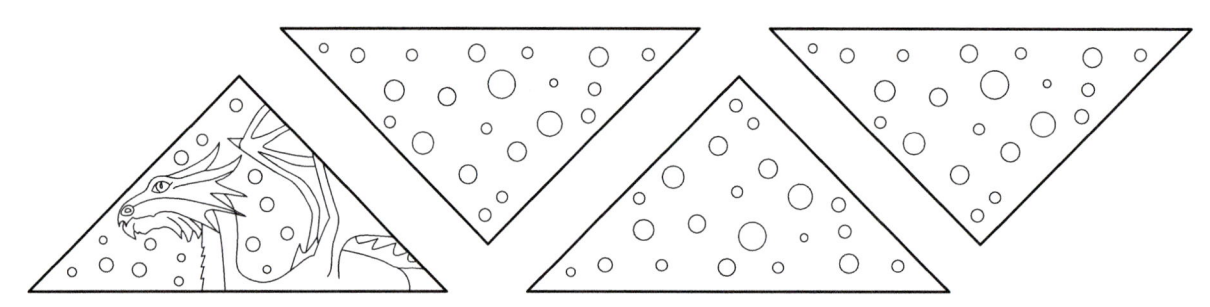

The task is to arrange the tiles in the outlines each time using every piece. The position of the head is not crucial. If you want to keep them as permanent pictures, glue the pieces to the template.

Let the children decorate each triangle, ensuring that one of them is the head and that they have the chance to choose their favourite shape for their dragon. They then stick their shapes into the outline provided in the resource sheets section.

Display them in the role play area and write children's comments about their own dragon. Older children can write their own.

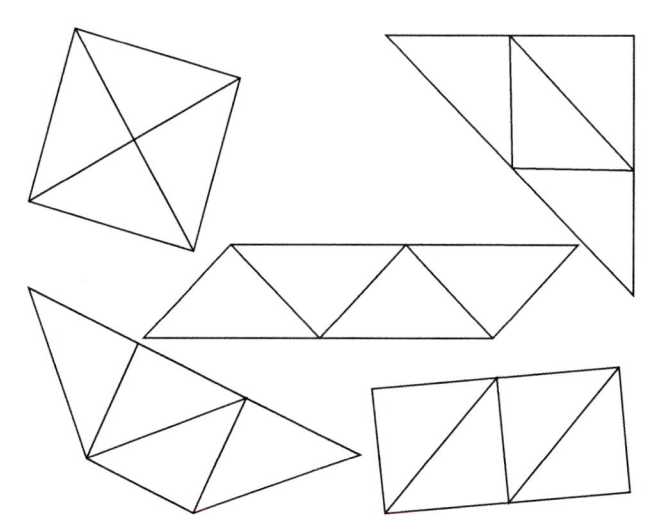

As an extension to this, the activity can be presented without the advantage of the triangle outlines.

Making models

Make models using interlocking cubes to represent the birthday presents that Charlie got for his birthday. You can also use empty cardboard boxes and cylinders from the centre of kitchen rolls. Have a wide range of different shapes and sizes for the children to choose from. Using newspaper as the cheapest option, ask children to wrap the present they have chosen. Ask questions such as '*How are you going to wrap your present? What will you need? How big does your paper need to be?*' **Hint:** You will need to think about how the paper is to be fixed to itself so that the present does not peep through. You could use glue, but this tends to be difficult with young children as the paper unwraps itself before the child can apply the glue. You could use clear tape, but there is the same problem as the glue unless strips are cut beforehand. Avoid making the strips too long or they will stick to themselves rather than to the paper. One solution is to use a wrist dispenser of clear tape. This is an elastic band that goes around the child's wrist. On the band is a tape dispenser of ready cut strips. These seem to work very well. They can be bought at most stationers or supermarkets.

Add the presents to the Charlie display. Use them as discussion points when reviewing how the children managed the task. Ask questions such as '*How did you wrap your parcel? Did you have enough paper? How did you stick the paper together? Was the paper you used too big or too small? Did you have any problems? What helped you solve your problem?*'

Development and variation

Focus on ordering wrapped presents according to their weight. You can use balance scales or digital scales showing grams.

Another way is for children to use their hands to feel the different weights and use that system to order the parcels. Do all children put them in the same order?

Once the contents of the boxes have been revealed, challenge children to put specific numbers of objects inside each one. Listen for reasoning that reflects the fact that smaller objects take up less space, and therefore more of them can be fitted into the box compared with larger objects.

Encourage children to predict how many of a certain object will fit in a particular box. Use questions such as '*Which do you think is the biggest box? I wonder which will be the best box for four small cars. Can you guess how many cubes will fit in this box?*'

Party hats

Plan and design made-to-measure party hats. Children can use what they learnt from previous activities about measuring heads to make a party hat that fits. Children need to work in pairs so that they can measure their partner's heads. Measuring your own head can be a bit tricky.

Once the hat is made, it can be decorated. This can involve creating a pattern that involves colour or shape or both.

Chapter 4: Dinosaurs and dragons

Dragon bunting

Design and make bunting that can be hung around the Charlie display. These are usually made using triangles, but that does not have to be the case. Choose a shape, ask children to draw a character from the story then stick or staple your shapes on a piece of flat ribbon or string, and there you have the perfect bunting for your party. Whilst doing this activity, children will need to be aware of not only the shape but also the size of their paper so that their character will fit into the space.

Making a book

Previous chapters have shown different ways to make a book. Some are suitable for children, whereas others are more appropriate for adults.

Most children love to tell a story. In fact, with some children it is difficult to stop them. Making a book is an alternative. They can then share their book with the class or a group or their family. Books have the benefit of having both a beginning and, more importantly, an end. Any extra ideas can become a second book in the series.

Start with a picture. Ask children to tell you about the dragons they have drawn. Ask open questions rather than closed where the children answer yes or no. For example, '*Your dragon looks happy. Why is he happy? Tell us some things that your dragon likes to eat. Why do you think Charlie likes to sleep so much? What presents do you think your dragon would like for his birthday?*'

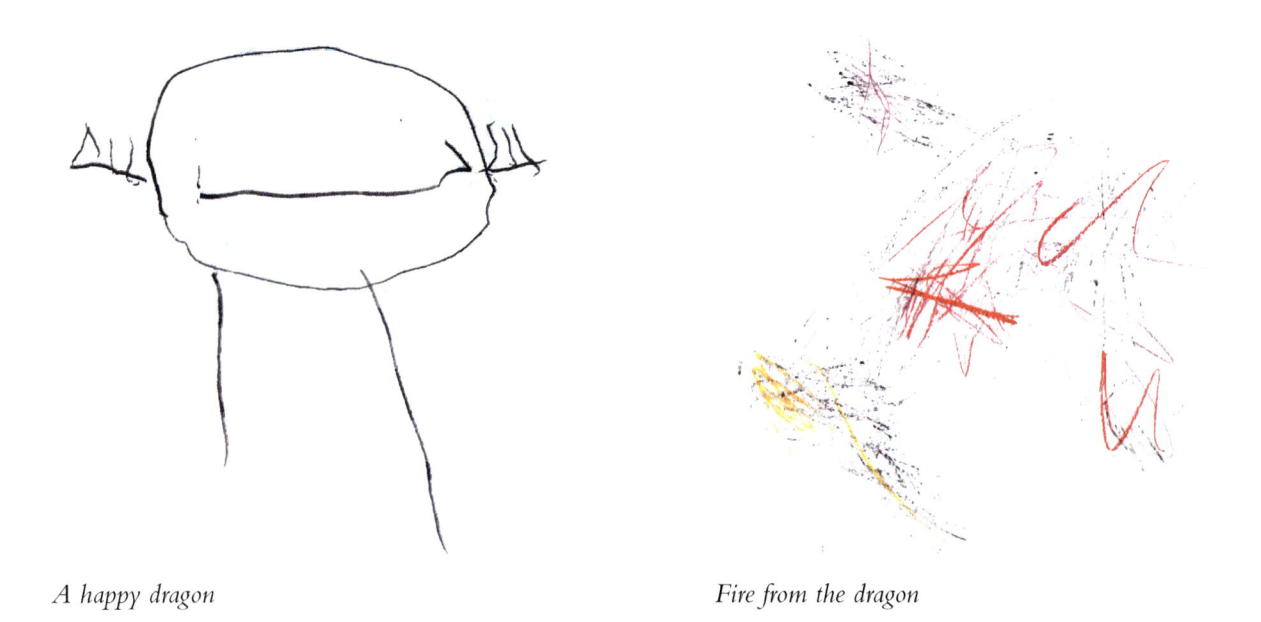

A happy dragon

Fire from the dragon

The books produced can be picture books or picture books with early writing. The main thing to remember is that the book contains the *child's* ideas and illustrations.

Discovery boxes

When putting together a discovery box, be aware that some children may not be able to use all of their senses, and so think carefully about what these boxes contain. The boxes should be put together to ensure that all children have access to something inside. Change these each week so that children stay interested and motivated.

For example, include magnifying glasses to look carefully at shells, sponges and pieces of wood that are on the floor of the cave.

Include reference books that show pictures for children to learn about caves. How are they formed? What creatures live in them? Investigate caves at the seaside and caves inland. How are they similar? How are they different?

Include stories which use languages other than English. Ask at your local library if they have any examples or go online.

Investigate flags from other countries that have a dragon on them. There are only three: Bhutan, Malta and Wales.

One of the boxes can include items that would be used for birthdays. This can lead to discussions about why we have birthdays. Be aware that in some religions or cultures, birthdays are not celebrated, but other things are. You could also include items for those occasions as well.

Including music

Music and maths are very closely related. Both involve pattern. Pattern is everywhere!

Listen to music that depicts animals. For example, how are animals depicted in the 'Carnival of the Animals'?

Listen to the music of Vivaldi to see how music is used to convey mood.

How might Charlie and the other animals move? Link these movements together as a dance sequence.

Make a fire breathing dragon. Start by painting a cylinder. Add eyes and nostrils. Glue strips of coloured paper (tissue paper is best) at the end of the cylinder. Make sure the paint is dry, then place the opening of the cylinder around your mouth (ensuring that your lips stay inside the opening to avoid moistening the cardboard getting coloured rings round your mouth). Now blow hard and the flames will shoot out in front of you.

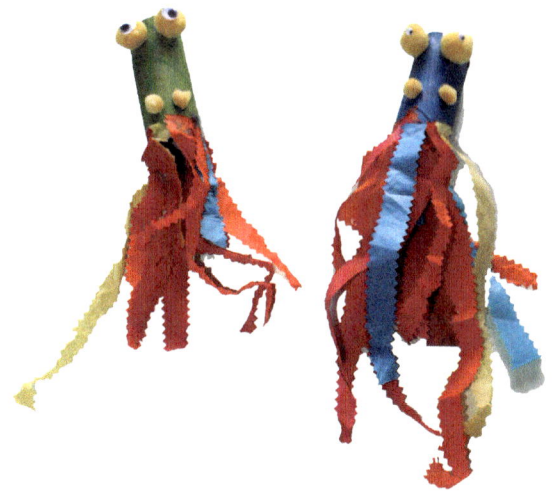

Add an investigation. *'I wonder which would give the best flames, gluing the strips inside the cylinder or around the outside? Let's try both and see what happens.'*

Design and make puppets

Sophie (age 5) designed this dragon puppet and it was used as the pattern for a sock puppet.

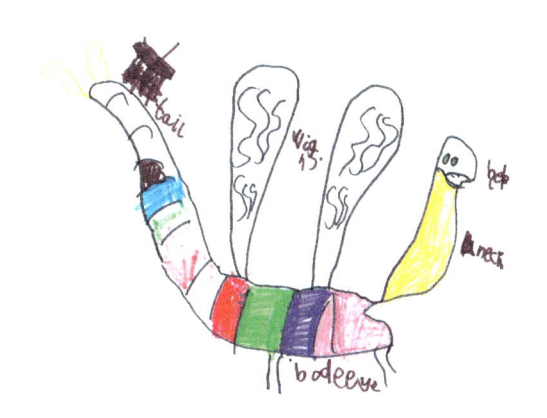

Put musical instruments in the cave for children to make night music or dragon-waking-up music (start quietly and build to a crescendo to demonstrate a roar).

Be dramatic. Choose different moods for the dragon: angry, tired, happy.

Games

Catch the Dragon's Tail

This traditional Chinese game is great fun for outside. You will need a large group of children – at least ten, but the more the merrier! The children can be any age, and adults can join in as well.

The children all form a line with their hands on the shoulders of the child in front. For younger children it may be easier if they hold hands instead. The first in line is the dragon's head; the last in line is the dragon's tail.

The dragon's head then tries to catch the tail by manoeuvring the line around in an effort to touch the last player. All the players in the middle do their best to stop the dragon's head without letting the line break.

When the head catches the tail, the tail player takes the front position and becomes the new dragon's head. All of the other players move back one position.

Dragon wing relay race

Cut the shapes of two pairs of dragon wings out of cardboard. Divide players into two teams and give each team a set of wings. Racers must hold their wings on their backs (or over their heads) and pretend to 'fly' to the finish line and then back to their teams, where they hand the wings off to the next player in line. The relay race continues until all players have taken a turn at flying.

Dragon egg hunt

Hide plastic Easter eggs around the inside or outside area. Send children on a hunt for these 'dragon's eggs'. You can also fill the eggs with trinket prizes for players to keep.

Developing mathematical vocabulary

Use the photocopiable sheet of the dragon outline provided in the resource sheets section on page 247. If possible, make a huge copy of it and put on a wall to start a display.

Talk about words that tell us about size. For example, you could have, '*big*', '*small*', '*huge*', '*tiny*', '*giant*' and '*as small as*'. Write the words inside the outline of the dragon.

'*What words could we use to describe dragons?*' Include words other than size words such as '*heavy*', '*noisy*', '*scary*', '*rough*' and '*smooth*'. Write the words around the outside of the dragon.

Involve the family at home. Challenge them to find other words to describe a dragon.

Act as a scribe to write children's suggestions to describe such huge creatures. Be aware that some dragons may be very small, so you may want to add a small dragon outline for small words.

Chapter 4: Dinosaurs and dragons   139

Harry and the Dinosaurs Say 'Raahh' by Ian Whybrow
Published by Puffin

Getting to know the story

Harry finds some old dinosaurs in his grandma's attic. He cleans them up and makes them his own, carefully (and accurately) naming each one. Harry and his dinosaurs go everywhere together. Today Harry's dinosaurs are acting strangely. They are hiding all over the house and refusing to come out. Could this be because Harry has to visit Mr Drake the dentist? At last, the dinosaurs are all persuaded to jump into their bucket, but will they behave once they get there?

Mathematical activities

How tall? How long?

In your outside area draw the outline of a dinosaur using chalk or rope. It can be on the ground or up a wall. Depending on space, you may need to find a species of very small dinosaur. Use non-standard units to measure the height and length of the dinosaur. Ask open ended questions such as '*What do you think we could use to measure the length of this dinosaur? If you lay on the floor next to the dinosaur, do you think you would be longer or shorter? What if I lay next to him? Why not make a guess and check if it works? Do you think I would be longer or shorter? What do we need to find out? Can you tell me what we have done so far?*'

Children can record what they found out using pictures, pictures and words, or just words. Whichever way they choose, they will be fulfilling the communication strand of problem-solving. Take photos of the children exploring the problem and use them as part of a discussion when you are back in the classroom.

Build a dinosaur using shapes

Using basic shapes, give children free choice about which to use to build up a dinosaur.
  For example:

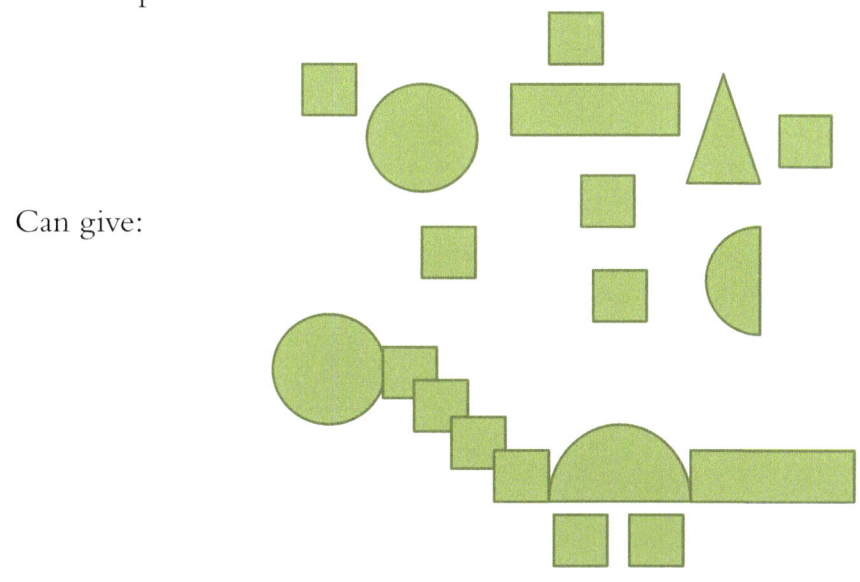

Can give:

Put a selection of shapes and colours in pots so that each pot has a different shape.

For younger children you may want to provide templates for them to match and cover. But once they get the idea of making a dinosaur, let their imagination run wild.

You may like to make your own Fuzzy-Felt shapes. Fuzzy-Felt is a simple fabric toy intended for young children. The toys consist of a flocked backing board onto which a number of felt shapes are placed to create different pictures. Felt pieces can be simple silhouettes or more detailed printed shapes. Fuzzy-Felt is generally for children over the age of three years, as the pieces may present a choking hazard. But if you make your pieces large enough they may suit younger children. Have an adult close by just in case.

Another option is to use a magnetic board and stick magnetic tape on the back of the shapes. In this case, use a firm card rather than paper. Magnetic tape is available in craft shops or you can order it online.

Time

Discuss the issue of time and when dinosaurs were on the earth. Make a very simple time line with dinosaurs on the left and people on the right. Fill in two or three other significant happenings along the rest of the line. It could be the birth of a baby, the building of your school, or the day human beings landed on the moon. If this was an accurate time line, each of these examples would be in the same space as the children but relax the rules this time. The important thing is that this happened *before* that and that happened *after* this. And dinosaurs were a long, *long* time ago, although we still have some species such as crocodiles that have descended from dinosaurs.

Counting back

Use number poems and rhymes for counting back, initially to and from five, but increasing to ten as children become more confident.

Poems

Five enormous dinosaurs

Five enormous dinosaurs,
Letting out a roar,
One went away,
And then there were four.

Four enormous dinosaurs,
Munching on a tree,
One went away,
And then there were three.

Three enormous dinosaurs,
Didn't know what to do,
One walked away,
And then there were two.

Two enormous dinosaurs,
Having lots of fun,
One ran away,
And then there was one.

One enormous dinosaur,
Chose a soft blue pillow.
He went away to sleep on it,
And then there were zero.

Five dinosaurs

Five huge dinosaurs,
Sleeping on a cave floor,
Woke up and started to roar,
'There is no room, no more, no more,
No more room on this floor!'
They tossed, and they turned and they pushed galore,
Till one poor dinosaur was pushed out the door.

(Continue counting down to one.)

One huge dinosaur,
Alone on a cave floor,
Woke up and started to roar.
'There's too much room on this floor, on this floor,
There's too much room on this floor!'
So he tossed, and he turned and he cried galore,
Till the poor dinosaur met his friends at the door.

'Come back dinosaurs, dinosaurs, dinosaurs!'
'Come back dinosaurs, dinosaurs!'
So, they all came back, and he cuddled with the four,
And there were no more roars galore.

Five dinosaurs went out to play

(To the tune of 'Five Elephants Went Out to Play')

One dinosaur went out to play,
On a bright and sunny day.
He had such enormous fun,
That he called another dinosaur to come.
THUMP! THUMP! THUMP!

Two dinosaurs went out to play,
On a bright and sunny day.
They had such enormous fun,
That they called another dinosaur to come.
THUMP! THUMP! THUMP!

(Count up till you get to five or to the number of children in your class.)

Going on a dinosaur hunt

(Children chant back each line after you say it.)

Going on a dinosaur hunt.
And I'm not afraid.
There's a tall mountain.
Can't go under it.
Can't go around it.
Guess I'll go over it.
Going on a dinosaur hunt.
And I'm not afraid.
There's a river.
Can't go over it.
Can't go under it.
Guess I'll swim across it.
Going on a dinosaur hunt.
And I'm not afraid.
There's some tall grass.
Can't go over it.
Can't go around it.
Guess I'll go through it.
Going on a dinosaur hunt.
And I'm not afraid.
There's a cave!
Can't go over it.
Can't go under it.
Guess I'll go in it.
It's dark and spooky in here.
It's cold in here!
I feel some scales.
I feel some big teeth!
OHH! It's a dinosaur!

(Children say the following with you.)

Run out of the cave,
Go through the grass,

> Swim across the river,
> Climb the mountain,
> Run home,
> Open the door,
> Jump into bed.
> I went on a dinosaur hunt,
> And I wasn't afraid!

Games

To help children develop their coordination, control and movement, use a dinosaur movement cube. This is made from a cube of any size, though I tend to use an empty tissue box. But make a larger one for outside use.

Each face of the cube has a picture of a dinosaur, so six different dinosaurs are needed. Each has an instruction. For example, 'Flap like a pterodactyl' or 'Run like a stegosaurus'.

Children take turns throwing the die and the rest of the class joins in with the actions. You will need a big space for this game.

To carry on this theme, use a tray or box of cubes and six small empty boxes with a dinosaur matching the faces of the die. This links with collecting data. After each throw ask a child (perhaps the child who last threw the die) to put a cube in the box that has the same picture as the one on the die face.

When all of the children have had a turn with the die, find out which dinosaur was seen the most.

Empty each small box of cubes. Count the cubes as you put them back in the box. Encourage children to join in with the counting. Write or tape the amount on the outside of the box. Do this for all six boxes. Line them in order from the least to the most amounts. It will look like a number line but with some numbers missing or repeated.

Use this to lead a discussion. *'Which dinosaur did we throw the most? Which dinosaur did we only throw (insert appropriate number) times? How many times did we throw the Tyrannosaurus Rex?'*

Use the cubes to build towers for comparison of height. Or make trains and compare lengths. Or use them to make a block graph.

Ask *'If we played the game again, do you think we would get the same answers? Why/why not?'*

The 'Like a Dinosaur' game can be played with two or more children, and it is suitable for young and older players alike.

Give the children plenty of space, put on some interesting dinosaur music and then ask them to move around in a certain manner.

You could ask them to:

- Stomp like a dinosaur.
- Roar like a dinosaur.
- Growl like a dinosaur.
- Run like a dinosaur.
- Chatter like a dinosaur.
- Scratch the ground like a dinosaur.

You can get as rowdy or noisy as you like and use up lots of energy in the process.

To calm the children down at the end of the game, ask them to 'sleep like a dinosaur' and give them a moment or two to rest.

Role play

You will need an old (or new if you have one) plastic fish tank or a builder's tray to create a living island for small world role play. You will also need newspaper, chicken wire, compost and quick growing seeds.

The living island

Scrunch up newspaper into large balls and build a mound on the bottom of the empty tank or tray. Cover the newspaper mound with small mesh chicken wire. Tuck the sharp ends of the wire under the rest of the wire. Pour compost all over the mound to create an island and push it down onto and into the spaces in the wire. Sprinkle a variety of seeds over the compost. Use a hand-held water sprayer to make sure that the entire island is damp. It will very soon start to grow, creating a living small world indoors or out. Use dinosaur models to inhabit the island. The island can be used for small world role play. Add short plastic tubes to become volcanoes. **Hint:** Cardboard is not as useful as it gets too wet and starts to disintegrate. Make boats to go on the water around the island.

Keep a photographic record of the island and make it into a book. Record the growth of the plants over time.

Make maps, guides and postcards for the island.

Write stories about 'adventures on the island'. Record some of the stories the children tell while they are playing.

Make dough or clay models. Make up stories about them, where they live and what they eat. Build an area that they can call home. Or use plastic models of dinosaurs, as clay and dough tend to crumble when they are wet – it depends on how enthusiastic the children are about watering.

Prop box

Include different dinosaurs, small wooden or plastic boats and writing materials for postcards. If you include packets of seeds, make sure that there is an adult nearby when the packets are opened.

Provide small boats for the water and maps of the island. You will also need some dinosaurs to inhabit the island.

Home/school links

Go to the library: What would your child like to find out about dinosaurs? Have a trip to the library like Harry and try to find out something new such as which dinosaur was the biggest or what they ate. Alternatively, you could use websites to find out more information.

Make your own story: Make your own dinosaur adventure. Encourage your child to arrange their dinosaurs (or other toy animals) in different places such as the bath, garden or park, and take photos of your child with them. You could print the photos so that children can stick them in a scrapbook or you might like to make a digital photo story of them. Children could compose captions for their photos. If they are beginning to write they could have a go at writing the captions themselves, or you could write for them.

Talk about the book: Children will be able to relate to Harry's feelings at different points in the story. Look at the pictures of the dinosaurs on the end papers together, and talk about, name and count them.

Make your own dinosaur friends

Mouseosaurus

Spikeosaurus

Giraffeosaurus

Wormosaurus

Fossils

Find, draw and make your own fossils by pressing shells into soft clay or dough.

Examine real fossils and talk about the shapes that you can see.
There are spirals (ammonites), star fish and any number of other shapes.

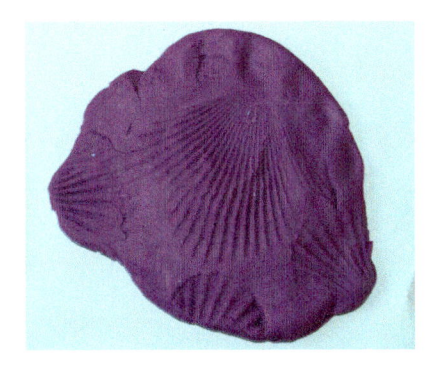

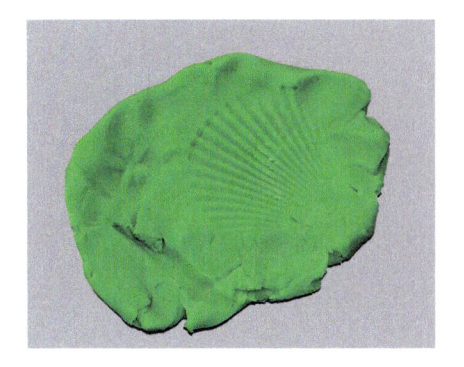

Paper plates again

You will need:

Paper plate
Card
Paint
Red paint (or any other colour)
Large bubble wrap

Instructions:

Paint half of the plate a dinosaur colour and leave to dry.
Paint the bubble wrap red (or your chosen colour) and press it onto the card. Repeat on the plate. Leave them both to dry.
Cut four legs, a tail and neck from the card.
Glue onto the back of the body.

This is a very simple dinosaur: a diplodocus in fact. But add or cut spikes and it becomes a stegosaurus. Turn the plate upright, add a longer tail, two long legs and two short legs, and it becomes the fiercest of them all, the Tyrannosaurus Rex.

Dinosaur diorama

Make a dinosaur scene with a cardboard box and some sticks, stones, shells, twigs, sand, polished stones or anything else a child would need to show their image of where dinosaurs lived. Each scene can be different. The children can work as pairs or individually.
   For example:

Paint or line the box with appropriate colours before getting the children to build the display. Use maths vocabulary such as *'on top of'*, *'beside'*, *'next to'*, *'behind'*, *'between'*, *'in front of'*.

Depending on your resources, make a special display of baby dinosaurs hatching from their eggs. I was lucky enough to know a potter who made these eggs for sale, and I got my set very cheaply (for nothing!) as they were duplicates.

Many have been broken over the years, but you could always encourage children to make their own set. There are several confectionary items in shops that use plastic eggs.

Use clay or dough to make the dinosaurs. You do not have to make a whole dinosaur; you just need a head to poke out.

Twins!

A new species

Use children's names to invent new dinosaurs. For example:

Jackosaurus
Vickiosaurus

Sophieosaurus
Thomasosaurus
Clareosaurus

Have the children draw what they think they would look like if they were dinosaurs today. Have the children tell about their new dinosaur. It is it big? Is it small? Is it short? Is it tall? Does it roar? Does it squeak? Does it stomp in a swamp?

In a Minute Mum by A. H. Benjamin and Nick East Published by QED Publishing

Getting to know the story

In a Minute Mum is a story about a little dinosaur named Rory that is always putting things off and always running late. It is driving his family mad! What will it take to make him change his ways? '*Have you ever put off an important task? Did it get you into trouble? How did it make you feel?*'

Rory's family asks him to help with simple tasks. '*Do you ever help with household chores? What do you do?*'

Mathematical ideas

Rory keeps saying 'just a minute' to his family. Do the children know what a minute is? Do they know how to tell the time? The concept of time can be difficult for young children to understand. A minute is such as short amount in which to do anything. Getting dressed, putting shoes on, or building a castle in the sand all take much, much longer than a minute.

Children enjoy the challenge of being asked to help solve a problem, so introducing story problems with a group of three- and four-year-olds is a good idea. It has the potential to provoke mathematical discussion, language and reasoning. And there may also be the opportunity to create a new problem at a different part of the story.

Children often enjoy putting similar items together in pots/baskets/trays. You could build on this by providing timing resources such as sand timers or digital timers that children could use to time themselves as they fill up the container.

Time to work with time

Place a variety of timing devices (such as different sand timers and digital timers) on a table or low cupboard near a collection of small easy-to-hold items such as marbles, shells, buttons, cubes and pencils as well as some containers big enough to hold several of the objects. Ask children how many marbles/shells/buttons they think they might be able to put in one of the containers before the sand runs out. They can only put in one at a time. Initially, use a one-minute timer. If you go for a five- or ten-minute timer, many of the children may have walked away by the time the sand runs out.

Chapter 4: Dinosaurs and dragons 149

Encouraging mathematical thinking and reasoning

Describing: Tell me about what you're doing. How many marbles did you get in that time? How many did you get in last time? What will you try next?

Recording: How will you remember how many marbles you managed to get in the pot that time?

Reasoning: Who has got the most marbles in their pot? How do you know? What could you do to make sure you get more marbles in your pot this time?

Opening out: What would happen if you used this different timer? What would happen if you only used one hand/used both hands? What would happen if you used this different pot? What would happen if you used, for example, buttons instead of marbles?

The mathematical journey

This story creates abundant mathematical possibilities from simple counting to different types of measures.

Start the session by asking children to tell you any words that they know about how we measure time. You may get answers such as '*day*', '*month*', '*year*', '*hour*', '*second*' or '*minute*'.

Link the word they know to activities that are personal to them at school and at home '*It's time for bed*'. '*It's time for your bath*'. '*It's time to tidy up*'. What else do they hear people say about time? Linking it with real life will make more sense for a lot of children.

Number: counting and cardinality – progressing from knowing some number words, to saying one number for each object, then knowing the number of the whole group. Managing relative number size and comparing numbers of objects.

Measures: comparing lengths of time from one minute through two minutes and up to five minutes using sand timers or digital clock faces. Measuring time and using everyday language to talk about time.

Capacity: developing an understanding that a large object takes up more space in a container than a small object.

Development and variation

How about asking the children how many marbles they could take out of the jar before the sand runs out? Following on from that, how long would it take to remove all the marbles? For older children who have, over time, developed a better understanding of elapsed time, turn the problem around and ask them how long it might take to put, for example, 12 marbles in the pot. This is more of a challenge as it requires them to find ways of timing themselves, which is where a digital timer might come in useful.

You could build on this idea further by making the most of opportunities to measure lengths of time which may come up in your everyday routine. For example, can the children tidy away in less time than they did yesterday? Can you get your coat on quicker than you did yesterday? Can you make a line at the door quicker than you did this morning?

Use different collections of small objects, such as marbles, shells, buttons, counters and corks as well as a range of different containers, for example, baskets, trays and pots. Use different tools for measuring time, for example, sand timers or easy-to-use stopwatches.

Leave paper, clipboards and pencils for children to record what they are doing and what they have found out, if they want to.

When we think of a minute today, we might think of a common expression, such as 'Got a minute?', 'Just a minute!' or 'In a minute'. But we rarely mean exactly 60 seconds.

How long is a minute?

Develop activities that demonstrate the exact length of a minute.

Ask children to place their heads on their tables. Say 'Go' and then use a clock, watch or stopwatch to measure exactly one minute. When children think one minute is up, they should quietly raise their hands without looking up. At the end of the activity, tell the children who were closest to the 60-second mark.

Try the activity again. Ask children to place their heads on their tables. This time, ask them to quietly sit up when they think exactly one minute has passed.

Have children working in groups of three and give each group a one-minute sand timer. Children should repeat these activities, timing each other with the one-minute sand timer.

Other, more energetic, activities can take place. For example, ask children to stand on one leg for one minute. Be aware that some children may need to hold on to a table or an adult's hand during this time. Does a minute *feel* longer during some activities than it does during others?

How to make a simple sand timer

A sand timer is a device that measures the passing of time. It consists of two halves of the same object made of the same material and size that are connected by a narrow hole. The bigger the hole, the quicker the sand will pass through.

You will need two clear plastic bottles that are the same shape and size. The shorter the bottles, the more stable the timer will be. Take the caps off, glue them together back to back and let the glue dry. Be careful not to get any glue in the middle of the lids or you will not be able to make a hole. Punch a hole through the middle of the glued together caps. (Best done by an adult!) Screw the cap onto the first bottle, just as you would normally do.

Make sure that the sand you use is very dry. If you use wet or damp sand, it will clog up your bottles. You could use coloured sand so that each different length of time will be represented by a different colour. You could add some glitter to the sand. Plain sand and gold glitter look good together.

Start filling the second empty bottle with sand. (Not the one that has the lid on it.) If you want the timer to be for a specific amount of time, then time yourself filling the bottle.

Screw the empty bottle onto the sand-filled bottle. Keep the sand-filled bottle on the table. Turn the empty bottle upside down. Screw the cap onto the bottle until it is tight.

Test your sand timer. Turn it upside down. The sand should flow smoothly from one bottle to the other. Check that it runs for the time that you want. Add or take out some sand as needed.

Wrap some strong tape around the necks of the bottles. Start at the bottom neck, work your way up past the seam and finish at the top of the neck.

Games

Stealing eggs from a dinosaur nest!

Play this fast-moving game where groups of children work as a team to 'steal' eggs from a dinosaur nest. You will find a photocopiable version of the game in the resource sheets section. Each line of chairs represents a team. If you have too few children, then play as individuals. Adults are welcome to join in! Encourage teamwork and make sure that children realise that if they do not obey the rules, then you will confiscate the eggs and return them to the nest!

Play dinosaur cards

A copy of this game can be found in the resource sheets section.

This matching game is very easy to understand. (With younger children do not use the whole of the pack as they often get fed up and leave the table.)

- Deal each player six cards which they do not show any other players.
- The first player places one of their cards, face up, in the middle of the table.
- The next player matches one of their cards to either end of the card just played by placing the two matching ends together.
- Players continue by taking turns to match one of their dinosaur cards to one of the two open ends of the line of cards.
- If a player cannot match any of their cards, they take one from the main pile and wait until their next turn.
- If there are no cards in the main pile, play passes to the next player.
- The game continues until nobody can match their cards, or someone uses up all their cards and wins the game.
- The winner is the first person to play all their cards or, if nobody can finish, the player with the fewest cards at the end of the game.

Investigating size and age

Present the children with a large egg (you may need to look for the type of egg that holds other eggs or gifts at Easter time).

Tell children the egg turned up in the classroom. Lead children in a discussion about it. '*What could be inside? What kind of animal could it belong to?*' (Large egg = large animal?) Compare the egg to a real egg and describe it – *thin shell, breaks easily, fragile*. What happens if you squeeze or drop a real egg? To prevent real eggs from getting broken, suggest that children write some notices to put next to or near to the eggs. For example: *Please take care of this egg, Handle/hold with care, Fragile, Precious, This is not a toy! Keep me warm, thank you*. Suggest some not-so-good-ideas to make children think – *Shake me, Please kick me*. Would these be good ideas? Discuss a safe place to put the egg.

Tell children you have been doing some research and you think this could be a dinosaur egg. Dinosaurs lived millions of years ago, so this is an amazing find. What can children do to help the egg hatch? What dinosaur do children think it could be? Ask children to share any dinosaur names they know. Do they have a favourite? Ask children to help write/spell the dinosaur names.

After a day or two, tell children that overnight the egg hatched! Introduce a toy dinosaur and give it a name. Do children recognise/know which dinosaur it is? It could be any of these:

Dinosaur facts

What dinosaurs are there? Discuss different types – flying, two-legged, four-legged, meat eating, vegetarian, and so on.

Were there any dinosaurs that lived in the water? Look in some informational books and use the contents or index pages to check. What facts can the children find out about the class pet dinosaur? Children can use the books to help them explore their own particular interests about dinosaurs. Encourage children to use the contents or index pages to make their research quicker.

Modelling

Make a dinosaur footprint in modelling dough or clay. Experiment with different tools to make marks. Sing 'Triceratops'. For the words and tune, visit the Kids Music Town website at kidsmusictown.com and go to Dinosaur Songs for Young Children.

Chapter 5: Bags, boxes and baskets

Why bags, boxes and baskets?

Children often enjoy guessing, counting and imagining.

Bags, boxes and baskets are excellent resources to help introduce estimation and measures.

They can develop the language of comparison and contrast such as bigger, smaller, heavier and lighter.

Depending on the activity, children can also use everyday language, such as '*curved*', '*pointy*' and '*straight*', to describe objects, then progress to using mathematical language such as '*circle*', '*square*', '*rectangle*', '*triangle*', '*oblong*' . . . where appropriate.

Mathematics

Calculating simple addition and subtraction problems

Comparing

Counting, understanding and using numbers

Discussing

Exploring and problem-solving

Describing shapes and measures

Matching

Reasoning

Communicating

Exploring and recording work

Making and testing hypotheses

Classifying

Collecting, organising and recording information

Choosing appropriate equipment

Being systematic

Making and testing predictions

Presenting results

Selecting materials and mathematics for the task

Recording systematically

Communicating clearly

Talking about work

Planning strategies

Checking results

Explaining and reporting to others

Ordering

Predicting

Discussing work with others

Recognising patterns

Generalising

Completing a task

Looking for connections

Looking for patterns

Asking questions such as 'what if?'

Estimating

Making sense of a task

Vocabulary

Counting numbers

Count 1, 2, 3 . . . 10

Comparing and ordering numbers

Adding and subtracting

Solving problems

Reasoning about numbers or shapes

Problems involving 'real life' or money

Measures

Measure, size, compare, guess, estimate, enough, not enough, too much, too little, too many, too few, about the same as

Length

Length, width, height, long, short, tall, high, low, wide, narrow, thick, thin, longer, shorter, taller, higher, longest, shortest, tallest, highest, bigger

Mass

Weigh, weighs, balances, heavy/light, heavier/lighter. Heaviest/lightest scales

Capacity

Full, empty, holds

Exploring shape and space

Shape, pattern, curved, straight, round, corner, face, side, edge, point, pointed

3D shapes

Cube, pyramid, sphere, cone, cuboid, cylinder

2D shapes

Circle, triangle, square, rectangle, star

General

What do you think?

Why do you think that?

What comes next?

Little Red Riding Hood

Getting to know the story

The story revolves around a girl called Little Red Riding Hood. The girl walks through the woods to deliver food to her grandmother who is not feeling very well. Her mother had ordered her to stay strictly on the path.

The Big Bad Wolf wants to eat the girl and the food in the basket. He secretly follows her, hiding behind trees, bushes, shrubs and patches of short and tall grass. He walks up to Little Red Riding Hood, who tells him where she is going. He suggests that she picks some flowers, which she does. But she goes off the path to find them. In the meantime, the wolf goes to the grandmother's house. He pretends to be the girl. He swallows the grandmother in one big mouthful (in some versions, he locks her in a cupboard and waits for the girl, disguised as the grandmother. This might be a better option for young children).

When the girl arrives, she notices that her grandmother looks very strange. Little Red Riding Hood then says, 'What a deep voice you have!' ('All the better to greet you with', says the wolf), 'Goodness, what big eyes you have!' ('All the better to see you with', responds the wolf), 'And what big ears you have!' ('All the better to hear you with', responds the wolf), and lastly, 'What a big mouth you have' ('All the better to eat you with!' responds the wolf). Just as the wolf is about to eat Little Red Riding Hood, a woodcutter comes to the rescue and with an axe, cuts open the wolf. Grandmother steps out unharmed. (Or he opens the cupboard door and she walks out.)

Mathematics

Sequencing the story

After telling the story, show pictures from the resource sheets section to illustrate the plot. You can use felt board or, by attaching magnetic tape, a magnetic board. Ask children to use the pictures to sequence the story. Use mathematical words such as *'before', 'after', 'along', 'through', 'inside'* and *'outside'*. You can also count the flowers that Little Red Riding Hood picked.

When sequencing the story as a group, use large pictures; with individuals, use smaller versions.

Making a book

You may wish to give children the picture outlines from the resource sheets section, ask them to colour them at home and then bring them back to school to be made into a book. This can be as simple as pasting the pictures into a ready-made book, or making books as shown in previous chapters.

Shapes and patterns

Use grandmother's bedroom, available in the resource sheets section. Discuss the various shapes to be found. Use the properties of the shapes as well as their names. For example: *'What shape is all over the chair (circle)? Tell me something you know about a circle. Look at the bed. What shape is on the bed cover (square)? Can you find another square in the picture? Look for a shape that has four sides and four corners.'*

You could ask the children to colour the shapes that are the same as each other in the same colour. For example, all the squares can be red, all the triangles can be blue and all the circles can be yellow.

Create different patterns for the curtains, rug, chair and bedspread in grandmother's bedroom. This could involve work on symmetry, shapes and colours. Use block prints, potato prints, hand prints, footprints or string stuck onto a wooden block. In fact, anything that will leave an impression when covered in paint will do. If you have large pieces of plain fabric, use them, after being printed, as curtains in the role play area, or as a bedspread in grandmother's bedroom.

Chapter 5: Bags, boxes and baskets

Investigating

Investigate Little Red Riding Hood's basket. What could be in the basket? List five things that Little Red Riding Hood could be taking to grandmother. Do all the children think of the same five things? List all of the possibilities and lead a class or group discussion about what they would choose out of the list for their grandmother and why. This can be recorded in a picture for a story of their own. This would be fulfilling the communication strand of problem-solving.

Food for grandmother

'I wonder if there are sandwiches in Little Red Riding Hood's basket. What do you think is in the sandwiches?' Choose two or three different fillings suggested by the children. **Hint:** Gummy Bears are not an option! Decide which fillings will be used.

For older children you can limit it to two or three ingredients that can be put together to make a sandwich filling. For example: cheese, egg and tomato. How many different sandwiches can be made? Ask children to investigate by using yellow (cheese), white (egg) and red (tomato) cubes. For example:

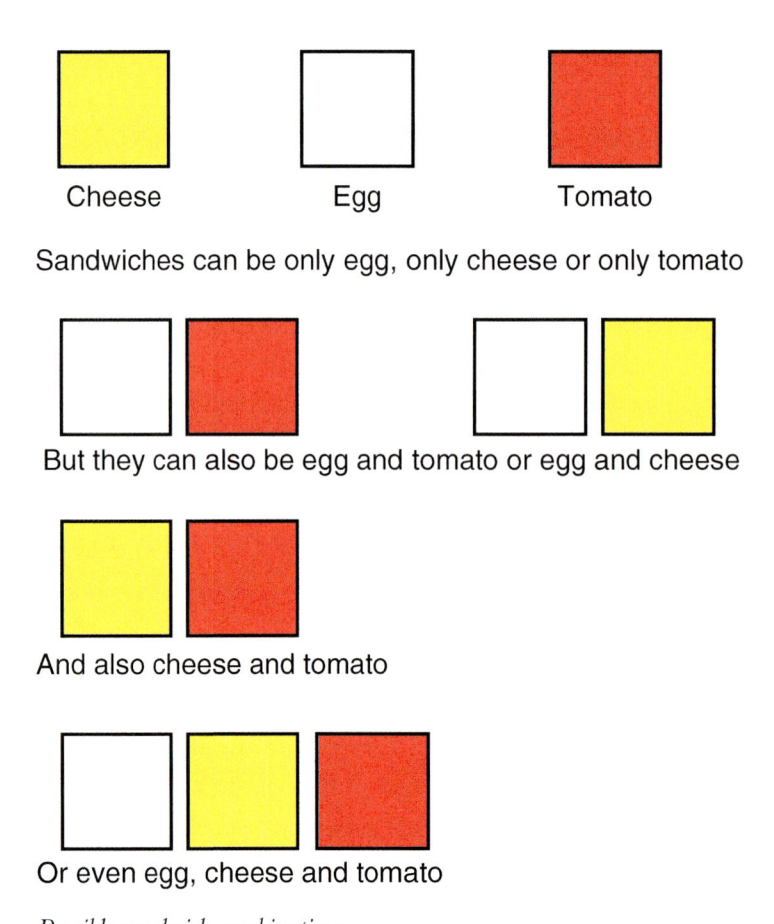

Cheese   Egg   Tomato

Sandwiches can be only egg, only cheese or only tomato

But they can also be egg and tomato or egg and cheese

And also cheese and tomato

Or even egg, cheese and tomato

Possible sandwich combinations

Can the children find any more? Have they found all the possibilities? Another strand from problem-solving!

Make some sandwiches and divide them equally into *halves* and *quarters*. Discuss the different shapes that can be made. Quarters can be triangles or squares. Halves can be triangles or oblongs.

Addition and subtraction

On the way to grandmother's house, Little Red Riding Hood picks some flowers for her grandmother. She picks *one* and then *another one*. How many does she have *altogether*? Stand plastic flowers in pots of wet sand. These can be a part of a trail or in the classroom on cupboards or tables or on the floor. When she has enough flowers, find a metal jug or bottle to place the flowers in. Count the flowers and then take one to put into the jug. How many are left? Continue until all of the flowers are in the jug.

Story boxes or bags

Why story boxes? The purpose of a story box is to create hands-on experiences for a child. Educators have long emphasised the importance of tactile exploration for young children. Choose versions of the Little Red Riding Hood book that have characters and items that are readily available. Remember that the complexity of the story and the number of items presented should be suited to each child. Often, simpler is better.

Place the book and items in a storage container or strong bag. Plastic containers are preferable as they are likely to stack, therefore giving you an opportunity to establish a story box 'library'. They are also sturdy enough to sustain the wear and tear of children's hands. Label the exterior of the container.

Share a story bag

For a Little Red Riding Hood bag, you will need, as basic equipment, a copy of the story and puppets or soft toy replicas of the characters in the story. This will depend on your version of the story, but in the more traditional versions the characters are usually Little Red Riding Hood, the mother, the grandmother, the woodcutter and the wolf. In addition, your bag could also include a small basket, fake flowers, the contents of the basket and books about wolves.

Choose a group of children to work with; the size of the group will depend on the intended activity and selected text. Seat the children around you, either at a table or on the floor, depending on your preference and class organisation. Children love guessing and surprises, and you can use this as a way of making the activity really exciting. Ask the children to guess what might be in the bag. They must listen to their friends in the group and try to give reasons for their guess. Next, give them a clue by producing a character. Children are usually very familiar with this story and are likely to guess what it is as soon as they have seen a character.

However, you can still get them to reflect and talk about it, and you need not tell them they are right straight away. Ask them if they still think the story in the bag is Little Red Riding Hood, and then produce another character and continue in this way.

Of course, they will soon realise they were right the first time, but lots of talk and discussion can be done, which will allow children to learn how to listen as well as how to talk. Get the children to use the characters from the bag to retell the story.

Add to the items in the bag over time so that the bag remains unpredictable and interesting.

Role play

This could be done with any part of the story. Going to grandmother's house would be a lovely way to introduce children to the role play by linking with something they are already familiar with. They can talk, discuss and plan what they would act like in this scenario by referring to what they know from their own family life. This could also be a good link to home, if you ask a few grandmothers to come into school to talk about their own house and their memories of their grandmother's house, and perhaps to bring some objects with them to share with the children. This could include a time line or even a family tree.

A 'walk through the forest' with Little Red Riding Hood would bring the outside in. Collect bits and pieces from walks the children have taken with their family as well as from any walks you have taken with the children. Feathers, leaves, twigs, pebbles and stones could all be collected. If you have little space, use a tabletop as your forest. Be sure to include flowers. These can be handmade, real or artificial. Plant seeds, like cress, which will grow quickly, or flower seeds, which take a little longer. In pots, plant bulbs, seedlings and bare-rooted plants ready to flower. Talk about how much compost will be needed for each tub. *'How much will each hold? How heavy will it be? Should we put the pots where we want them to be before we put the compost in? Why?'*

Trails

Direction and position

Make a track for Little Red Riding Hood from her house through the woods to grandmother's house. This can be done in the classroom using directions such as *'left'*, *'right'*, *'straight on'*, *'forward'*, *'back'*, *'under'*, *'over'* and *'around'*.

It can also be done outside using trees, bushes, paths, play equipment and large cardboard boxes for houses.

Use a large picture of the wolf's head (cut out) and hide it somewhere along the trail. Where is the wolf hiding? Use position words such as *'behind'*, *'under'* and *'next to'* as the children travel the trail. If a child spots the head before anyone else, they can take it and put it in a new position. Encourage them to use sentences and position words such as '*I found it behind the bush. I'm putting it on top of the bin*'.

Put together a scavenger hunt for when children work their way around the trail. You may need to prepare this in advance, as not all of the items will be naturally found in your outside space.

Give each child or pair of children a basket to carry, which can be filled with their finds. A list of items to be found could include two different types of grass, leaves from three different trees, three smooth stones, a pine cone, acorns, flowers (real or artificial), something red, a feather, wood, a small stick, something shiny, something white and something soft.

Spread these items out along the trail so that not all the feathers or stones or leaves are together; otherwise there will be a stampede of children rushing to pick them up.

Small world trails

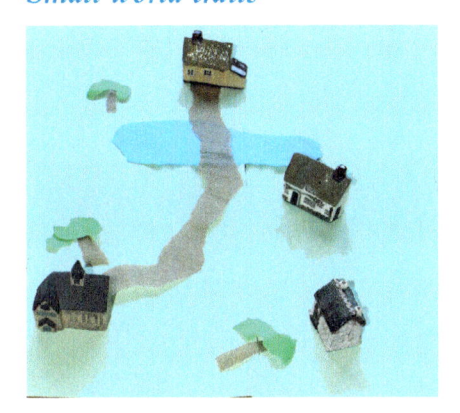

Games

Kim's game

One of the ways children learn is through play. A child who is playing is refining learning skills that continue to develop during childhood and beyond.

Play 'Kim's game' (named after the Rudyard Kipling novel *Kim*) with the items from Little Red Riding Hood's basket. This game is commonly played with young children, as it promotes the development of memory and concentration and observation skills, which are useful for all areas of learning.

To play, put five or ten familiar objects from around the classroom on a tray – they could be things like a pencil, a paintbrush, some cotton wool and a toy. Ask the children to look carefully at them for about 30 seconds. Then cover the tray with a cloth and ask them to tell you what they remember.

Another way of playing the game is to cover the things, take one thing away and ask the children to spot what is missing. You can put more things on the tray as their focus and memory improve.

Board games

You can use any of the pictures in the resource sheets section to create board games of Little Red Riding Hood's journey to grandmother's house. You will find a full-size photocopiable version of the game in the resource sheets section.

The rules should reflect the skills to be reinforced or developed, such as counting or colour recognition.

Puppets

Lolly stick puppets

You will need five lolly or art sticks, one each for the mother, grandmother, Little Red Riding Hood, the wolf and the woodcutter.

Use the pictures from the resources sheets on pages 251–252 to create the characters.

Discuss with the children how to set up a puppet theatre. What do you need to know or find out about?

For a very simple theatre you will need:

> A big cardboard box.
> Two lengths of material for curtains. Tea towels will do.
> Masking tape.
> Scissors.
> Optional extras: paint, tinsel, fairy lights.

Cut out the base and back panel of the box so that you just have a stand-alone stage frame: one long side and two short sides as flaps to keep it upright.

Out of the long side, cut a rectangular hole through which the puppets can be seen, leaving up to 20 cm around each side and the top. This measurement depends on the size of the box. The two side panels should allow the theatre to stand up by itself. Make sure the hole is centred with equal distance from the edges of the box.

Attach curtains to the backstage top of the hole using your two tea towels. Use masking tape or a large stapler to fix them in place.

Prop your puppet theatre on a table and put on a show.

Hint: String fairy lights or tinsel around your stage arch to make it really fancy.

Shoe boxes

Shoe boxes are so often thrown away by either the seller or the purchaser of shoes. But they are so very useful for so many things.

A hinged shoe box as shown in the photo can be used as the backdrop for many stories.

Place a smaller box inside the larger box. This can become grandmother's house.

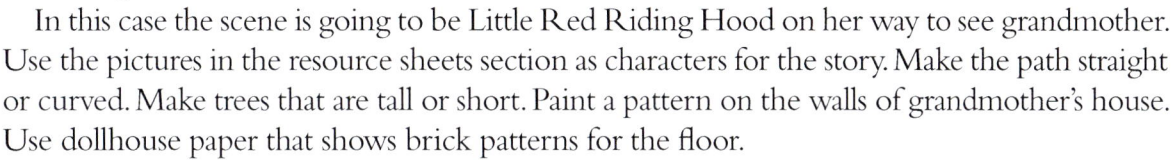

In this case the scene is going to be Little Red Riding Hood on her way to see grandmother. Use the pictures in the resource sheets section as characters for the story. Make the path straight or curved. Make trees that are tall or short. Paint a pattern on the walls of grandmother's house. Use dollhouse paper that shows brick patterns for the floor.

Once finished, this can be a static scene made by one or two children and other pairs can make a different scene from the story so that the boxes can be sequenced. Or it can tell the whole story by adding other characters. Glue blocks behind the characters so that they stand up and can be moved around.

Cardboard tubes

Although not technically a bag, box or basket, I have included these as they are so useful.

Again, these are very easy to make. All you need are five cardboard tubes and tissue paper of relevant colours for the characters. The activity is the same for all characters; only the colour of the paper changes.

You will also need *circles* for faces and bits for wool for hair and whiskers.

Discuss how *large* the paper needs to be so that it rolls all the way around the *cylinder*. Little Red Riding Hood needs a pointed hat, but the other characters have both ends of their paper tucked inside the cylinder.

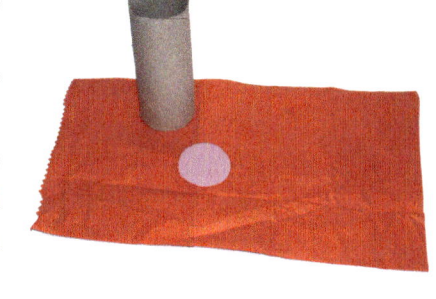

Draw a face on a circle and glue it onto the character. Add hair and accessories as you like.

You then have finger puppets to go with your puppet theatre.

Chapter 5: Bags, boxes and baskets

Baking

Making shortbread for grandmother

My grandmother always made shortbread for her grandchildren when we visited in the summer holidays. I still make it regularly when my grandchildren visit me.

You will need the following:

225 g of softened butter
125 g sugar
250 g self-raising flour (you can use plain flour but the biscuits will be denser)
50 g cornflour

What to do:

Cream the butter and sugar until light and fluffy. Start with an electric mixer, then pass the bowl round a group of children so they can all have a stir.
Gradually add the flour and cornflour. Remind children to stir slowly, otherwise the flour will go everywhere except in the bowl!
Roll the dough into a rectangle approx. 20 cm × 2½ to 3 cm.
Chill for 20 minutes. This gives just enough time to wash up!
Preheat the oven to 325°F/170°C (gas mark 3/fan oven 150°C).
Cut the dough into 5 cm slices and place apart on baking parchment. Prick with a fork.
Bake for 10–12 minutes or until set.
Remove onto wire racks to cool.

Once the biscuits are cooled they need to be shared equally between the children. How best to do this? It is not a good idea to actually share the biscuits to start with. Count how many biscuits there are and substitute them for counters or cubes. These are much easier to handle and will not get broken or eaten.

Once the cubes/counters are shared out equally, the children need to make a box so they (the biscuits, not the children) can take them home safely. Younger children can choose a box from those provided. It is interesting to see which box they choose. Some children think that the bigger the box, the more biscuits they will get! You may need to remind them that the biscuits have to fit in the box so that they do not move around too much or they will get broken.

Here are some of the recordings made by children after they had sorted through junk modelling boxes and chosen one which they wanted to make.

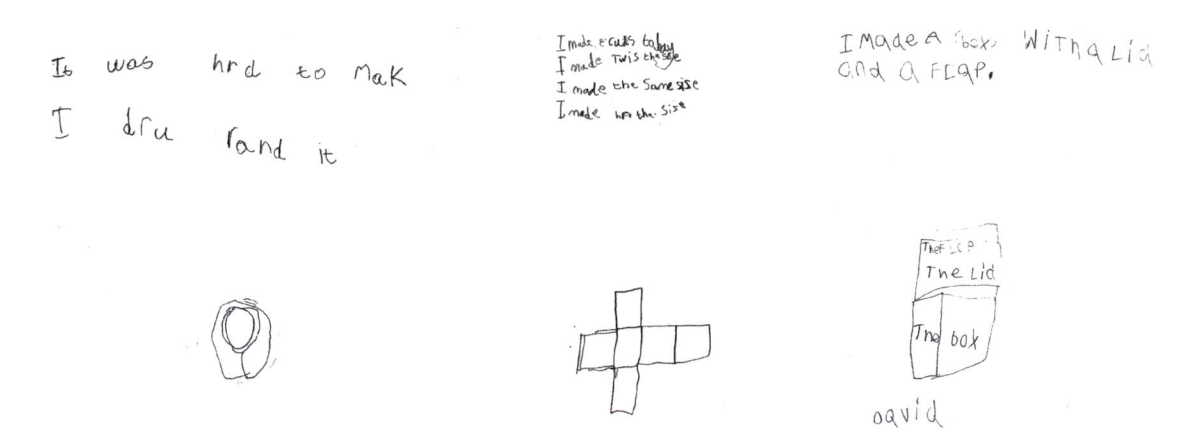

Home/school links

Ask family members to collect cylinders (kitchen roll middles are good because each, cut in half, can give two puppets), shoe boxes and scraps of paper or material which can be used to dress puppets.

Arrange a puppet show in the classroom, perhaps at the end of the day, to present to family as they collect their children from school.

The Lighthouse Keeper's Lunch by Ronda and David Armitage Published by Scholastic

Getting to know the story

Every day, Mr Grinling the lighthouse keeper rows out to his lighthouse to clean and polish his light to make sure it shines brightly at night. Every day, Mrs Grinling packs a lunch basket for him, which she sends on a wire from their cottage across to the lighthouse. At lunchtime he tucks into a delicious and well-deserved lunch, prepared by his wife. But Mr Grinling is not the only one who enjoys the tasty food. One day Mr Grinling's lunch does not arrive because a group of greedy seagulls have eaten it. Mrs Grinling unsuccessfully tries various strategies to keep the seagulls from eating his lunch. Will Mrs Grinling think of a way to stop the greedy seagulls from stealing the lighthouse keeper's lunch?

Although the text is easy to read, some of the vocabulary is quite complex (e.g. *industrious, concocting, varmints, baffle, brazen, ingenious*). But this can lead to some interesting discussions.

Mathematics

Problem-solving

An object will remain stationary unless a push or a pull is applied.

The degree of a push or a pull may bring about a change in the movement of an object. The push or pull may speed up or slow down.

You will need a ball of string, balloons (different shapes), drinking straw, tape, a paper cup (Mr Grinling's lunch box), a timer and a clothes peg.

After reading the story, discuss the ways that Mr Grinling could get his lunch even faster to stop the seagulls from eating it. '*Mr Grinling has a problem. How can we help him?*' Make a note of all ideas and encourage the more far-fetched ones. These can be added to a lighthouse display later.

Make a 'rocket' to deliver his lunch.
Here's how:

1. Tape one end of a length of string to a chair and pull the other end through a drinking straw.
2. Attach the string to another chair so that the string is taut.
3. Blow up the balloon but do not tie it or let the air out. **Hint:** Use the clothes peg!
4. Keeping hold of the balloon, attach it to the straw using tape.
5. Start the balloon rocket at one end of the string and let it go!
6. Children can discuss and record what they have seen.

Investigate how far the balloon rocket can travel. When you attach a paper cup (Mr Grinling's lunch box) to the straw at the front of the rocket, will the rocket still move? Does the addition of Mr Grinling's lunch box slow the rocket down? Can you time how long the balloon rocket takes? Try using different shapes of balloons. Does this change the time it takes for Mr Grinling to get his lunch?

Now, have children design a device which will stop the seagulls from stealing the lighthouse keeper's lunch.

Talk to the children about the problem Mr Grinling has with the seagulls. '*What can he do about it?*'

Work with small groups of children to talk through some of their ideas. Ask them to work in pairs to design something that will help Mr Grinling. Make sure you have all the resources they need and have talked about ready so that each pair can get started. When all of the devices have been made, have a large group meeting so that the pairs can tell the whole class what they did, why they did it and how it will help to keep the seagulls away.

Children can also create a different kind of lunch basket that will keep the seagulls out. Ask the children to design a seagull-proof basket. Some children may prefer to work with a friend, others may prefer to work on their own.

Make sure you have plenty of boxes, string, tape and scissors ready.

Shape

1   Initially, introduce shells through a simple 'invitation to explore' activity. I like to lay a variety of shells on a tray and provide the children with magnifying glasses so they can explore them in whatever way they want to. After they have a chance to explore the shells for a while, I suggest a few ways to play with them.

The shells can be ordered by size.

They can be sorted. Leave this fairly open so children can make up their own minds about what principle to follow. It can be by colour, size or texture. Discuss the different ways of sorting.

2   Listen to the shells to see if they make sounds. The children love to do this and generally they can 'hear the sea' in most of the shells, although the smallest do not seem to work!

Safety tip: Be careful if you are using quite small shells and asking children to put them near their ears. Pushing the shells inside their ears will not help them hear better!

You can also smell the shells, but they have usually been washed well, so that is not as effective as one might like. I have always stopped at actually licking the shells to find out what they taste like. But you can also use your sense of touch to decide if the shells are rough or smooth. Sort them using a simple version of a Venn diagram.

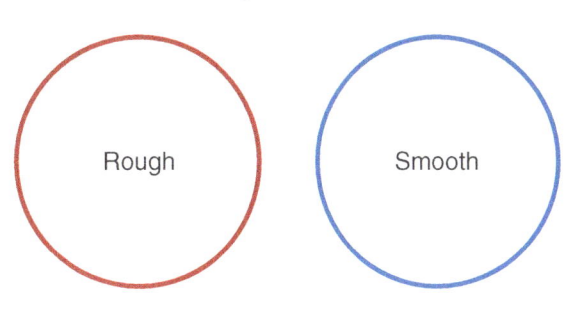

3 Take a photo of each type of shell that you have. Make them into cards so that children can match the real shell to a 2D representation. Bury the shells in sand in a small tub and children can become shell explorers. Use a small scoop to find the shells. Match their shape to a ready prepared picture.
4 Placing shells and mirrors on a tabletop will lead to an independent activity that encourages quiet exploration.

More shapes using cylinders

Start a collection of cylinders. They can be tall or short, fat or thin.

To make the lighthouse, wrap the cylinder in white paper and tuck the ends in. The wrapping needs to be quite tight so that it does not unroll. You can add a bit of glue where the paper overlaps to make it secure.

Just as when making Pooh Bear's bees, cut strips of red paper to wrap around on top of the white paper to make the stripes on the lighthouse. If they are too long, cut a piece off.

Make a cone for the top and draw a door at the bottom. Staple or glue to blue paper. Or, to make it appear to be on rocks, paint the back of a paper plate a rock colour and glue the base of the cylinder onto it.

Yet more shapes using triangles, circles, oblongs, squares

You can either pre-cut the shapes you want the children to use or ask them to draw around, then cut out the shapes themselves. Provide glue or glue sticks and backing paper. Voila: an instant display of lighthouses. Put the table with the cylindrical lighthouses in front of the display of shapes on backing paper and you have a really stunning display.

Sequencing

Write a set of instructions that teach someone how to make a delicious sandwich for Mr Grinling's lunch.

Retell the story from the point of view of one of the seagulls.

Prop box

There are so many different opportunities for a role play area that you may need several different prop boxes.

1 Mrs Grinling's kitchen: a wall clock, paper plates, cups and dishes, play cutlery, a checkered table cloth, a basket, some play fruit, a toaster, a kettle, play cakes and bread and biscuits and a basket.
2 The lighthouse: table cloth, basket, play sandwiches, cakes and fruit, pictures of boats for the wall, model boats for shelves, magazines about boats, a few shells.

Role play

Mrs Grinling's kitchen

Children love taking on different roles in imaginative play. Play kitchens are a particularly popular resource for pretend play, as it gives children the opportunity to imitate situations that they are familiar with.

Kitchen role play is not just a fun activity for children; it also benefits a child's development. Young children learn through play and are always exploring and experimenting.

Kitchen role play widens a child's vocabulary as they begin to learn the names of new objects and foods, whilst also using new verbs such as 'cook' and 'stir' and opposites such as 'hot' and 'cold'.

Kitchen role play enhances a child's cognitive ability and problem-solving skills. If problems arise, such as a spoon or plate going missing, it forces children to come up with a solution – whether that is substituting the fork for something else or going out of their way to find the lost item.

Play kitchens also help to improve a child's numeracy skills. Children can count how many plates they need, weigh ingredients or count how many minutes the food needs to be in the oven, which enhances their mathematical learning while they play.

Play kitchens give children the opportunity to identify new objects and food. You can stock play kitchens with a variety of items, which also gives children the chance to categorise the different food types and utensils as well.

There are lots of opportunities for measuring and counting to be done and plenty to chat about as they prepare their meals.

The kitchen can be small and basic or it can be more open with table and chairs. You can add things like weighing scales, timers, recipe cards, or mixing bowls and spoons.

Set the table for one, two or more people. Match the number of plates to the number of cups. Add cutlery: knives, forks and spoons. Set the kitchen out as a snack area so children can choose their own snack.

Once sitting around the table, role play can include the different characters in the story (Mr and Mrs Grinling, Hamish the cat, the seagulls). A discussion can focus on how they were feeling at different points in the story.

Games

Using the hexagonal grid available in the resource sheets section will be a new experience for a lot of children.

It can be made larger or smaller, according to the age and ability of the players.

Draw the lighthouse on the left-hand side of the grid. Anywhere will do. Draw the Grinlings' house on the right-hand side of the grid. Again, anywhere will do. Draw a seagull in some of the spaces and baskets in other spaces. These can be as many or as few as you like.

There are several variations of this game so it will suit all ages and abilities.

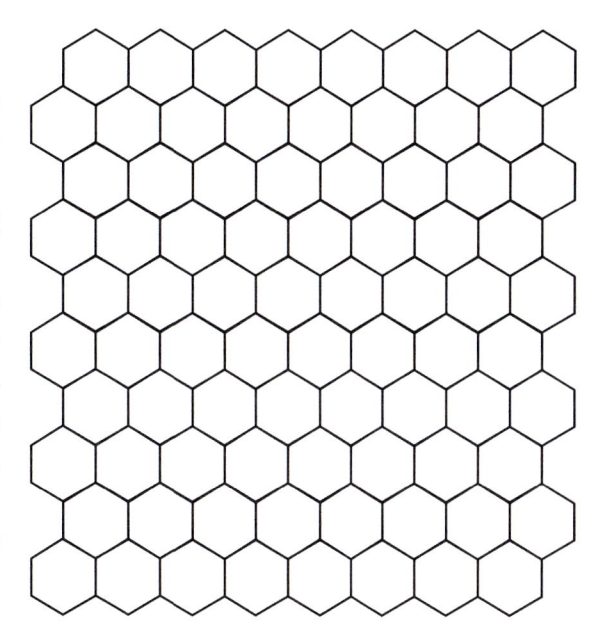

1. Both players start at the lighthouse and see who the first to reach home is. Players take turns throwing dice with suitable numbers on the faces. After each throw, players can move to any touching hexagon in any direction; the same number of spaces as the number on the dice. The first to arrive home is the winner.
2. Play starts as before, but if a player lands on a seagull, they miss a turn.
3. Play as in Steps 1 and 2 above, but if a player lands on a basket, they have another turn.
4. Have two starting places. One player starts at the lighthouse and travels home. The other player starts at home and travels to the lighthouse.
5. If following Step 4, any player who lands on the same space as the other player can send that player back to their start.

(Step 5 has the potential to make the game last a very long time!)

Home/school links

A story bag is a way for young children to experience a story. It is a tool to enhance the learning of concepts. It is a fun, interactive learning experience for children and adults alike.

In the bag can be a copy of the book, a woolly hat, some shells, a book about lighthouses, a game to play, a basket, a toy cat and any puppets that you may have. Ask for parent feedback on the contents of the box and what they would like added.

Hands-on experiences help to provide meanings to words. Add a list of appropriate vocabulary and questions.

Handa's Surprise by Eileen Browne
Published by Walker Books

Getting to know the story

This story is about a little girl, Handa, who lives in an African village. One day, she is carrying a basket of fruit on her head to her friend Akeyo, who lives in a neighbouring village. She does not notice the succession of animals who, one by one, take a piece of fruit from her basket until there is nothing left. A monkey grabs the banana, an ostrich the guava, a zebra the orange, an elephant the mango, a giraffe the pineapple, an antelope the avocado and a parrot the passion fruit.

Fortunately, there is a last-minute twist in the plot which means that Akeyo is not disappointed. All is solved when a goat charges at a nearby tangerine tree and provides a big surprise for Handa. When Handa reaches her friend Akeyo, Handa is astonished to find her basket full of tangerines, but Akeyo is delighted, as tangerines are her favourite fruit!

Mathematics

Mass

Ask children to share what they already know about weight, then work together to *compare* the *mass* of several pairs of fruit. Do all the bananas weigh the same? How about all the oranges?

Gather together a selection of different fruit and vegetables. You will also need some weighing scales. These can be balance scales or digital scales, depending on the stage of learning of the children.

First you need to find out which is the *heaviest* and which is the *lightest* so you need to *compare* and then *order* objects according to weight. To begin with, use non-standard units to explore the concept of mass.

Show children how balance scales work. Explain that you are going to use it to compare the mass of some objects today.

Have on a table or floor a basket of fruit and a basket of vegetables. Take something out of one of the baskets, and then ask a volunteer to take out a second object from the other basket. Place both objects in the middle of the group and ask children to pair-share which of the two they think is heavier. After a few moments, invite volunteers to share their thinking with the class.

Ask your helper to compare the two objects by holding one in each hand. Which one feels heavier? Explain that you are going to use the scale to check and ask children to show with their arms how they think the scale will look after you have placed one of the objects on each side of the scale.

What happens when you put one fruit on one side of the balance?

Repeat with other pairs of objects in the basket. Be sure to use the terms '*heavier*' and '*lighter*' throughout the discussion and encourage children to do so as well. If two of the objects drawn from the basket turn out to *balance* each other perfectly on the scale, take the opportunity to discuss the idea that some objects weigh the same amount.

Can you put them in order from lightest to heaviest?

Balance a basket

How easy is it to walk whilst carrying something on your head? Using a small basket with a few soft items, or a cushion, children can practice walking whilst holding their load on their heads. This can become a game, with someone trying to take an item without being noticed.

How far can each child walk before the basket falls off? Mark the endpoint for each child and then use non-standard as well as standard methods of measuring. You can cut strips of paper for each child and let them compare their own strip with their friend.

Data handling

Pictogram

Use the same fruits as in the story for data handling activities. Prepare some pictures of each fruit beforehand, enough for the children in each group.

Prepare some fruit for tasting. Put a little of two or three types of fruit onto separate dishes and provide children with spoons or forks.

Ask each child to taste the fruits and decide which they like the best. (Check for dietary issues first.) They take a picture of their favourite and place it on a grid. This will gradually build up a pictogram to show which the favourite fruit in the class is.

For example:

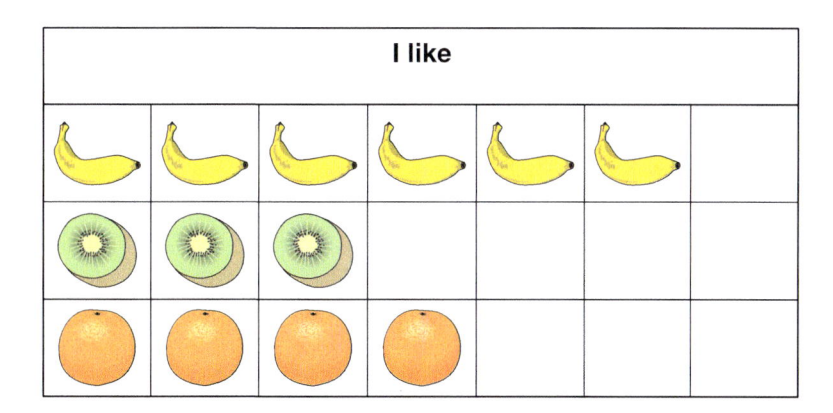

Discussion can follow about which was the favourite fruit, which was the least favourite fruit, how many groups of fruit there were, how many altogether, and so on.

How many bananas? How many kiwis? How many oranges? How many altogether?

On another day, repeat the activity using two or three different fruits from Handa's basket.

Tallying

If the children have been looking at tallying as a way of recording, one idea for practising this is also shown here.

You can leave the tally column empty or you can fill in two or three of them as an example. It depends on the children and what you want them to do. Is it an assessment or is it a fun activity? It could, of course, be both!

Match the tally pattern with the numbers shown on the dice. Talk about ordinal numbers as being first, second, third and so on. The banana was the first fruit to be taken; therefore, it matches with the 'one' spot. Guava was the second fruit to be taken, therefore that matches with the 'two' spot. And so on until the sixth spot. Sorry about the passion fruit. Not enough spots!

Position, direction and movement

Draw a simple map showing Handa's route to see Akeyo and add pictures showing the events which took place along the way. This is a perfect way to sequence the events of the story as well as sequencing the animals and the fruit using both ordinal and cardinal numbers.

Using maps

The story is based in southwest Kenya. Can you find this on a map or in an atlas? Can you find out more about the country? How is it similar to or different from where you live?

Is a home link possible here? Do you have any families who have lived in or visited Kenya?

More sequencing

Make a zigzag book

Using card or paper, children can make a zigzag book and draw the story with each scene of the story on a different page. Then they can add their own writing to tell the story, using the repeated phrases or in their own words.

Using pattern

Make a feature of the patterns on a zebra, a dwarf crocodile and a giraffe to create artwork.

Emphasise the vocabulary of pattern such as '*shape*', '*pattern*', '*curved*', '*straight*', '*flat*' and '*round*'.

Baking

Banana loaf (or muffins if you prefer)

As always, check for allergies and other issues with food before baking.

You will need:

115 g butter (room temperature)
2 very ripe bananas
150 g light brown sugar
2 large eggs
225 g self-raising flour
1 tsp baking powder
2 tbsp semi-skimmed milk

What to do:

1. Preheat the oven to 180°C/350°F (fan oven 160°C/gas mark 4). Grease the loaf tin and line with baking parchment.
2. Mash the bananas. Put the butter, brown sugar, eggs, flour, baking powder and milk in a large bowl and beat using an electric hand whisk for one minute (or two

minutes with a wooden spoon) until blended. Add the banana and beat for 30 seconds or until mixed in. Spoon the mixture into the prepared tin. Level the top.
3   Bake for about one hour (less if making muffins) or until well risen and golden brown. Check after 45 minutes. If the top is browning too much, lay a piece of foil over it. To see if the loaf is done, insert a fine skewer in the middle; it should come out clean.
4   Leave the loaf to cool in the tin for a few minutes. Run a palette knife around the edge of the tin, turn out the loaf, peel off the lining paper and finish cooling on a wire rack.
5   Eat and enjoy!

Prop box

Collect picture and information books that are set in East Africa. Introduce the children to the Story Giraffe – a soft toy who chooses a new favourite book from the box to read each day. Children will look forward to coming in and looking to see which book the Story Giraffe is reading to itself in the role play area. This will quickly become the book that everybody wants you to read to them and to read for themselves.

Add photographs, postcards and brochures from a travel agency, music and animal noise CDs and any models the children may make or bring in from home.

Role play

Journey into Africa

Transport your role play area to Kenya by lining it with African print material, clothes and artefacts such as musical instruments, bowls and baskets.

Pin up photographs or postcards of some of the animals and landscapes that are native to Africa and display these alongside any African models or artefacts that you or the children might have. You might even consider playing an audio CD (quietly) of African birdsong occasionally or animal noises in a jungle.

When you introduce *Handa's Surprise* into your setting it is important to offer the children opportunities to recreate and explore the story lines for themselves. You will notice children beginning to do this independently. Listen in as they play and you are bound to hear them trying out the language from the book and gradually absorbing it into their own. Closer observation will help you pick up on the ways in which they are spontaneously playing the story. Weave this into the provision, working with the children to create a role play area linked to the book.

Could you act out the story and take digital photos to retell it to the children or to parents? Involve children in sequencing the story.

The fruit shop

This can be a real-life introduction to money and the addition of money.

Before setting up the shop, do a 'favourite fruit' survey. This can be done in a similar way to the tally chart of Handa's fruit.

Use fruit that is in plentiful supply at the time of year you want to do it. You can link it with 'buying' fruit at snack time. In this way, each child gets to eat what they like rather than what you want them to eat! Not ideal for every day, of course. (Check with the children's parents or guardians about any banned fruits.)

A table or cupboard top, some colourful bowls and fruit are really the basics for the fruit shop. But to make it more authentic, add a till, some purses containing low-value coins and pads of paper for shopping lists. You can also add signs such as '*Welcome to our shop*' and '*What would you like to buy today?*' And add some baskets so that children can collect their shopping. I do not usually advocate using plastic but, in this case, you may want to add plastic fruit. I have found that using real fruit for shopping tends to end in a few stray apple cores or half-eaten bananas.

Add large pictures of the fruit on offer and price them. Older children can then choose any two items and total the cost.

Games

In this game children will compare the weights of various pairs of objects. You will need a weight spinner, available in the resource sheets section, and six, eight, ten or twelve common classroom or household items of varying weight on a tray or in a basket.

Gather children so that they can see and hear how to play the game. Place the balance scale and tray of objects so that they can all see. Show them the spinner you have prepared. Point out that one side says 'heavier' (illustrated by rocks) while the other says 'lighter' (illustrated with feathers).

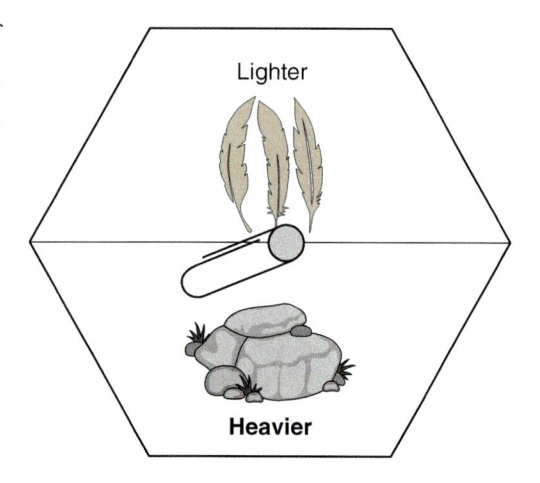

Choose an object from the tray and put it on one side of the balance scale. (Choose an object that is lighter than some of the items on the tray, but heavier than others.)

Now explain that it is the children's turn to choose an object, but they have to spin the spinner first. If it lands on 'heavier', they have to choose an object from the tray that they think is heavier than the one you just selected. If they spin 'lighter', they have to find an object that they think is lighter than yours. Pass the spinner to one of the children sitting near you and ask him or her to spin it. When it stops spinning, ask the class to read it.

Ask the children to look at the objects on the tray. Do they see any they think would be heavier than the item you have already placed on one side of the balance scale? After some discussion, ask one of them choose an item and place it on the other side of the scale. *Is it heavier? How do you know?*' If it is, remove both objects from the scale and put them together to one side. If it is not, ask children to experiment with other objects until they find one that works, and then remove both objects from the scale to put to the side.

Repeat the previous steps, but this time, let the children choose an object from the tray first, while you spin the spinner and do what it says.

Continue the game, taking turns with the class to set the first object on the scale or spin the spinner, until all the objects have been removed from the tray. If you or the class spins something impossible, take another turn. You can keep children's interest high by periodically changing the objects on the tray (or asking children to gather new collections).

Home/school links

Send the Heavier/Lighter game home to play. Give detailed rules of how to play and add some ideas for items to put on the tray. You may also need to add relevant vocabulary and questions to ask the children. For example, *'How do you know that this is heavier?'* This will reinforce the work done in the classroom as well as encouraging parents to play with their children.

Not all homes have balance scales so include these simple instructions of how to make your own set.

1 Use a hole punch to make two evenly spaced holes in a large paper cup. Make the holes close to the rim of the cups.
2 Cut two pieces of string of equal length, about 30 cm long. Use thick strong string, as long as it fits through the holes, which will make the balance more durable.
3 Tie the ends of the string through the holes in the cups. Use one piece of string for each cup. That will give you bucket-like handles.
4 Using a notched clothes hanger so that the paper buckets do not slip off, hang the cups on opposite sides of the clothes hanger in the notches. Both cups should be hanging at the same level. If one is lower than the other, you will need to adjust the string handles.
5 Hang your balance scale on a door knob. These are generally low enough for children to reach.
6 Collect small items from around the house that will fit in the cups. Investigate what is heavier and lighter.

Not a Box by Antoinette Portis
Published by HarperCollins

Getting to know the story

A box is just a box . . . unless it is not a box. From mountain to rocket ship, a small rabbit shows that a box will go as far as the imagination allows.

Inspired by a memory of sitting in a box on her driveway with her sister, Antoinette Portis captures the thrill when pretend feels so real that it actually becomes real – when the imagination takes over inside a cardboard box, and through play, a child is transported to a world where anything is possible.

Bunny has fun with a cardboard box but some people just don't understand. When repeatedly asked why he is playing with the box, Bunny makes it clear that the box can become whatever he wants it to be, whether it is a rocket, robot, or racing car. It is his Not-A-Box!

The story repeats the line 'It's NOT a box'. Repeated lines provide great predictability, especially for emergent readers.

Mathematics

This story is a good one for practicing positional words such as '*in*', '*on top*', '*beside*' and '*behind*'. This vocabulary can be reinforced when the children are engaged in their own 'not a box' activities.

There are opportunities for practicing predicting skills by looking at the details in a picture for clues. This leads nicely into a '*What do you think?*' type of question mentioned later in this chapter. When asking 'what do you think?' you are encouraging children to develop flexible thinking and creativity. A 'what do you think?' question cannot have an untrue or wrong answer. It is a matter of opinion that you are asking the children to express.

As Bunny continues to say 'NOT a box!' throughout the book, there will be plenty of times when you are using negation (the concept of 'not'). Very often we ask children to '*find the red car*' or '*put the blue ball in the tub*', but we are not so used to saying '*find a car that is not red*' or '*put a ball that is not blue in the tub*'.

Solving problems

Reasoning is a large part of problem-solving. This can be about numbers or shapes. But in this story you will be asking children to think about capacity (how much something holds) as well as volume (how much space something takes up).

Measures

Length

When looking at or choosing boxes, consider the *size* and *compare* them by using *length*, *width* or *height*. '*This box is longer than this box*'. '*This box is shorter than this box*'. '*These boxes are the same length as each other*'. '*Find me a box that is not as long as this box*'. '*Find me a box that is not as short as this box*'. '*Find me a box that is about the same length/height/width as this box*'.

Turn the boxes so they are vertical and talk about '*taller than*' and '*shorter than*'.

Find boxes that are the same length but have one that is *wider* than the other. Which means you will also have a box that is *narrower* than another one.

Other vocabulary that you can use is that of direct comparison such as '*longest*', '*shortest*', '*tallest*' and '*highest*'.

Mass

When using the words of mass you can either compare empty or filled boxes. You can use the same boxes but fill them with different objects, some lighter than others. This will lead to using the words '*weigh*', '*weighs*', '*balances*', '*heavy/light*', '*heavier/lighter*', '*heaviest/lightest*' and '*scales*'. The scales can be balance or bucket scales or scales that show grams. Use the boxes for a display and write the words on cards placed next to the longest box or the heaviest box.

Capacity

Start with a 'discover capacity' activity. You will need five or six empty boxes, all different but not too big. Choose boxes that have a predominant colour or turn them inside out, re-stick and then paint them. Include at least one small one. You will also need items such as dry sand (wet sand would make the cardboard soggy), beads, cubes and feathers (be aware of allergic reactions). You can buy treated or fake feathers online, which would do just as well. Use one small box to fill each of the other boxes in turn. Count how many times the filled small box fills each of the coloured boxes. Make sure you have a large board or flip chart to record the results. For example, see the table at the right.

Colour of the box	How many?	
	Guess	Actual
Blue	2	3
Red	3	5
Yellow		
Green		

Volume

Volume is the amount of 3D space something takes up. You will need a collection of small, medium and large objects. As with capacity, start with a 'discover volume' activity. This time, give each pair or small group the same size box as everyone else in the class and the same objects. Small cereal boxes are fine. The idea behind this activity is to introduce children to the concept that the larger the object, the fewer of them will fit in the box. And the smaller the object, the more will fit in the box. (Avoid sand this time unless you are prepared to count the grains!)

When children have finished the activity, begin a discussion starting with '*What did you find out?*' rather than '*What did you do?*' You already know what they did because you asked them to do it!

Exploring shape and space

What is a box? It can be a rectangular shape in 2D ☐ or ☐ or a cuboid in 3D ☐ or ☐.

3D shapes

Talk about the parts of a 3D shape.

Faces are the shapes surfaces.
Edges are the line segments where two faces meet.
Vertices (corners) are the places where three or more faces meet.
Cylinders and cones are a bit different!

A cylinder has two flat ends that are usually circular and one curved surface. The curved surface is not a face.

A cone is a 3D shape that has a circular base and joined to a point by a curved side.

2D shapes

Circles are 2D shapes made by drawing a curve that is always the same distance from the centre.

They are impossible to make using straight lines.

Use lolly sticks or matchsticks with the heads already burnt to make 2D shapes. Using three sticks, what shapes can you make? Using four sticks, what shapes can you make? Remember that all four-sided shapes are quadrilaterals and can be regular or irregular.

For example, here are two quadrilaterals:

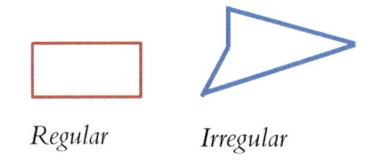

Regular   Irregular

Use pipe cleaners that will bend easily to make a shape. You can use one pipe cleaner for each shape or a pipe cleaner for each side of a shape.

Use shape cutters to make geometric shapes with modelling clay or cookie dough.

Make shape collages. These can be random pictures or towers as in the Rapunzel story.

Feely bags

Feely bags are good for exploring shapes. Put a small selection of shapes into a bag. Children, without looking in the bag, use their fingers to feel as much of the shape as they can. Start a discussion by asking '*What does it feel like? Does it have pointy corners? Does it feel round?*' With these clues, can the rest of the class guess the shape? Add more shapes to the bag as the children become more familiar with the activity as well as the names of the shapes.

Testing a shape

As children learn more about 3D shapes, let them explore how they move and interact with each other. Set up a simple ramp, not too high and not too long, and test each shape to see if it rolls down the hill or slides down.

You can also test each shape to see if it can be stacked easily on top of another shape. Explore the children's understanding of why a shape does or does not roll, slide or stack.

Prop box

The prop box just has to be full of boxes of different sizes, shapes and colours. Add to them regularly as they will not last for long, but find interesting shapes as well as the more usual shapes.

Ask for donations from home. People are usually only too pleased to donate boxes, especially after a birthday or Christmas.

Add the story *Not a Box* and any other stores that involve boxes, such as *My Cat Likes to Hide in Boxes* by Eve Sutton.

Role play

Hand this over completely to the children. Allow them to be creative, imaginative and free.

For play to allow imagination to take over, a child can be anywhere at any time that they choose. Anything is possible.

Trails

A fun way to start learning about shapes (at home or at school) is with a 'shape hunt'. Children can explore and identify shapes in their own environment and everyday life. Older children can take a clip board, a pencil and a checklist of shapes to record their findings.

Photographing the shapes that you find is a good idea, as younger children tend to forget what they have seen.

You can look for 2D shapes or 3D shapes or both. Encourage children to look up as well as down. There are some amazing drain covers! And electricity pylons are more interesting than you may think.

Games

This is a game that most children love and get really involved in. It is a 'What could it be?' game where children have to guess what is hidden in a box and give reasons for their thinking.

Choose two or three boxes of different shapes and sizes. You will need a selection of objects which differ in size, weight and rattling ability.

Try to select items that the children are used to seeing in the setting, or have experience of from elsewhere.

Put different small objects in each box and cover the box with a lid. Give each box a shake so that children hear a rattling noise. Discuss what might be inside. *'Tell me (a bit more about) what you think is inside the box. How big is it/are they? How many of them are there, do you think? Draw a picture of what you think is in the box'.*

Share the drawings and ask each child to say what they think is in the box and why. *'Why do you think is inside? What do you think it is that size? Why do you think there are that many?'*

Use everyday language to describe and compare quantity, size, weight, capacity and position.

Make a display of 'I thought that . . .' using the pictures that have been drawn.

Children may like to become the teacher and find another box that could just hold a . . .? Leave the decisions up to them. Some may need support in finding and using their own box to question others about. Ask questions such as *'How many . . . could you fit inside?'* or *'Here are some other different boxes. How many . . . could you fit into each of them?' 'Guess how many pencils will fit into this box'.*

Puppets

Have a collection of empty cardboard boxes suitable in size to fit on a child's hand. Undo each box along the stuck seams and turn then inside out. Re-glue them along the same seams so that the inside of the box is now outside. This surface responds better to glue and/or paint as it is more absorbent.

Each child now has their own empty box ready to decorate in any way they want to. It can be a car puppet, a person puppet, an animal puppet or a 'glue as much as you can, including glitter, on the box' puppet!

Share the finished puppets with others in the class.

Home/school links

Start collecting or ask parents to collect medium or large cardboard boxes. They need to be big enough for a child to get in and out of. They also need to be big enough to be decorated with pictures, photos or materials that show what the box is.

Take a series of photos of what the 'not a box' becomes.

Just like the little bunny in *Not a Box*, they will discover how the simplest of things can be the most inspiring.

Encourage adults to be creative with their child. Remember that it is the child's box to do with what they will. It can be anything (within reason!). Be prepared to provide some resources for children to take home if needed. A suggested list to get you going includes scissors, markers, crayons (especially red crayon), construction paper, glue sticks and any other leftover arts-and-crafts supplies you have.

Have a Not a Box parade and be sure to have special Not a Box snacks at your event to keep everyone's imaginations in full gear.

Chapter 6: Minibeasts and woodland animals

Why minibeasts and woodland animals?

Minibeasts, like mathematics, can be found everywhere.

This is a great theme for getting the children outdoors, really exploring and developing their observation skills.

Turn some of your outdoor area into a minibeast haven. If you are adding a pond or even a bowl of water, be aware of safety issues for young children.

Where to look for minibeasts

- Worms: water a grassy area and stamp your feet to bring worms to the surface.
- Woodlice, earwigs, beetles and millipedes: look under stones, under or in dead wood, in damp shaded areas, especially around the base of trees.
- Dragonflies: try looking near ponds, rivers or water.
- Bees, hoverflies and butterflies: on and around flowers, bushes and shrubs.
- Spiders: you can find these everywhere. Look for their webs in the mornings if there is a dew or frost overnight. Take photos so that you have something to discuss back in the classroom.
- Slugs and snails: look in damp shaded areas and surfaces, particularly after rain or at night. Or just follow their silver trails. Each snail has a spiral shell which starts at a central point and coils around. They are also easily seen on nautilus shells and ammonite fossils and the threads of screws.
- Ladybirds: often found on plants and sometimes trees. Ladybirds are a type of beetle and can have up to 20 spots. Usually these spots are symmetrical across the body.
- Ants: often burrow into the ground under rocks or a fallen tree to build a nest.
- Look for tadpoles in ponds, ditches and slow-moving streams beginning in the end of March.

Woodland animals

A lot of these are now not confined to only woodland and, with proper feeding, will come quite close to a window or door.

The two stories in this chapter centre on a hedgehog and a squirrel.

Mathematics

Ordinal and cardinal numbers

Comparing and ordering numbers

Adding and subtracting

Using measures

Exploring patterns, shape and space

Using the language of position, direction and movement

Choosing appropriate equipment

Being systematic

Making and testing predictions

Presenting results

Selecting materials for a task

Exploring and recording work

Making and testing hypotheses

Recording systematically

Communicating clearly

Talking about the work in hand

Planning strategies

Making and testing statements

Explain how or why something works

Explain and representing results to others

Thinking logically

Ordering

Predicting

Recognising patterns and relationships

Generalising

Completing a task

Interpreting mathematical information

Looking for connections

Looking for patterns

Asking questions

Estimating

Making sense of a task

Choosing ways of modelling a problem

Trying alternative strategies

Vocabulary

Counting numbers

1, 2, 3 . . . 10, count, 1st, 2nd, 3rd . . . 10th

Number, zero, count

Comparing and ordering numbers

Counting on, sequencing, enough, too many, not enough

Adding and subtracting

How many? How many left?

Measures

Length

Long, just over, just under, height, bigger than, thinner, short, fat, thin, long, measure, as long as, shorter than, taller than, how far?

Tallest, shortest, widest

Mass

Weigh, grams

Chapter 6: Minibeasts and woodland animals

Capacity

How much? How full? More

Time

After, before, fast, slow, Monday, Tuesday, Wednesday, Thursday, Friday

Exploring patterns, shape and space

Symmetry, pattern

2D shapes

Spiral, straight, sides, corners, edges, triangle, circle, square, centre

3D shape

Cylinder

Position, direction and movement

Left, right, next to, beside, above, below, near, far, opposite

General

What do you think?

Why do you think that?

What comes next?

What is the same?

What is different?

Snail Trail by Ruth Brown
Published by Andersen Press

Getting to know the story

Slimy Snail sets out on an adventure, up a hill, through a tunnel, and on and on. When he finally comes to rest in a dark cave, we take a look at the trail he left and discover just where he has been travelling. Children will get a sense of perspective – a high bridge to a snail is just the handle of a trug to us. A big and fast slide to Slimy Snail is just a spade to us.

Mathematics

Spirals

A *spiral* can be a curve which turns around some central point, getting further away or closer as it goes.

Or you can make a spiral with straight lines. This is an example of an *open spiral*.

Mathematics is a very creative subject. It involves spotting *patterns*, making connections and using what you already know in new contexts.

It would be a good idea to either have a large whiteboard or use cubes to make a spiral with *straight sides*.

If you have rods that are an equivalent length to the number they represent, you can use these too.

Look around your classroom and at home to find where spirals have been used in the real world. You may find table mats or small door mats, or even coasters to put your mug on.

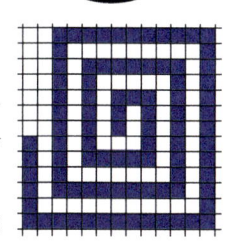

There are spirals all around us – from screws to the pattern of segments in a pineapple, or the way leaves are spiralled round the stem of a plant.

Twirly whirly twizzlers

Did you ever make twizzlers as a child? Start simple with a four-hole button and a piece of string. Thread the string through two *opposite* holes of the button. Tie the end of the string together. Spin the string, pull it and the button will whirl round.

Progress to a small piece of cardboard and some string. Cut a 5 cm circle out of cardboard. Punch 1 hole 2 cm each side from the centre, giving 2 holes for string to be threaded through. Thread the string through the two holes and tie the ends together. Create two loops at the ends for your fingers. Spin the string as before and then pull and release and the cardboard will spin.

To make it extra special, draw a spiral on each side of the piece of card. The twizzler will work and you can experiment to see what visual effects can be made. Make links to colour mixing too, by colouring the spirals differently.

Immerse children in the world of spirals. There are many practical activities that will allow children to see, find and make spirals.

Use a collection of shells to *sort* those with spirals and those without.

Look to see if all the spirals go the same way. Some will go to the *left* and some will go to the *right*.

The objects in the basket that are not shells, such as a starfish, cannot go into either of the sorting baskets.

This is an early introduction to Venn diagrams where objects are sorted initially into two separate circles.

Use the spiral shells when making snails with dough.

Chapter 6: Minibeasts and woodland animals   183

Ask children to make spirals by rolling a strip of paper around a *cylinder* or, for narrower strips, around their friend's finger.

Add features to transform the spirals into the shells of snails.

Collect autumn leaves to place the snails on in a tabletop display.

Paint paper plates with fairly thick glue and ask children to make a spiral on it.

Again, add features to make these into snail shells.

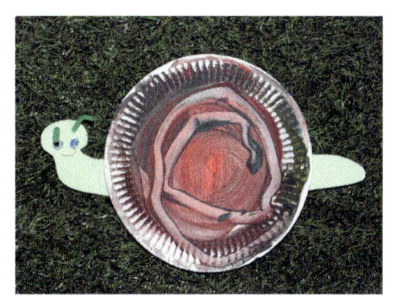

Some children will do their spirals to the left and some will do them to the right. Use this to prompt a discussion. '*What do you notice about the direction the spirals are going? Are they the same or are they different? What is the same? What is different?*' Add the finished snails to the tabletop display.

Give each child in a group a different colour dough. Ask them to roll their dough into a long snake.

Then, starting at one end, roll the dough into a spiral almost to the end. Leave the end part of the snake as a head for the snail

Each group can then arrange their snails in order of *height*. With older children discuss the reasons why some snails are *bigger than* others. It could be that some children had *more* dough. Or maybe the snakes were rolled *thinner* before being made into a spiral. Does a short *fat* snake make a shorter snail? This could turn into an investigation as other options are explored. Make a set of snakes that are *short and fat; short and thin; long and fat; long and thin*. '*Which snakes do you think will make the tallest snail? Which will make the shortest snail? Why do you think that? Explore using your snails. What did you find out?*'

Printing with spirals

You will need soft dough so that the impressions show quite clearly.

These were done using spiral pasta.

Sequencing

The sequencing images in the book can be used to help children understand the story. They can also be used to story map the images. This involves using long paper on the floor and you or the children draw the story in the sequence and then walk along it together.

Chapter 6: Minibeasts and woodland animals

Number and speed rhymes

When reciting the poem below, continue down to no sleeping snails, changing the colour of the bird each time. You can use the snails as a number line, taking one away each time, or you can choose five children to curl up like a snail and be taken away by another child who is wearing or holding a colour that matches the bird.

Five garden snails

Five garden snails sleeping in the sun
Along comes a yellow bird and flies away with one.

Four garden snails sleeping in the sun
Along comes an orange bird and flies away with one.

Three garden snails sleeping in the sun
Along comes a green bird and flies away with one.

Slowly, slowly

Slowly, slowly very slowly creeps the garden snail
　(walk fingers up arm)
Slowly, slowly very slowly up the wooden rail
Quickly, quickly, very quickly runs the little mouse
　(move fingers quickly up and down arm)
Quickly, quickly very quickly round about the house

This is a lovely poem to get children moving around, each being Sammy Snail.

Sammy Snail

Sammy Snail is slowly moving
See him slide across the grass.
He leaves a silver path behind him
We all know when he has passed.

Sammy Snail is never worried
Though he wanders far and wide.
For on his back his house he carries
And when he's tired he pops inside.

> *The snail*
>
> The snail he lives in his hard, round house,
> In the orchard, under the tree:
> Says he, 'I have but a single room;
> But it's large enough for me'.

> *Snail*
>
> He cannot fly.
> He cannot hop.
> He cannot run at all.
> But you should see
> The way he goes
> Slowly up the wall.
>
> He cannot skip
> Or race about.
> He has one way to go;
> And as I watched him
> I must say
> He's good at going slow.

Each of these poems can be written and illustrated by the children as part of a classroom display. Use a brick pattern which shows how a wall is built. Put the snails in different positions on the wall and add the poems.

Use positional vocabulary such as *'on top'*, *'above'*, *'below'*, *'bottom'*, *'next to'* and *'beside'*.

Investigating

Baking

Use a very simple biscuit recipe.

You will need:

125 g soft margarine or butter
125 g sugar
250 g plain flour
1 egg
1 tablespoon cocoa powder or drinking chocolate
Optional: pinch of salt

What to do:

1   Beat the margarine and sugar together.
2   Beat the egg and add this to the mixture.
3   Sift in the flour (and salt if used).

4 Mix to form a ball of dough.
5 Break the ball in half and add cocoa powder to one half.
6 Break each half into pieces and roll into snakes.
7 Flatten the snakes and put a cocoa one on top of a plain one. Roll into a spiral.
8 Lay them flat onto a greased baking tray in a moderate oven (190°C, fan oven 170°C or gas mark 5) for about 15 minutes.

For snack time, make spiral sandwiches. Ask children which flavours they would like. Make a graph or pictogram of the different flavours and how many of each you made.
Add a few spiral crisps or cooked spiral pasta.

Snails and circles

Mandala has become a generic term for any diagram, chart or geometric pattern that represents the world abstractly or symbolically. Familiarity with the philosophical writings of India prompted Carl Jung to adopt the word 'mandala' to describe these circle drawings.

The mandala activity here shows a rotational pattern of snails with a spiral at the centre. It is a good starting point for children to see and understand the meaning of *rotational symmetry*.

A shape has rotational symmetry when it still looks the same after some rotation.

A mandala is a geometric design mainly used in Hinduism and Buddhism to help meditation.

And you and the children can make your own! You will need paper or card and pens or pencils in many colours.

Cut out a circle from paper or card and mark the centre.

Starting at the centre, draw patterns (of any type of symmetry for older children). Colour in the patterns as you build up the design. Keep adding patterns as you move further from the centre.

You can paint a background pattern using two or three colours in rotation such as blue, red, yellow, blue, red, yellow. This can be as circles of increasing size or as stripes around the radius (the centre point). When the paint is dry, repeating patterns can be added on top of the paint.

Prop box

You can use these items:

- Fiction and non-fiction books on minibeasts
- Plastic examples of minibeasts
- Shell with spirals
- Smooth shell with no spirals
- Autumn leaves, real or paper
- Magnifying glasses
- Tweezers
- See-through specimen boxes with lids
- Small rubber gloves

Role play

Create a cosy, creepy corner where the children can crawl inside to look at fiction and non-fiction books on minibeasts. Have spiders hanging from glittery webs. Have snails on the walls, across the floor and in a small outdoor garden made of artificial grass and real flowers growing in tubs and buckets. The snails can be paper, card or dough. They can be made of interlocking bricks or painted to decorate the outside area. They can be small, huge or somewhere in between.

Link this area with a 'Minibeast Investigation Lab'. This can be set up on a table or cupboard top. You will need see-through tanks with lids, magnifying glasses, reference books or books made by the children about what they have found out about snails and spirals. Include some plastic minibeasts and tweezers. Also think about dress-up clothes such as goggles, lab coats and small gloves.

Include the collection of snails that you have brought together so the children can see the similarities and differences between snails. Add some spiral shells into the tanks as well as fresh grass every day and stones or pebbles.

Trails

Exploring snail art

Ask the children to bring in some snails from their gardens.

Place a piece of black card or paper in the bottom of a box.

Place the snails in the box and watch the silvery trails appear on the paper. When there is no one near to watch the snails, put a lid with holes in over the box. They may not move very fast, but they do move and could end up anywhere. But if they escape, just follow their trails.

Show children how to make their own snail trails. Have a shallow dish and put some silver paint in the bottom. The children put their index finger into the paint and then press that finger onto black or very dark green paper or card. When the paint has gone from the finger, dip it in the paint again and carry on.

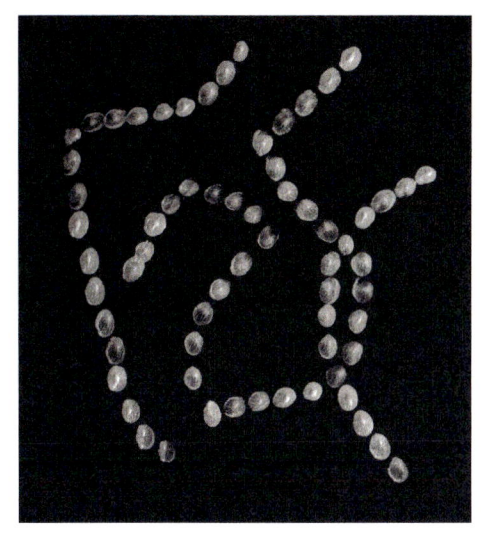

See what patterns the children make. You may get a line, a circle, a spiral or random walks. Avoid making the paper too big so that the resulting pattern can be used as the front cover when children are making books about their snails.

Games

Hopscotch snail layout and game play

This game can be played inside using a large piece of paper, or outside using chalk on a flat surface.

With chalk, draw a circle on the ground that is large enough in which to stand. Draw a large spiral shape outward from the circle. Divide the spiral into sections, trying to keep them all the same size. There should be at least ten sections, but it can be as large as you want. Start at the first outside section and number the sections consecutively beginning with '1'. Label the centre square 'Home'.

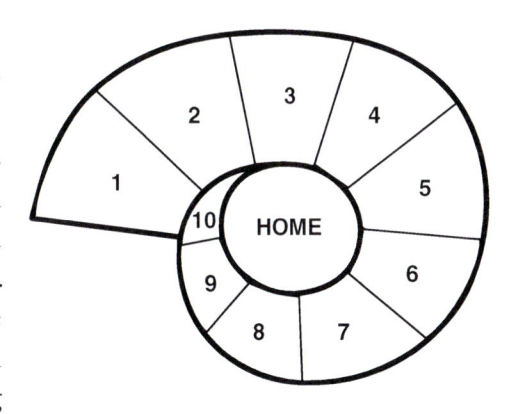

The first player starts at Box 1. The player hops on one foot on each section around the entire spiral to the centre then back. Some children may need to rest in the centre before starting their journey back.

The player cannot switch feet, step on a line or step outside the box. If a player does any of these things, they lose a turn. But tweak the rules a little for younger children.

If the player makes it out successfully, they can pick any section and put their name in it.

The next player does the same thing but must hop over any square that has a name in it. Younger children can jump rather than hop.

A player may rest on two feet in any square that has their own name in it.

The game is over when players can no longer make their way through the snail.

Blowing through a spiral maze

To set this game up you need a large piece of paper, an extremely long thin snake made from dough – although this can be lots of shorter snakes joined together – a small plastic ball and a straw.

Using the dough snakes make a round spiral on the paper. Leave a big gap between each of the lines.

Put the ball at the beginning of the spiral at the outside edge between two tracks of dough.

Gently blow through the straw until the ball, following the spiral, makes its way to the centre.

Once children are confident with the game, use sand timers to see if they can get the ball to the centre before two minutes has elapsed. Or one minute for those that have a lot of blow! But it takes skill and patience.

A snail trail

Prepare a track for the snails. This can be on paper in the classroom or chalked on paving outside.

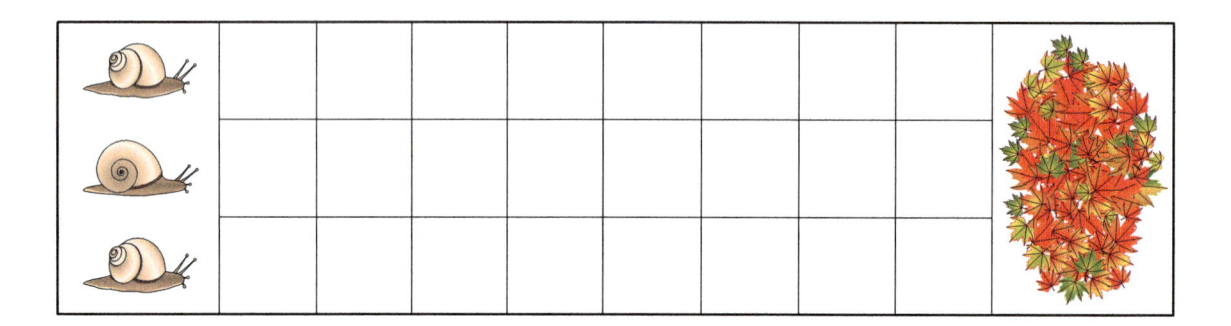

The aim of the game is to get your snail to the pile of leaves.

Each player places their own snail model at the beginning of the track. Each player takes it in turn to throw a 0, 1, 2, 0, 1, 2 die. That player moves their snail the same number of places as is shown on the die.

This involves recognition of number, understanding of zero and counting on.

For older children you can:

- Add more sections to the track.
- Add numbers to the track.
- Change the die that is used.
- Put obstacles on the track such as a leaf. If a snail lands on a leaf, that player misses a turn.

The advantage to adding numbers is the conversation you can have with players. For example, *'You are on number two. You have thrown a three. What number will you land on? You are on eight. How many more do you need to get to the leaves?'*

If you make the track into a ten frame for two players, you can use and reinforce number bonds to ten. You will need counters to cover the sections that the snails have covered.

Players can see how many spaces they have covered as well as how many they still need to cover. The two numbers will always total ten.

Puppets

Make finger puppets using coloured pipe cleaners. You need two of the same colour and one of a different colour.

Put the two that are the same colour together and twist them around your finger as a spiral. When you get to the end, separate the two pipe cleaners and they become the antennae. Glue some googly eyes on the end of each. Roll the leftover pipe cleaner into a spiral and attach it to the pieces wrapped around your finger. Add eyes and you have instant pipe cleaner finger puppets.

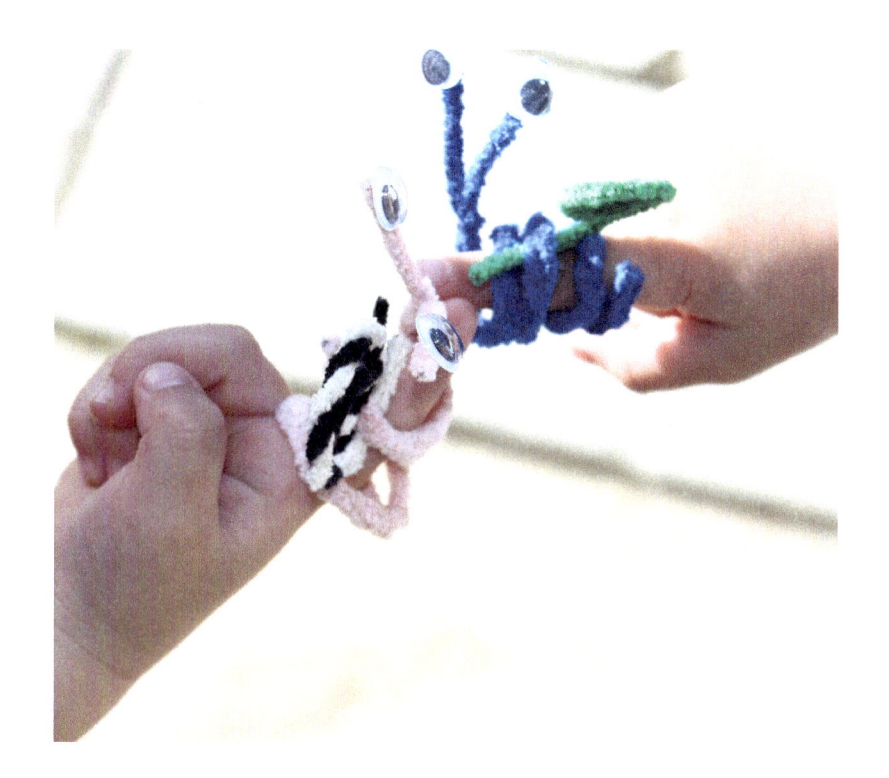

Home/school links

Ask parents to help their children to become snail detectives at home. Emphasise the safety aspect (for the snails!) and the best way to bring them into school.

Send a game home for family members to play together.

Superworm by Julia Donaldson
Published by Scholastic

Getting to know the story

Superworm is long and strong and a real hero as far as all of his insect friends are concerned. He always comes to the rescue when there is trouble. When Baby Toad is in danger of being run over on a major road, he turns himself into a lasso and scoops the baby away from the oncoming wheels. Another time, Beetle falls into a well and

Superworm transforms himself into a fishing line in order to save him. In fact, Superworm can pretty much turn himself into anything and that makes him a very useful and helpful friend.

Unfortunately, there is a mean Wizard Lizard living nearby and when he hears about Superworm's powers he orders his servant crow to find and capture him, which he does. The lizard then gets Superworm tunnelling in the soil in order to find lots of hidden treasure for him. All of Superworm's insect friends are unhappy when they find out what has happened and they are determined to help set him free. Will they be able to come up with a cunning plan and save their own special superhero? Here is a poem from the book:

Superworm is super-long.
Superworm is super-strong.
Watch him wiggle! See him squirm!
Hip, hip, hooray for SUPERWORM!

Mathematics

Magic potions

Develop a magic potion that will save Superworm.

Mix different colours using water and food colouring. Be aware that some children may react badly to some colours if they drink the water. Check with their parents or guardians first.

You can use four or five colours, making them lighter or darker according to how much food colouring you add. Make sure that you use jugs that are easy to pour from and do not fill them too full.

Talk about '*how much*' and '*how full*' as the children are doing the activity. Some children may be able to use spoonfuls for adding colour to their potion while others will need just '*one* shake' of the food colouring bottle. Or, if you have any, use plastic pipettes for drawing the colour from the bottle and squeezing it into the water.

Fizzy potions

Many people call this a science experiment. I call it maths because of the sequencing of ingredients, which uses ordinal numbers and the amounts of each. But it could be either or both!

You will need bicarbonate of soda; white vinegar; washing up liquid; food colouring; glitter flakes for added drama; a small glass jar and a tray or large dish ready to contain the inevitable overflow from the jar; and, of course, a magic wand.

> *First*, half fill the jar with vinegar. Using a small jar means that there is some vinegar left for someone else.
> *Second*, stir in a few drops of your chosen colour.
> *Third*, add a big squeeze of washing up liquid and a good helping of sparkly glitter or confetti.
> *Fourth*, add a teaspoon of bicarbonate of soda and start to stir with the handle of the magic wand.

The potion will bubble and froth, fizzing over the top of the jar and making a sparkly mixture.

Magic colour-changing potion

I will admit before we start on this one that there may be a little more science to it than maths, but the activity is one that develops awe and wonder in small children. To them, it really is magic!

You will need one red cabbage; bicarbonate of soda; white vinegar; clean empty jars; water; teaspoons.

Make some cabbage water by pouring boiling water over a whole red cabbage and leave it to soak for about half an hour, although this can be longer. This water can be prepared at home and brought into school, but it is much more fun for the children to take some active part in the activity from the beginning.

Pour the cabbage water into four empty jam jars. Why is the water blue? A good discussion point. Once the cabbage water is in the jars, add varying amount of water to each jar so that it becomes diluted. This should give you four jars of varying density of colour.

Start involving the children at this point rather than having them as spectators. Pour some white vinegar into a small container. You need to do this four times. Ask four different children to add the vinegar to the cabbage water and give it a stir. Be ready to be amazed! The blue cabbage water turns pink! And because of the different amounts of dilution there will be a range of pinks.

Choose four different children to add a spoonful of bicarbonate of soda to the pink water and give it a stir. A few bubbles later, the pink changes to different shades of purple.

You can keep on adding vinegar and bicarbonate of soda as before to see what happens. You will need to tip a little of the potion away now and then to accommodate the added vinegar.

How about keeping one jar of each colour and labelling them? The colour may give an indication of the contents. Use the now-lidded jars as part of a Superworm display.

Making worms

This very simple activity that uses strips of gummed paper that are used to make paper chains. But by asking the right questions you can involve children in a wealth of mathematical vocabulary.

Make your own Superworms. Make *long* worms, make *short* worms and make colourful worms. Make a worm that shows a *pattern*. What can you *measure* with your worm? Is it *as long as* your table? Is it *shorter than* your shoe? Lie down on the floor. Is your worm *longer than* you? *How many* worms are the same *length* as you?

Put all the worms end to end. *How far* do they go? Can you make a Superworm that is *taller than* your teacher? Make a Superworm *taller than* your friend.

What is the *shortest* worm you can make? *How many* links did you use?

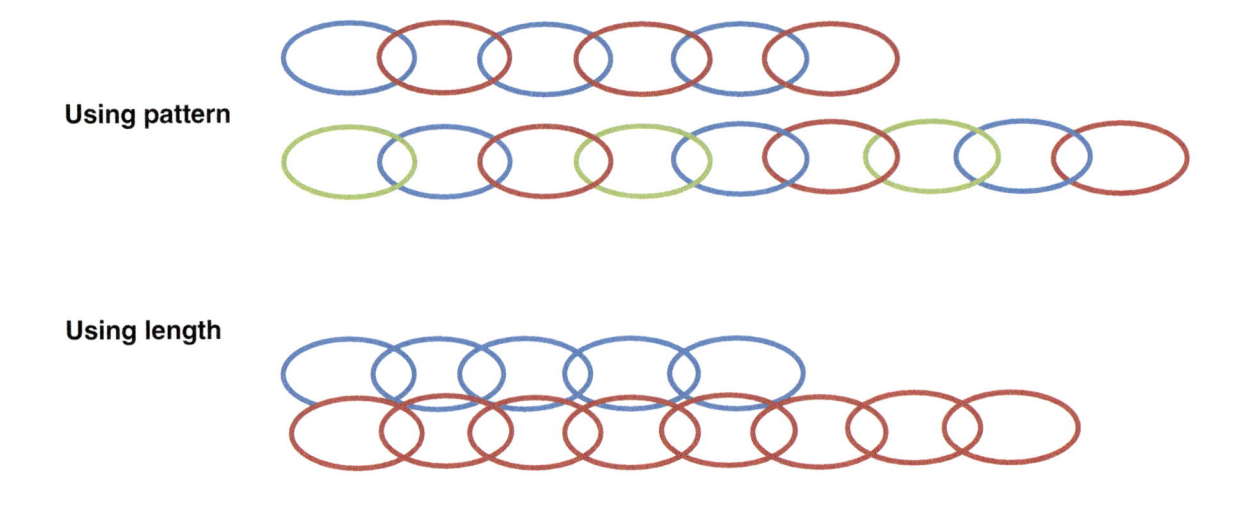

Using pattern

Using length

Using and making maps

Find Superworm

Children are often fascinated by maps and plans. The ability to read and understand a map is a valuable skill, and it can start when children are very young. Although they may not be able to make much sense of drawn maps, there is a lot of associated work that can be done which will build their visualisation skills about where objects and places are in relation to each other.

All young children develop and use their own mental maps throughout their early years: the route from where they are to their favourite toy, getting from one room to another, the route from downstairs to their bedroom upstairs.

When working with or developing maps, keep in mind what mathematics you want to promote. What will the children learn? What mathematical processes can be developed? How can the work build on and support the mathematics the children already know? What opportunities will the work provide for the development of problem-solving skills?

Getting ready for maps

After telling the story of Superworm, work together to draw a picture of the journey that he follows. Use words such as '*after*' and '*before*' when *sequencing* the story.

Go for a walk and pay close attention to what you see and where you see it. This can be indoors or outdoors, but try not to include too much or the children will forget much of it. Together, draw a picture of the walk. Ask prompt questions such as '*What did we see first?*', '*What came next?*', *Where did we see the butterfly?*'

Following a map

Go through the story again and pick out the important features for the class map. Draw a large map with sheets of paper joined together. Large newspapers are good for this activity as they can be painted over and appropriate pictures stuck on them. These will cover a lot of the print. Discuss with the class what pictures (animals, friends, minibeasts, flowers) need to go on the map and where they need to be put. Each child can take responsibility for painting one of the ideas for the map. This way it becomes much more of a community project. Use vocabulary such as '*next to*', '*beside*', '*above*', '*below*' when placing the pictures.

When everything is in place and glued on and illustrations are done, follow the map to find where Superworm is being held by the wizard. Talk through the 'walk' using vocabulary to promote sequencing (*first, second, third*) and position (*near, far, behind, beside, high, low*).

Other parts of the story can be made into maps, such as the journey to the well and the journey to the road. Give children large A3 size paper for them to make their own maps. Ask them to share their maps with others in the class. They can also be used as part of a Superworm display.

Minibeast hunt

Set up an area which has a builder's tray (a large shallow tray) or old plastic fish tanks.
Set the challenge: *Can you find Superworm's friends?*

Fill the tray or tank with leaves, twigs, fir cones, acorns, grass and any other material you can find, but keep it natural, not plastic.

Provide magnifying glasses and collection pots, tweezers and goggles.

And, of course, supply a large collection of imitation minibeasts which can be hidden in the tray. Children can use tweezers to find as many minibeasts as they can in one minute. They can lay out their finds, count them and group them into sets (has wings, has six legs, can fly and so on).

They can discuss their findings with their friends and finally can record, by drawing, their own collection.

Search for Wizard Lizard's lair

Follow the clues in the book to find out where it might be. What do the pictures show (small cave-like area with grass, small stones, bush and a wild rose at the entrance)?

Link this with the role play area and ask the children what they think the lizard would want in his lair. Use their ideas when filling a prop box and setting out the actual area to be used.

Planning

Develop a plan to save Superworm

Work together as a group to make a plan to save Superworm. This works better if you have not already read the story beyond 'Action! Quickly! At the double! Superworm's in frightful trouble!' But if you have already read the whole story through, talk about the plan that the animals made. '*Was it a good plan? What made it a good plan? What was the best part of the plan? Did the plan work?*'

Then suggest that children make a different plan of their own. As a whole group, discuss ideas given by the children. In pairs or small groups, give children the materials they need to make their plan work.

Design

Make a superhero cape

Transform yourself into a superhero just like Superworm. Design a cape and add effects.

You will need to find out *how long* you want the cape to be. How *wide* does it need to be? How will you attach it to your clothes? Do you need a *long* piece of ribbon or string? Can you use pegs and peg it to your clothes? Which is the best way? What happens to the cape when you run *fast?* Does the cape move? Does it still move if you walk *slowly?*

Build a worm farm

You will need to collect an equal amount of sand and soil. Involve children in checking that the amounts are the same. Use balance or bucket scales. Use old leaves to put on the top which have been left from previous activities or go outside and collect some. Have some fresh water in a jug and, if possible, some grass clippings. And, of course, most importantly, some worms.

Observe the changes over the weeks. After two days, the worm tunnels can be clearly seen through the sand. After a week there is definite movement of the sand, soil and grass.

Chapter 6: Minibeasts and woodland animals

Instructions:

- Add a layer of gravel or small stones to the bottom of the jar; this should help with drainage. Add the soil and sand in equal layers.
- Add a little water – not too much.
- Find some worms and gently put them on top of the soil.
- Add the leaves and grass clippings to the top.
- Make some holes in the lids and put it on top of the container. I used a small plastic sieve that was usually in the water tray as a lid as it could be easily lifted on and off by the children.

Remember to keep the wormery out of direct sunlight. Putting it in a cupboard would be better.

Start a wormery diary and check the changes on a daily basis. Each child can make their own diary and draw pictures to track the changes. Include the days of the week in their diary so you have a record of when the changes happened.

Over time you should see the sand and the soil get mixed up as the worms burrow down. The leaves and grass should be pulled down into the soil so it all gets mixed together.

Make magic flowers

If you were a wizard, what would you do? You can use natural resources that you have already collected to make a magic flower. Or a very simple way is to make one with a circular paper plate, tissue paper circles and glue. Make available all of the materials so the children can choose their own.

> First, start with the circular plate and turn it upside down. The underneath surface will take the glue better.
>
> Then scrunch up tissue paper circles, one circle at a time. These can be all the same colour or a range of colours.
>
> Glue the first one in the middle of the paper plate and then arrange the others around the centre one. Make sure each is stuck fast before going on to the next one.
>
> Or you could go really wild and use squares of paper instead of circles so you have two different shapes to talk about.

Job done! Add a stick or a strip of strong card for the stem and 'plant' it in a small container full of dry sand. You could also place the flowers in small jars or bottles, but do not water them if you have used cardboard for the stem. It will get a bit soggy!

To make it really as magical as possible, get out a glitter bottle. Spray the flower with spray adhesive and sprinkle glitter liberally. Spray glue is a bit more effective than using glue sticks as the glue stick tends to tear the paper.

Make a well

Using materials available, make a well just like the one in the story. Tell the children how the well would have been used.

Chapter 6: Minibeasts and woodland animals

Using interlocking cubes or bricks, make wells of different 3D shapes. You can make a cube or cuboid.

Is it possible to make a cylinder using bricks with straight edges? Explore what the children can make.

Have a selection of empty boxes of different shapes. Can these be made into wells? Allow children to explore the boxes and talk about them. Prompt them if needed with words like *'corners'*, *'edges'*, *'triangle'*, *'six sides'*.

Dig for treasure

Fill a tray with sand or soil mixed in with leaves, fir cones and acorns. When they are all mixed together, hide some treasure. This can be anything that you have around the home or the classroom. I would not recommend sweets. Small LEGO or plastic toys would be good. Something shiny and something in the jewellery department goes down well. Lots of shops sell party bags with small items inside. Provide a range of tools, including tweezers, for the children to use in order to find the treasure. The treasure can then be classified by the children in their selected way. They can tell you the reasons for their classification or they can draw pictures as a way of recording their finds. These can be shared with the rest of the class later.

Making a spider web

Ask children what they already know about a spider web. Previous stories have looked at spider webs, so some children may know a lot already.

Many spiders build webs specifically to catch insects to eat. However, not all spiders catch their prey in webs, and some do not build webs at all.

Webs allow a spider to catch their food without having to use a lot of energy by chasing it. It is an efficient method of gathering food. Every web begins with a single thread, which forms the basis of the rest of the structure. After building all the radius threads (the threads that go outwards), the spider lays more non-stick silk to form a *spiral*, extending from the centre of the web to the outer edge of the web.

Using glue

Using PVA glue and non-stick parchment paper, make a spiral by putting some glue into a small container with a nozzle. 'Draw' the radii first then go around them in a spiral to the outside edge. Whilst the glue is still wet, add glitter and leave it all to dry. Peel the webs off the paper.

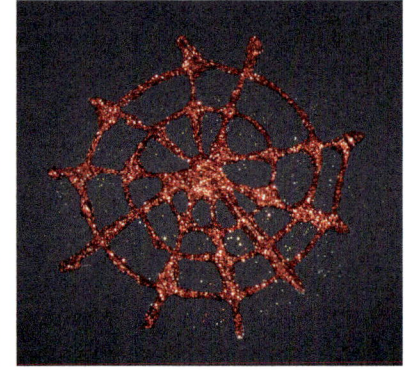

These webs are more successful if you use textured paper. This can be bought at art or craft shops.

The webs pictured here have been put onto black paper so that they are more visible, but they can hang on threads and move in the wake of a gentle breeze or even as children walk underneath.

Using pipe cleaners

Use three pipe cleaners, which bend easily. Make the frame of your web by twisting two pipe cleaners together at the centre of each stick to form an **X**.

Twist the third pipe cleaner down the centre of the **X**.

Spread the sticks out so that there is the same distance between them. This makes the web framework.

Twist on a new pipe cleaner about 3 cm from where all the sticks join at the centre. This starts the spiral of the web.

Weave the pipe cleaner around the framework of the web. Each time you reach a framework thread, twist or loop the capture thread around it once to secure it.

Keep weaving in the same way to create a spiral. Every time a pipe cleaner runs out, simply wind on a new one where the previous one ran out and keep weaving.

Using paper doilies

Use white doilies as they are going to be painted over. These 'webs' are going to be for the wizard's home, as they are magical in shape and not the conventional spiral. Examine the doilies before the children start using them. *'What do you notice about this doily? Can you see a pattern? Tell me what pattern you can see. What happens to the pattern when I turn the doily round like a wheel?'*

Place the doily on a piece of white paper. Using any colour (they are magical after all) and a stubby brush, dab the paint through all the holes, almost as though you are stencilling.

Remove the doilies carefully and look at the wonderful, colourful webs. Talk about the different shapes and patterns that the children can see.

Making spiders

Children are often surprised when they learn that a spider is not an insect. Insects have six legs but spiders have eight.

Using paper plates

Using paper plates is the simplest way. Children paint a plate with black paint. They also paint a piece of A4 paper with black paint. When the paint is dry on both pieces, cut the paper into eight strips and paste them on to the back of the plate. Using sponges of different shapes, dip them in paint and splosh them on to the spider to make a pattern.

This spider was made by four-year-old Oliver. He wanted a spider that was a bit different!

Using fir cones

You will need a fir cone for each spider and four pipe cleaners for the legs. Attach the legs by weaving them into the fir cone so that each end is about the same length. Bend them a little and, presto: A spider! Depending on the type of fir cone, you can have spiders of various sizes, from small to enormous.

Prop box

Depending on the role play area, there will be different props in the prop box. Scenario 1 is the outside area where Superworm helps and plays with his friends. The cover of the book gives a good indication of what this area can contain. The props for this can be imitation minibeasts, spiders, web making materials, flowers and imitation or child-made caterpillars. Add a few frogs and some snails and the box will be full. But you also need to squeeze in Superworm.

Inside Wizard Lizard's lair is a totally different prop box. This one will contain dark creatures, mainly black. You will need a crow (make a headband with a crow picture stuck onto it), some oak leaves (real or paper), a lizard and treasure props such as small buttons, half a cork, a pretend toffee and a plastic fork. And do not forget a magic flower. This can be made from dark blue crepe paper.

Add fiction and non-fiction books about worms, spiders, bees and other bugs. You may want to also include lizards and crows!

Role play

A small pop-up blackout tent would be ideal for the lizard's lair. Add a tree made of boxes piled on top of each other and add some oak leaves to it.

You could also have a basket with shiny things such as Christmas baubles (plastic, not glass), silver and gold tinsel, shiny boxes and a jewellery box full of 'treasure'.

A backdrop of a Superworm display would look good with a foreground of fake grass, flowers in pots, both real and child-made, and a wealth of insects, bugs, frogs, snails and anything else that you have or that can be made. Suspend a sun from the ceiling and build a well of blocks. Leave the rest for the children to source and then incorporate into their play.

Trails

Make a magic potion using natural materials. Go outside to collect some mysterious, unusual or attractive bits and bobs.

Use a large basket into which the children put what they have found. This can be a community resource for bringing back into the classroom. You could 'plant' some items around the trail so the children can find them and add them to the basket. Along with leaves, acorns and fir cones, you could add weeds, grasses and flower petals.

Each pair or small group can add ingredients to a bowl, stir with a stick, add a little water and maybe some food colouring to make their special potion. Now make a wish!

Decant each child's magic potion into lidded jars and label them accordingly. You can call them 'Autumn Leaf Brew' or 'Scary Spider Potion'. Children will come up with some good ideas of their own.

Within the trail, set up a potion-making station. There will need to be an adult present at all times at the table. Add old recycling boxes and packets, bits and pieces left over from a craft activity – in fact anything you can find, as well as what the children find. This will encourage creativity and open-ended play. There is no right or wrong way to use the materials and no prescribed outcome. It all depends on child choice.

Young children get to practise and improve their pouring skills, experiment with colour, explore the concepts of floating and sinking and, depending on what is available, see what water displacement is all about.

Chapter 6: Minibeasts and woodland animals

What do you need?

Here are some of the things that can be added to your potion station: old plastic bottles and jars, a small jug of water (but have spare water on hand for refilling), paint or food colouring, glitter or sequins, grass, weeds, flower petals and other plant bits (check for child allergies beforehand), straws or sticks for stirring and old shirts or aprons for protection.

Setting it up is easy. Cover the table with an old towel or shower curtain and set out the potion materials. It would be a good idea if each different ingredient is in its own bowl or pot. Then leave it to the children. At first, they may try to cram the largest amount of everything into their jar, but over time they do get more selective.

Games

Worms

This game links with this worm poem.

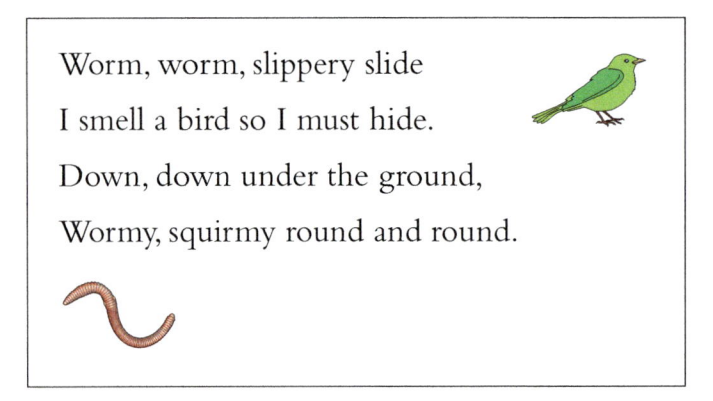

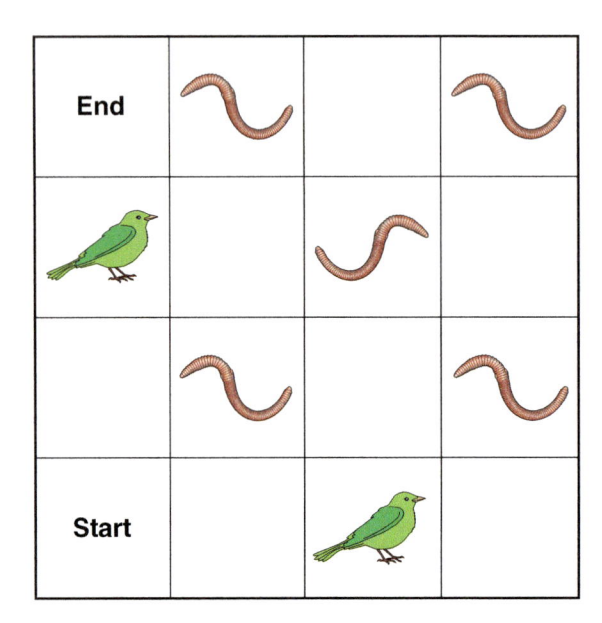

> Worm, worm, slippery slide
> I smell a bird so I must hide.
> Down, down under the ground,
> Wormy, squirmy round and round.

This is a game for two players.

Each player has a counter or cube which is used as their playing piece. They take turns throwing a 1, 2, 3, 1, 2, 3 die and move that many spaces in the grid. If a player lands on a worm, they have another turn. If they land on a bird, they miss a turn. The first player to reach the end is the winner.

Chapter 6: Minibeasts and woodland animals   203

There are no numbers on this grid, but they can be added if you want to. The worms are placed so that the players follow the direction the worms are facing. This encourages moving in the right direction at the end of a row. This pattern of movement is copied in lots of board games such as Snakes and Ladders.

Variations:

- The grids can be made larger for older children.
- The rules can be changed as long as the players know the new rules before they start to play. For example, each time a player lands on a worm they collect a counter. At the end of the game the player with the most 'worms' is the winner.
- Increase the number of birds.
- Add numbers to the grid.

Spider web maths

You will need a die per pair and a handful of counters.

This is a game for two players.
Players choose which web they want to work with.
Each player takes turns to throw a die. This can be 0, 1, 2, 0, 1, 2, or 1, 2, 3, 1, 2, 3 or 1–6 depending on the experience of the children. These can be conventional spot dice or picture dice.
Each player has three turns throwing the die, taking the matching amount of counters and placing them on their own spider web. After three turns each, put away the spare counters. Find out who has *most* or *least* by each player lining their counters side by side using one-to-one correspondence. The person with the longest line has most; the shortest line has the least.

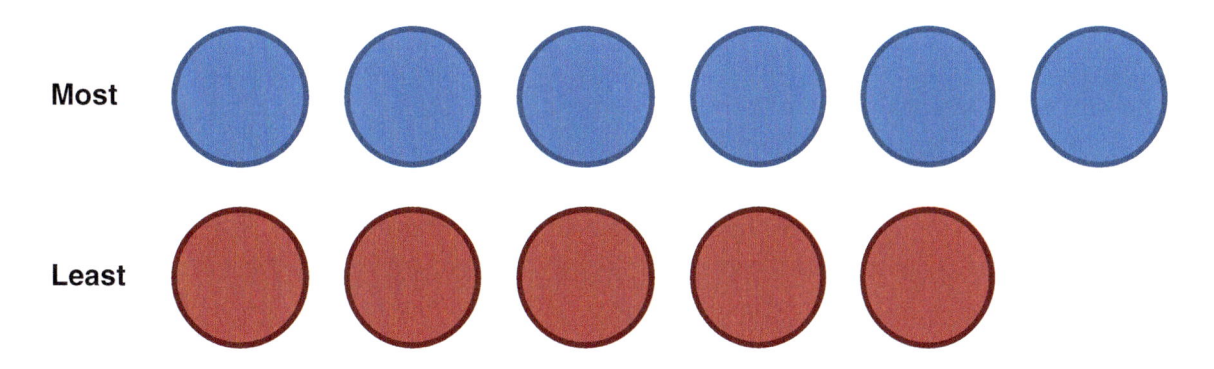

Most

Least

204 Chapter 6: Minibeasts and woodland animals

Children do not need to be able to count to play this game as no numbers are used. But those who can count can compare quantities and talk about them: '*I have six counters, you have five counters. Six is more than five, so I have the most*'.

Roll a spider

Usually, this game is played by rolling the numbers in order before the parts are drawn to make the spider. But with younger children, I tend to waive this rule.

But any of the insects or creatures in the story can have their own 'Roll a . . .' game as long as there are six things that can be drawn.

Dice	Part	Label
6	◯	Body
5	◯	Head
4	⌒	Legs
3	⌒	Legs
2	⌒	Legs
1	⌒	Legs

Home/school links

Ask parents if they can supply a plastic jar or bottle so that a wormery can be made in school. The only rule is that there has to be a fitting lid.

If a few worms could also be added, that would be a bonus.

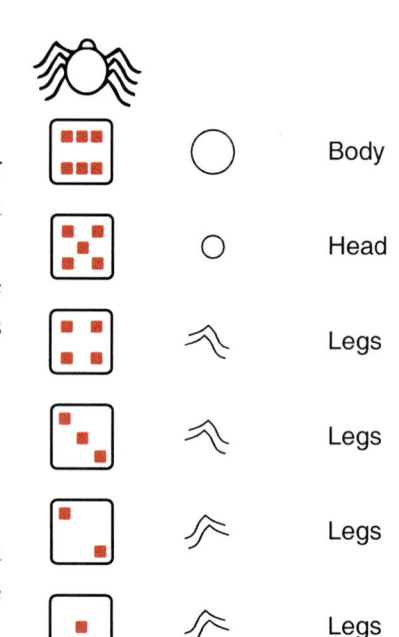

The Very Helpful Hedgehog by Rosie Wellesley Published by Pavilion Books

Getting to know the story

Isaac is a hedgehog who has only ever been alone, and that is the way he likes it. One day an apple falls from a tree and sticks onto the spines on his back. He wiggles and jiggles, but he cannot get it off. As he struggles to remove the apple, help comes in the unexpected form of a donkey who cannot reach the apples that fall outside of his paddock. Isaac learns that it is better to have a friend and to be helpful than to be on your own all of the time.

Mathematics

Pattern

Prepare a blank hedgehog outline and give the children a tray of fairly thick brown or grey paint and a set of objects which they can use for making patterns. I have used forks, pasta, strips of card (using the edges for spikes) and a comb. You will find a sample outline in the resource sheets section.

The object of this is to encourage the children to imagine, make and see a prickly pattern on their hedgehog. Different patterns can be discussed and featured on a hedgehog wall.

Chapter 6: Minibeasts and woodland animals   205

Matching

These matching games can be made very easily using a grid as the basis. You may want to start with a 2 × 2 grid and build up to the 4 × 4 grid. Cut along the lines of the grid and ask the children to match the pieces of hedgehog to make a complete picture.

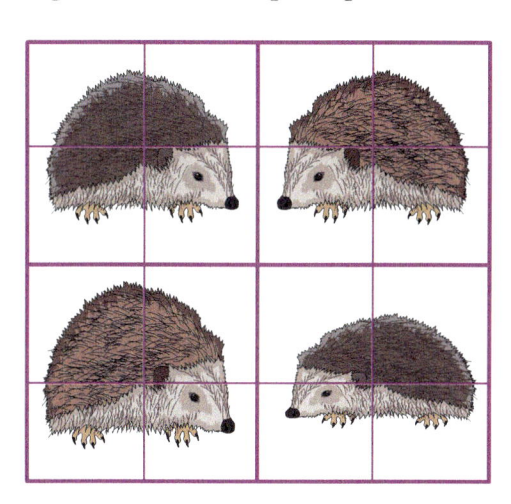

Number sticks

Use dough or air-drying clay and make the shape of a hedgehog. Start by rolling the dough into a ball. Make two slight indentations for the eyes and pinch the end for a nose.

Use a craft stick to make holes for other sticks, being sure to wiggle it a bit to give extra space. Paint some craft sticks bright colours and write a number at one end.

When the dough/clay is dry, paint it. Poke the appropriately numbered sticks into the previously made holes.

There are many simple questions that will show you the children's understanding of our number system. *'Find a number more than three. Find a number less than seven. Take out your favourite number. Why do you like that number best? Find me the number that is the same as your age'*. By keeping the questions fairly open, it gives children more choice and fewer opportunities to be wrong. *'Show me number five'* is a closed question, which has the potential to have a wrong answer.

Measuring using the length of a hedgehog

You can ask children to make a hedgehog out of dough or air-drying clay or you can provide them ready-made. An alternative is to give children cut-out cardboard hedgehogs to use as a measuring tool.

Prepare some recording sheets for older children.
For example:

I am measuring	How many hedgehogs?
My arm	🦔 🦔 🦔
My shoe	
My leg	
My friend	

The recording can be pictures of hedgehogs, numbers or tallying. Discuss with the children what they did when they were measuring and how they worked out the answer if a measurement was '*just over*' or '*just under*' the length of the hedgehog.

All about a hedgehog

The body of adult hedgehogs ranges from 14 to 30 cm long, and their tail can add 1 to 6 cm.

When they are born (there can be up to seven babies in a litter), their spines are soft and short. But soon after birth, their spines harden, becoming stiffer, sharper and longer.

Babies stay in the nest until they are about three weeks old. By that time, their eyes are open, their spines are effective and they can safely follow their mother outside the nest as she looks for food.

Hedgehogs love to eat insects, small mice, snails, lizards, frogs, eggs and even snakes.

What a lot of number information!

Each of these facts can be used for a fact-finding wall, which can have examples of all the different type of hedgehogs so far produced as well as posters, baskets of books and the facts themselves.

Number mats

Print some number mats with a large hedgehog and a number in the centre. The mats can be laminated to ensure they have a longer life.

Give children a numbered hedgehog and a pile of pegs. Ask them to put the same number of pegs on the hedgehog (as spines) that match the number on its body. This involves recognition of numbers and counting the correct number of pegs. Change the numbers as the children need more challenge.

Prop box

You may include:

> Fiction and non-fiction books that include hedgehogs.
> Different textures that can include pine cones, horse chestnuts (both outside shell and inside conker), fabrics that are rough or smooth, sandpaper, leaves.

Chapter 6: Minibeasts and woodland animals   207

Fiction and non-fiction books that feature donkeys.
Fresh apples that will need to be replaced daily. Use them at snack time so they are not eaten during the day!
Photographs of each child with a friend.

Role play

Catering for both a hedgehog and a donkey can be a bit difficult. But putting the donkey on the wall and the role play area in front solves that!

Or you can use a table or cupboard top and have a small world role play area. Talk with the children about what needs to be provided. Read the story again and pick out what the children think are the important features.

Collect seeds from an apple and plant them in pots. These can provide a background. Don't forget to water them regularly and you may be lucky enough to grow your own (very small) apple tree.

Trails

Make a maze

Many children may not know what a maze is, so construct them in the classroom or outside using chairs, big blocks, sticks or benches. Explain that the children can't go over or under the wall and they can't knock the wall down. Start with a very simple maze and gradually make it more difficult.

Design a simple maze for Isaac to walk through. This can be done on the floor, on a tabletop or on paper. It can be made using chalk outside that the children can walk around or bricks and blocks as before. Test the maze first to make sure that there is actually a way out!

'*Isaac needs to get home but there are walls and bushes in the way. He can't go over them, he can't go under them and he can't go through them. Find a way for Isaac to get home.*'

Games

A simple track game is easy for children to follow. Extend or reduce the track as appropriate for the players.

Collecting for Isaac's tea

Isaac is very hungry. He has collected a lot of apples for the donkey. Now he wants to find food for his dinner.

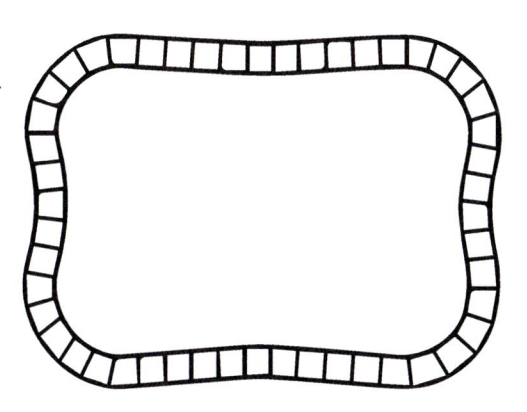

Within the track, draw two or three of the following: minibeasts, mice, snails, frogs, eggs. In the centre of the track put a selection of counters for each animal. For example, black for insects, grey for mice, brown for snails, green for frogs and yellow for eggs. These can also be made from squares or circles of coloured cardboard.

Decide where START is on the board and take turns to throw an appropriate die. The players work their way round the board and if they land on a picture space, they can collect the matching colour counter. You may want to colour the section where the animal is to match the colour they need to collect.

Have a recording sheet for each player so they can place any counters they have collected in the matching space.

For example:

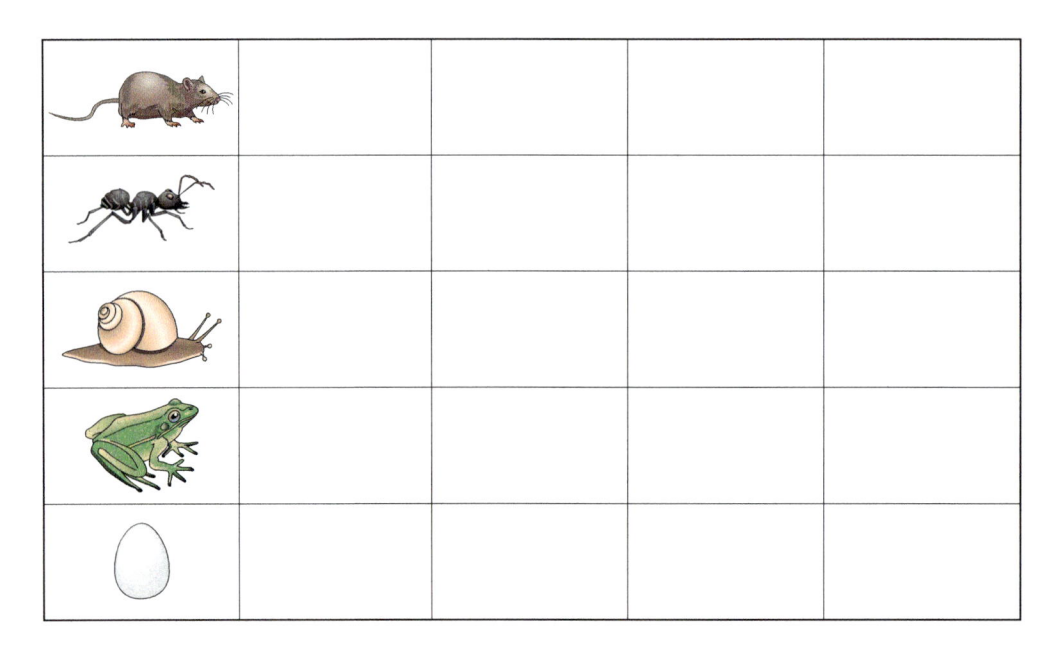

When each player has reached the start section, play is stopped.

The recording sheets can be used as discussion resources for looking at *how many, more than, altogether*.

Puppets

Have some cut shapes prepared to fit over a child's finger. These can be made from paper, card or fabric. If using fabric, I have found that felt is best as it doesn't fray round the edges.

If you have a pair, use pinking shears, as these work well for cutting the prickles. Or you may have a set of crazy cutter scissors that will do the same thing.

Each child will need two shapes or to fold the paper in half and, keeping it folded, cut one shape, but don't cut down the fold.

Chapter 6: Minibeasts and woodland animals   209

Home/school links

Take the clay or cardboard hedgehog that was used for measuring home, and find things that are longer than, shorter than and the same length as the hedgehog around the home. Make a record of what has been measured and bring it back into school for a class discussion.

A blank hedgehog game is included in the resource sheets section.

By now, children should be used to playing board games. Send this one home and ask children to work with their brothers, sisters, adults and other family members to make a game that can be played back in school. Offer some guidance to go with the game.

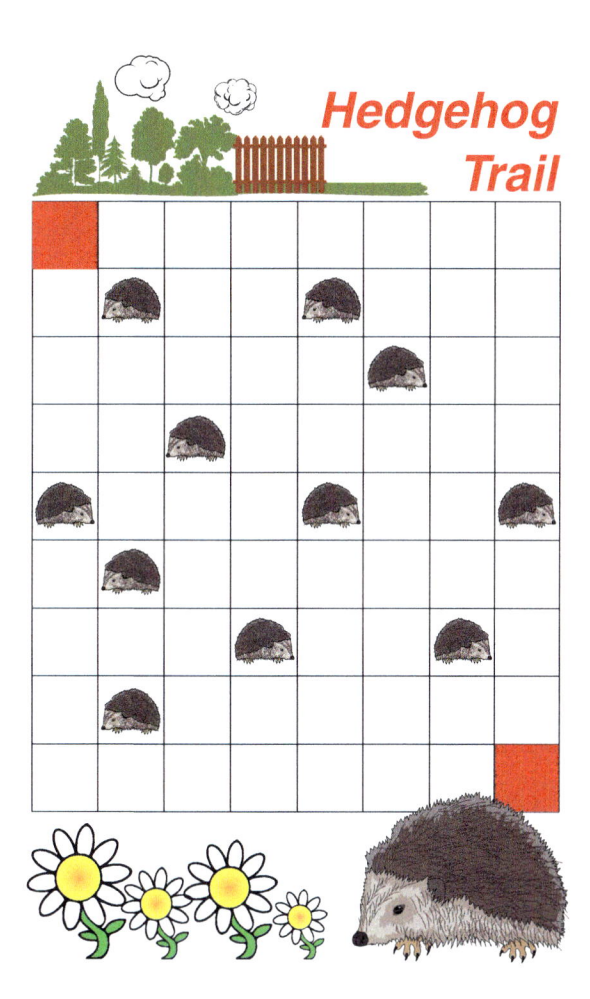

Squirrel's Busy Day by Lucy Barnard
Published by QED Publishing

Getting to know the story

Squirrel is collecting acorns in his red trolley. He is so busy he doesn't have time to play with rabbit or mouse, to talk to badger or give some time to any of his friends. Squirrel's trolley is soon so full of acorns that it is very heavy. When pulling the trolley up a hill, the handle breaks and the trolley careens down a hill crashes and sends all the acorns flying. All of his friends come to help him find his acorns and bring them home. Squirrel is very thankful for his friends' help and decides he can make the time to play with his friends after all.

Chapter 6: Minibeasts and woodland animals

Mathematics

Using number rhymes

Find as many autumn/squirrel/acorn number rhymes you can. I tend to put mine on paper and laminate them so they last a lot longer. I also have storage boxes made from shoe boxes that I paint and label. These are then ready for annual repeats of any topic I do and can be easily added to over the years.

For example, a short rhyme can include counting back and counting on, using a number line, and recognising the last number as the quantity.

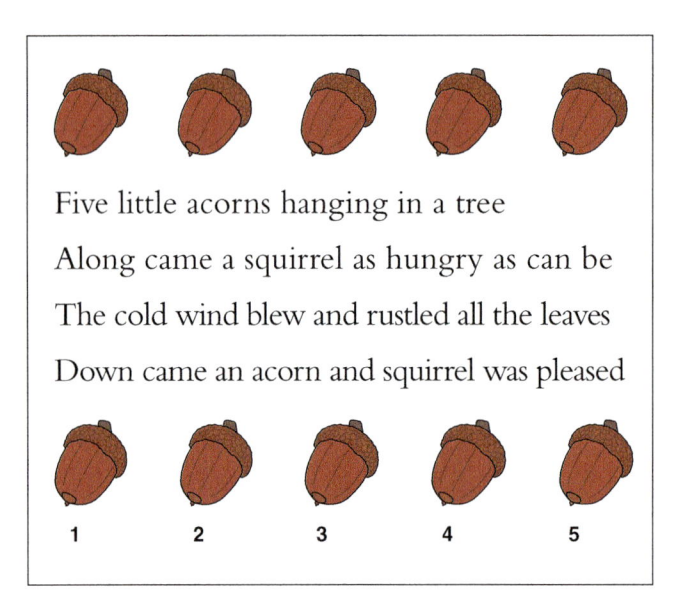

Five little acorns hanging in a tree
Along came a squirrel as hungry as can be
The cold wind blew and rustled all the leaves
Down came an acorn and squirrel was pleased

1   2   3   4   5

Squirrel dough mats

These are easy to make and easy to use.

Decorate the mat with autumn leaves. I have put 20 leaves around the edge of my mats but you can have more if you like, or just go up to ten. Never miss an opportunity for counting or partitioning. *'How many leaves are along the top row? Count them. How many would there be if two blew away? Cover three of them with the acorns. How many can you still see along the top row?'*

Each mat has a number and the number of acorns matches that number.

Children are asked to use acorns or dough spheres to cover the acorns and then count them. '*Count the acorns; point to them as you count. 1, 2, 3. And what number is this (point to the number)? If there are 3 acorns, what do you think this number is?*' After a while, ask the children to put the appropriate number of acorns along the bottom of the mat without counting the acorns at the top.

The illustrations on the mat can change to involve any of the friends that are in the story.

You can make a set for older children of odd and even numbers or numbers to 20. I would recommend that you use a different animal for each different set you make. Putting them away in the right set is so much easier than trying to sort lots of squirrels.

Make an autumnal minibeast habitat in a tray or shallow tank

When putting this together look, feel and talk about shapes, textures, patterns and smells. You can use compost, wood chippings (any spirals there?), stones, gravel, fir cones, acorns, twigs, leaves, small logs and minibeasts. Put magnifying glasses and tweezers nearby.

Sort and match collections of plastic minibeasts.

Count the minibeasts that have been found. How many legs do they have? How many spots are on the ladybird?

Record the minibeasts that have been found on a graph. Add together the amounts to work out the total number of minibeasts.

Use cubes to measure the length of large plastic bugs. Find the longest and the shortest and order the bugs according to size.

Weigh the bugs, finding the heaviest and lightest.

Use images of butterflies and ladybirds to explore symmetry in the real world.

Look at and talk about patterns.

Use the nuts and seeds as painting materials.

This picture shows what Jack did by putting a conker in different dishes of paint and then rolling it round and round the paper. When he got fed up with rolling, he used it for dabbing and then splashed a bit!

Chapter 6: Minibeasts and woodland animals

Other things to talk about

'Can we find more leaves like this one? Or this one?'

'I wonder why this is so prickly. I wonder what the nut inside looks like. Is that prickly too?'

'This leaf is smooth round the edge, this leaf is jagged. Let's sort the leaves by their edges.'

'These acorns have come out of their cups. Have we got enough cups here to fit all the acorns in? Have we got too many cups?'

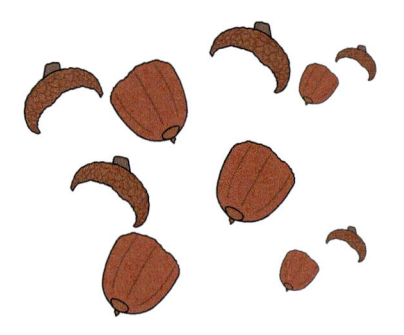

'This leaf is made of smaller leaves. This one isn't. Let's look for more leaves that are made up of smaller leaves.'

Design and make

Make mini beasts from mixed media including mixing paints to match the colours of real minibeasts.

Paint or use collage to create minibeast patterns.

Design and build a bug house as a class project

You can make a simple wooden box and fill it with different materials or, as a more ambitious project, use pallets which will make a multi-story hotel that you can fill with all sorts of natural materials. You can build your bug-hotel any time of the year. You can choose any of the following: old wooden pallets; strips of wood; straw; moss; dry leaves; woodchips; old terracotta pots; old roofing tiles; bricks, preferably those with holes through them; old logs; bark; pine cones; sand; soil; hollow bamboo canes; dead hollow stems cut from shrubs and herbaceous plants; a sheet of roofing felt; planks of wood; and whatever else you can find – preferably natural materials.

Choose a suitable site that needs to be level and firm. Using pallets, you can build a strong, stable framework, but I wouldn't go more than a metre high. Put the first pallet on some bricks on the ground. Fill the gaps so that there are different nooks and crannies, crevices, tunnels and cosy beds.

When you think you have gone high enough, put a roof on to keep it relatively dry.

Design and create, in a shoe box, individual habitats for a chosen minibeast.

Make autumn shakers by putting different objects such as acorns, conkers and sycamore seeds in different lidded pots. Ask the children to listen to the differences in the shaker noises. What happens if you put more seeds in? Does the noise change?

If you have an outside area and there are trees there or nearby, don't keep sweeping up the leaves and composting them. Not yet, anyway! Instead, build a huge pile of leaves that children can run through, throw in the air and squeeze into bags, boxes or baskets. Put equipment around such as scoops, dustpans, brushes, large and small boxes, a long-handled broom or even toys such as a large truck with a scoop. Watch the joy on the faces of the children as they attack the leaves with great gusto. Later, talk about how many leaves may be in each container or how much a container can hold.

Press seeds, leaves and grass into dough to make a pattern.

Look for shapes and patterns

Cut an apple vertically. Cut another apple horizontally. What can you see?

'Tell your friend what patterns you can see. Choose two leaves that look different from the collection of leaves. Tell your friend what you can see. What is the same and what is different?'

Make a feely box by cutting a hole in the side of a shoe box. Put in two seeds (for example, an acorn and horse chestnut seed) and discuss with the children what they can feel. Encourage words such as 'hard', 'soft', 'smooth', 'rough', 'big', 'small'.

Trails

Design and make a simple tabletop maze using sticks and twigs. Put some acorns in the middle.

Can squirrel find all of his acorns?

Make mazes using LEGOs on a base board

This maze was made by three-year-old William. He tested it by rolling a small ball through it. It was made using baby LEGO.

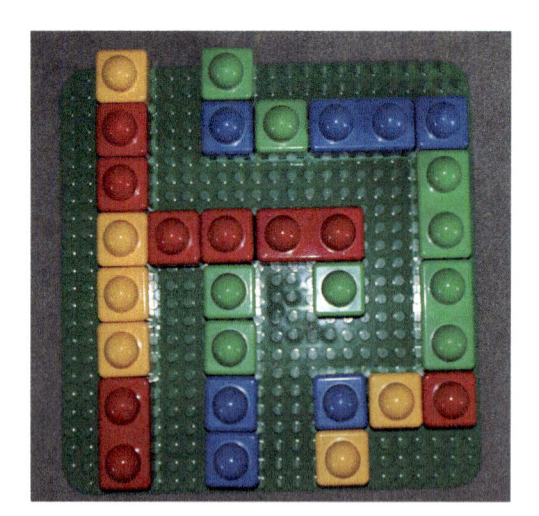

This maze was made by four-year-old Henry. He used Duplos. When I asked where the entrance and exit were, he smiled and said that it was a secret and that was why his maze was so good!

After some discussion (persuasion!), he decided that the entrance and exit are represented by the blocks that are slightly sticking out; one along the bottom and the other on the right-hand side.

Prop box

You can collect:

- Soft toys that match the animals in the story. These can be large or really quite small. Charity shops and jumble sales are very good sources of these. My charity shops have me on speed dial and let me know when anything I need comes into the shop.
- Fiction and non-fiction books about the woods or woodland animals.
- Finger puppets of the animals.
- Acorns and a red trolley. This may be a bit big for a box but is essential for the story.
- Twigs, leaves and acorns for the floor of the area. I wouldn't recommend sticks, as they can become out of hand and revert to being swords! Twigs are more child friendly.

Role play

If you are using leaves and twigs over the floor, I suggest covering the floor first. Use an old blanket, a bed sheet or slip-proof plastic sheets like a small tarpaulin.

Home/school links

Encourage families to contribute to the collection of leaves, seeds and nuts.

Resource sheets

Chapter 1 resources

© Janet Rees

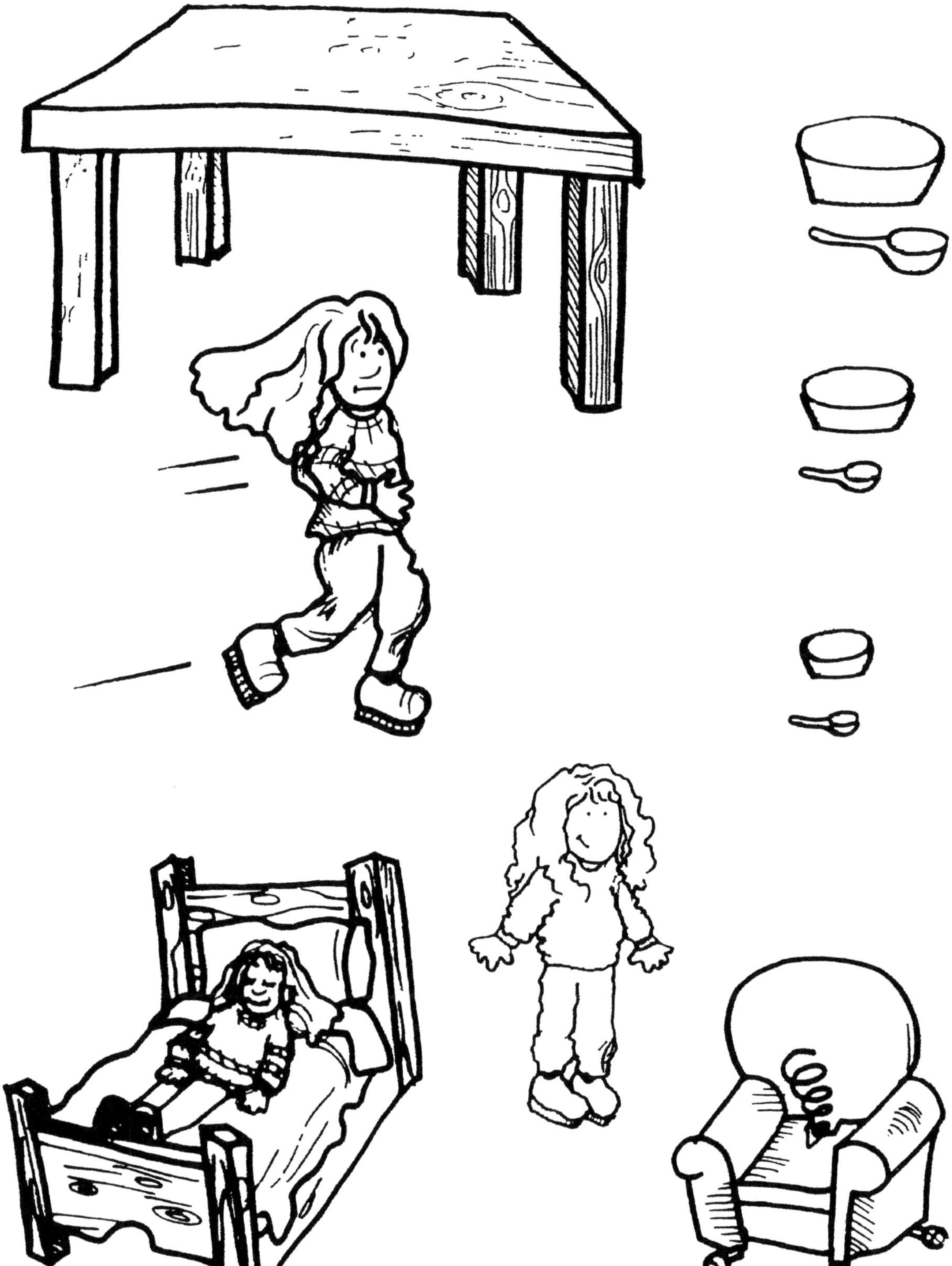

© Janet Rees

© Janet Rees

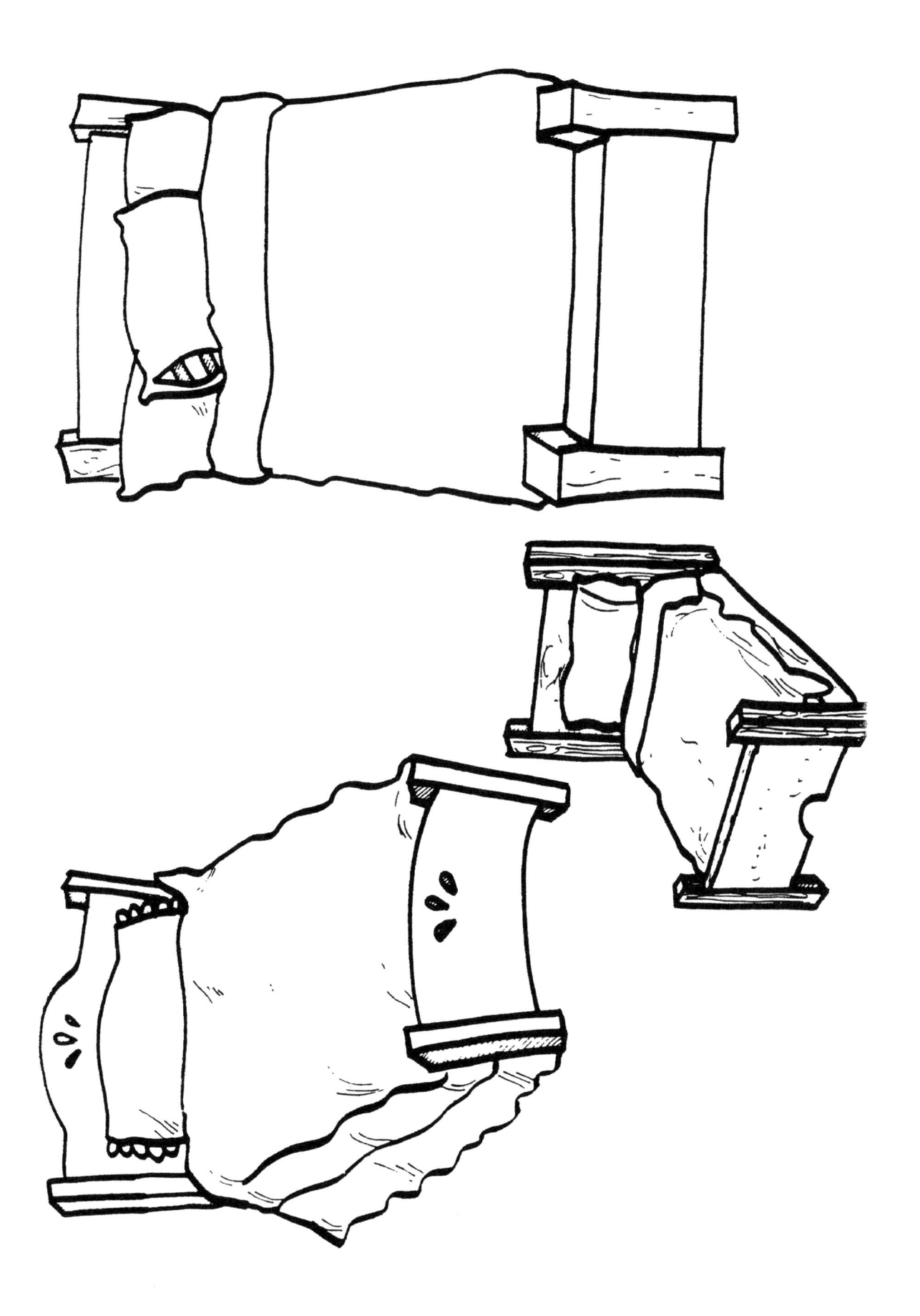

225 g flour

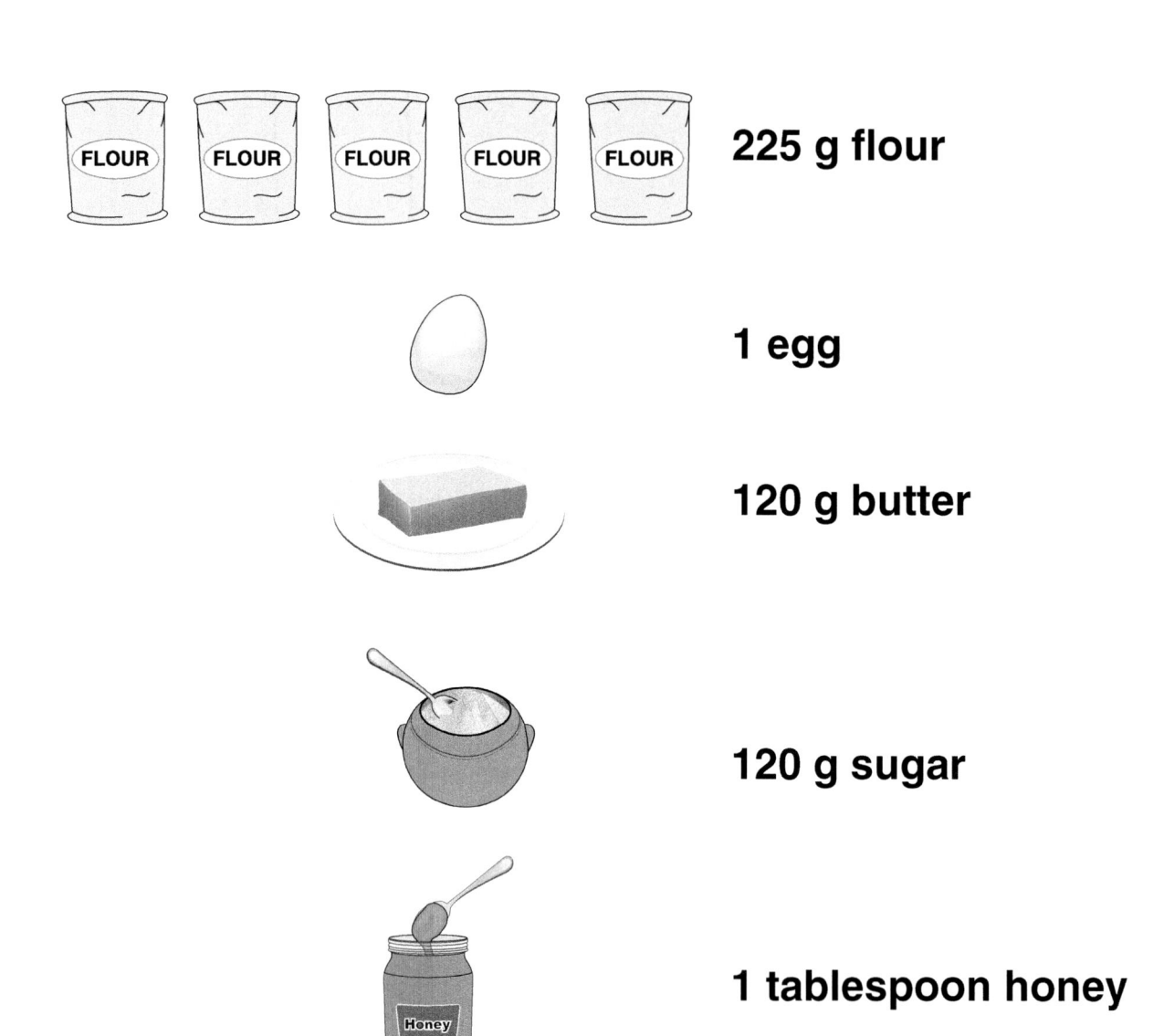

1 egg

120 g butter

120 g sugar

1 tablespoon honey

HONEY

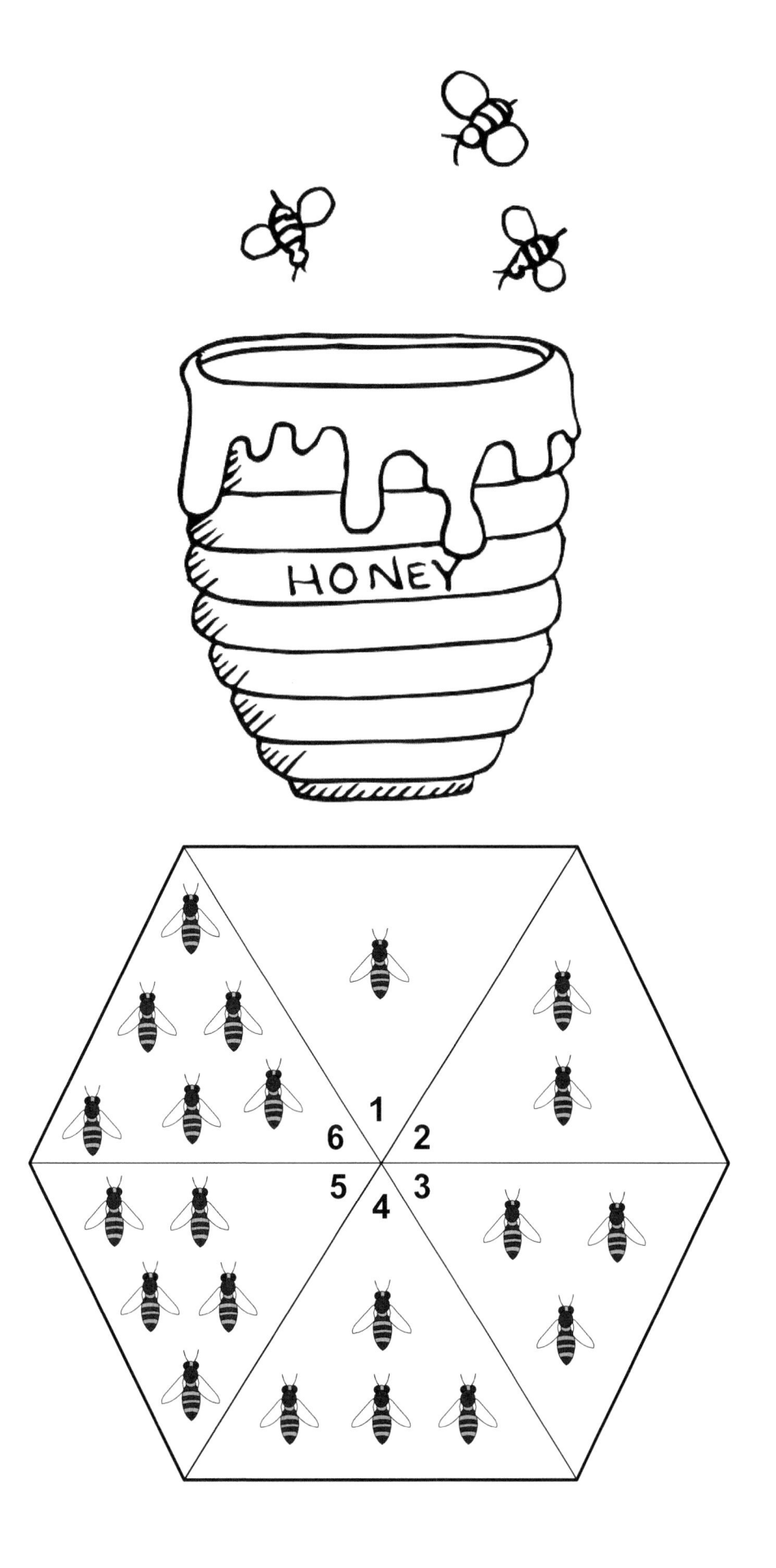

1
6 2
5 3
4

© Janet Rees

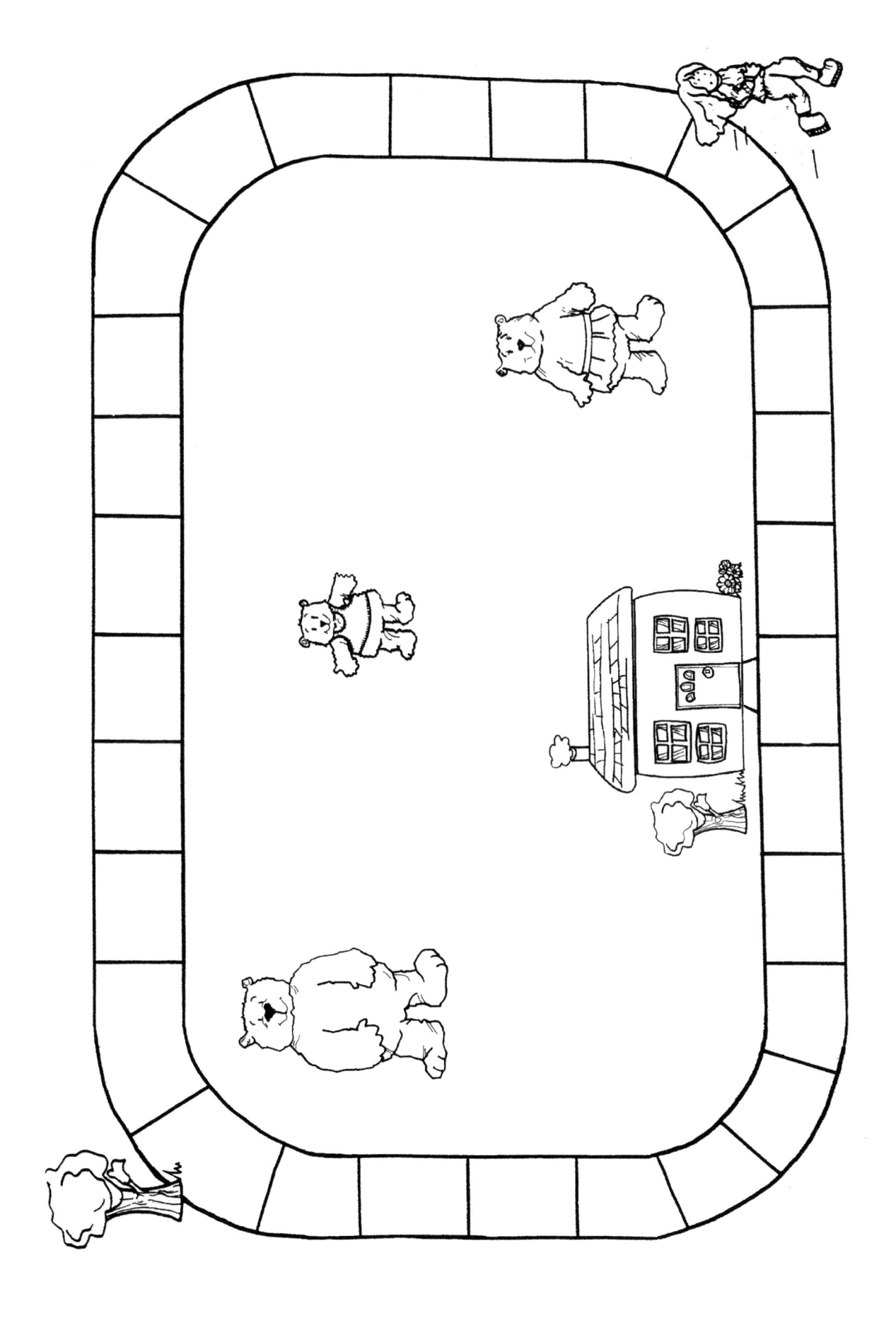

Making dough

Ingredients

2 cups plain flour

1 cup salt

1 cup water

1 tablespoon cooking oil

A jug

A mixing bowl and spoon

Instructions

Mix the dry ingredients together in the bowl.

Pour the water and cooking oil into a jug and stir together.

Add the oil and water mixture to the dry ingredients and mix them together with the spoon.

Knead the dough to make it smooth.

Cut out biscuit shapes and place them on a baking tray.

Bake on a very low heat until they are hard.

Chapter 2 resources

© Janet Rees

© Janet Rees

© Janet Rees

© Janet Rees

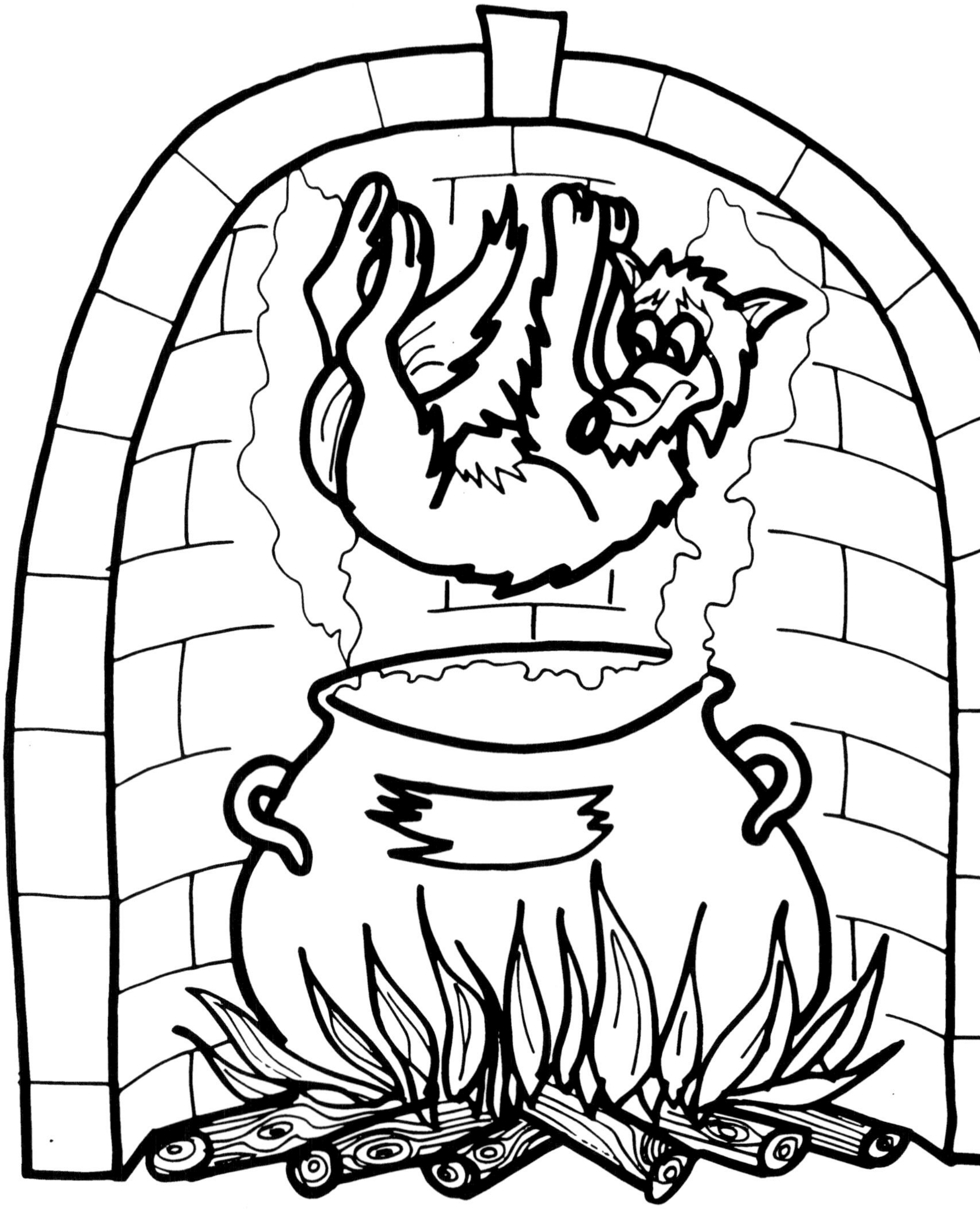

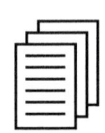

© Janet Rees

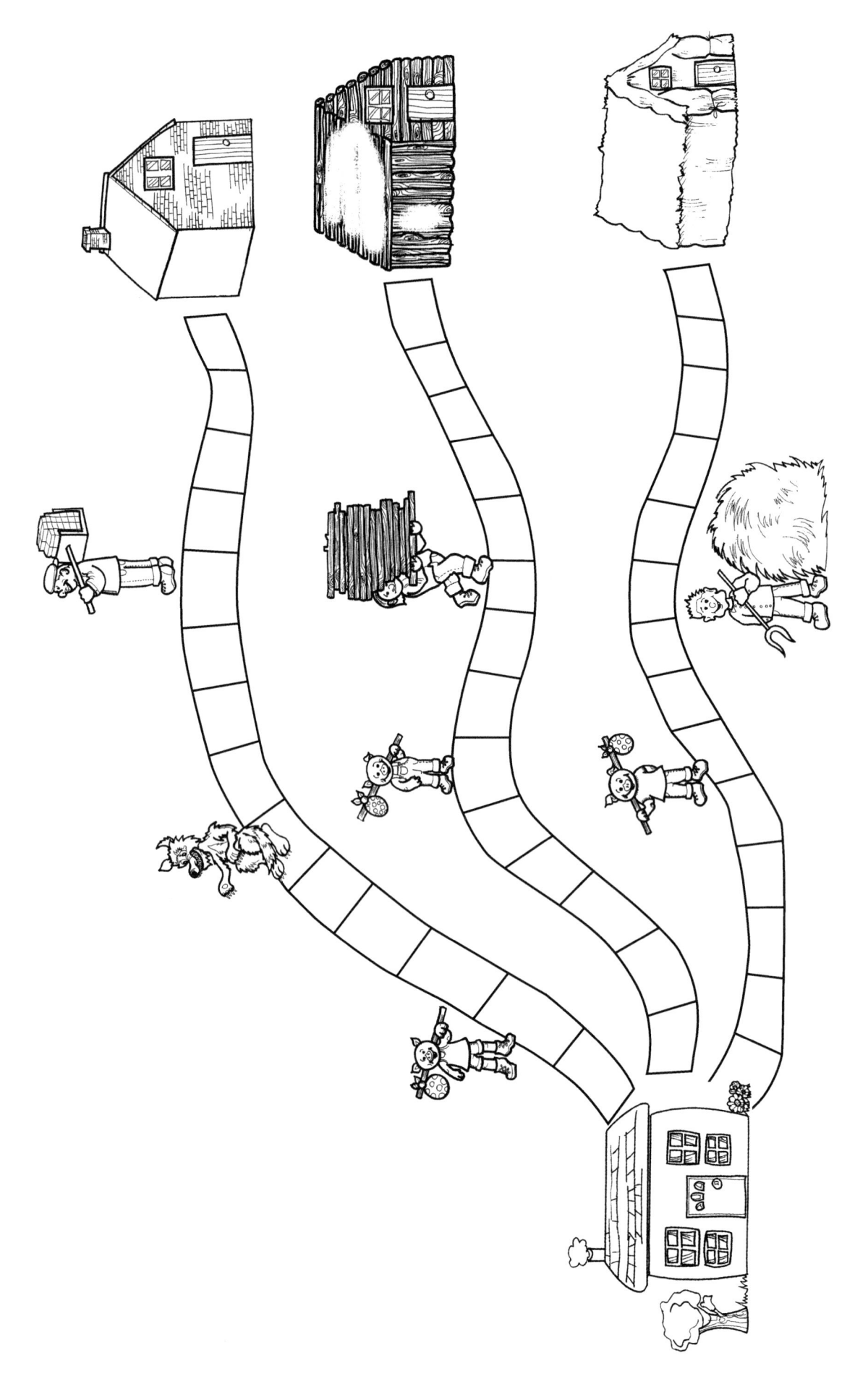

© Janet Rees

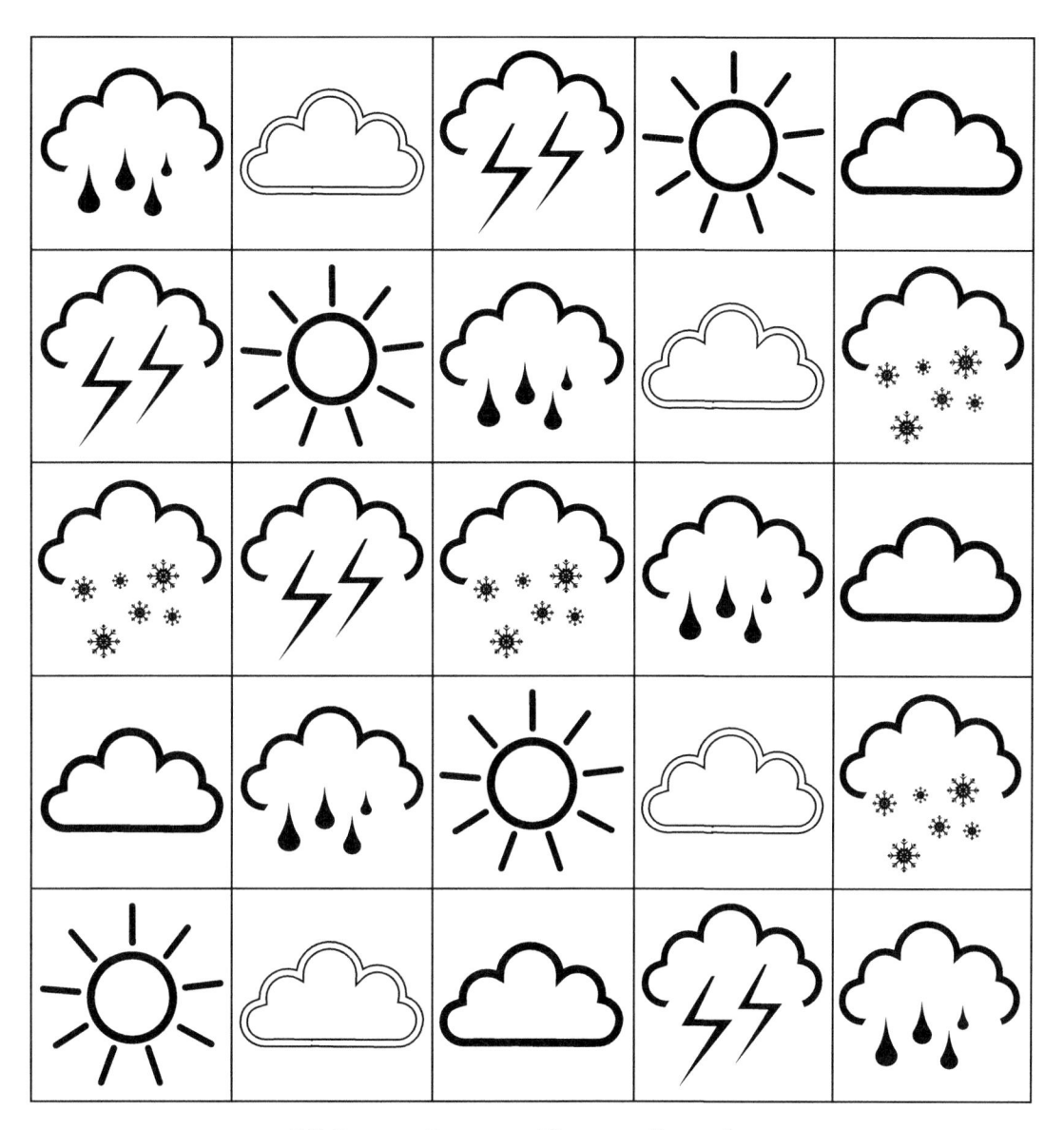

Weather Symbols

1. What country do you want to go to? _____

2. Where do you want to stay?

A town ☐

The seaside ☐

Country ☐

3. Do you want to stay in a

Tent ☐   Caravan ☐

Cottage ☐   Hotel ☐

How long do you want to stay? _____

How many adults?
How many children?

Chapter 3 resources

© Janet Rees

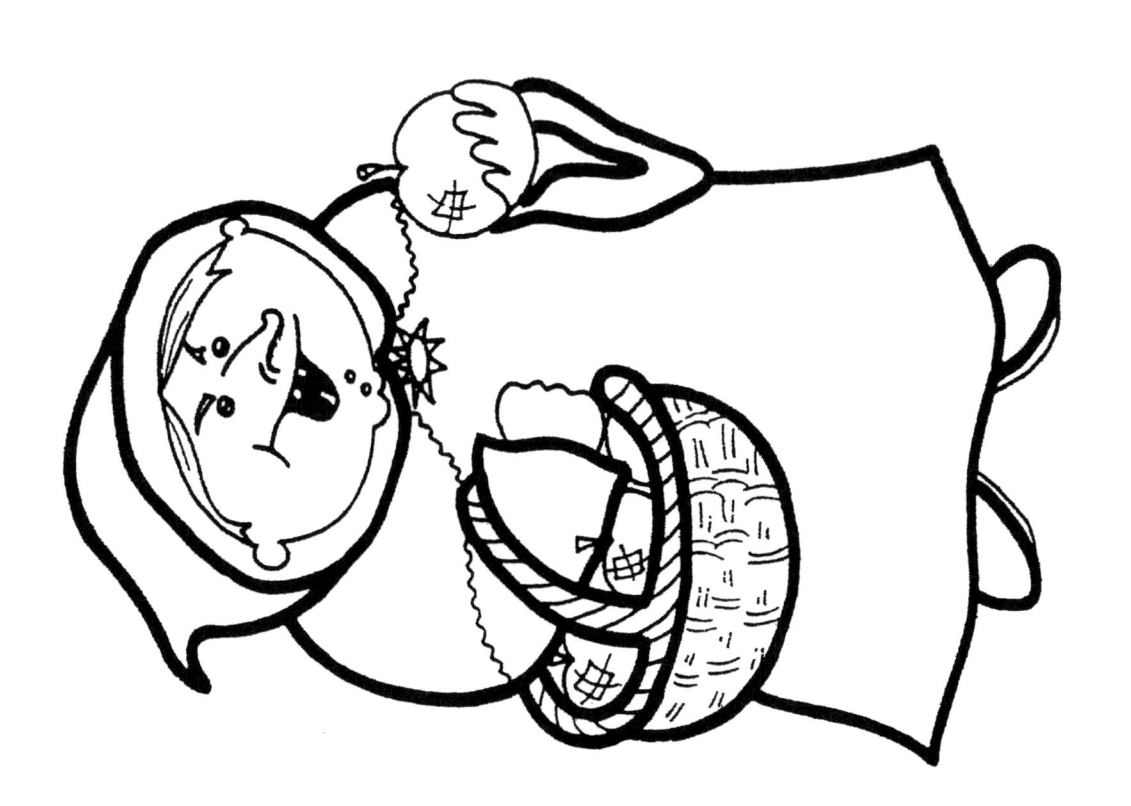

© Janet Rees

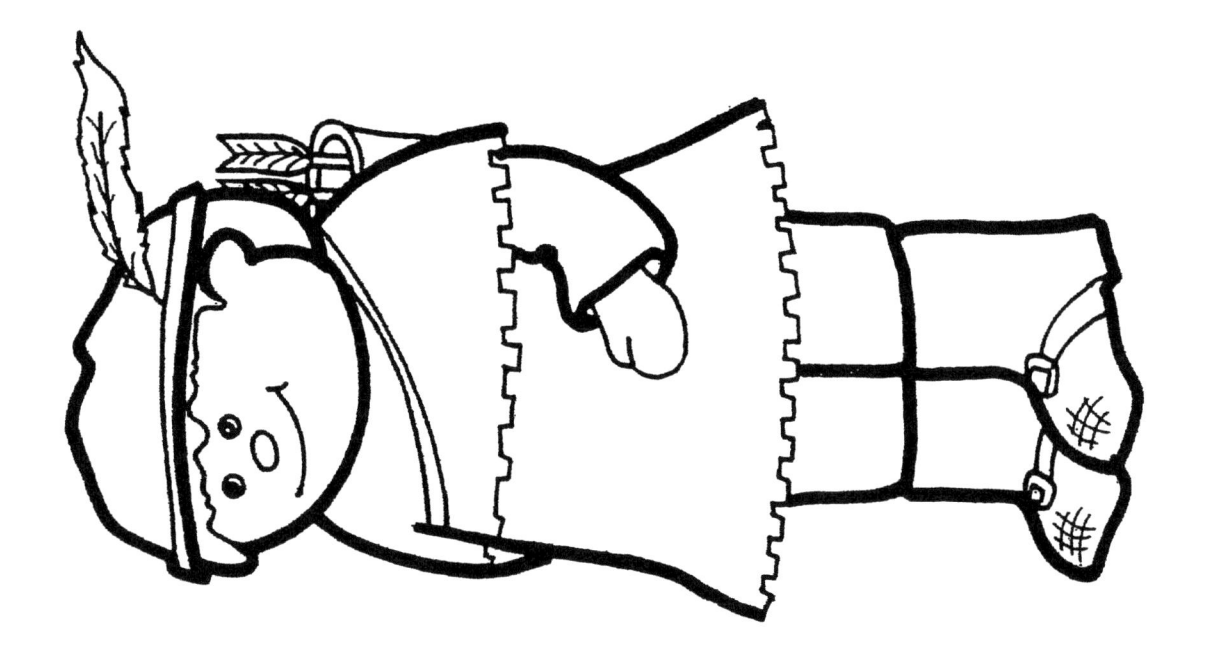

© Janet Rees

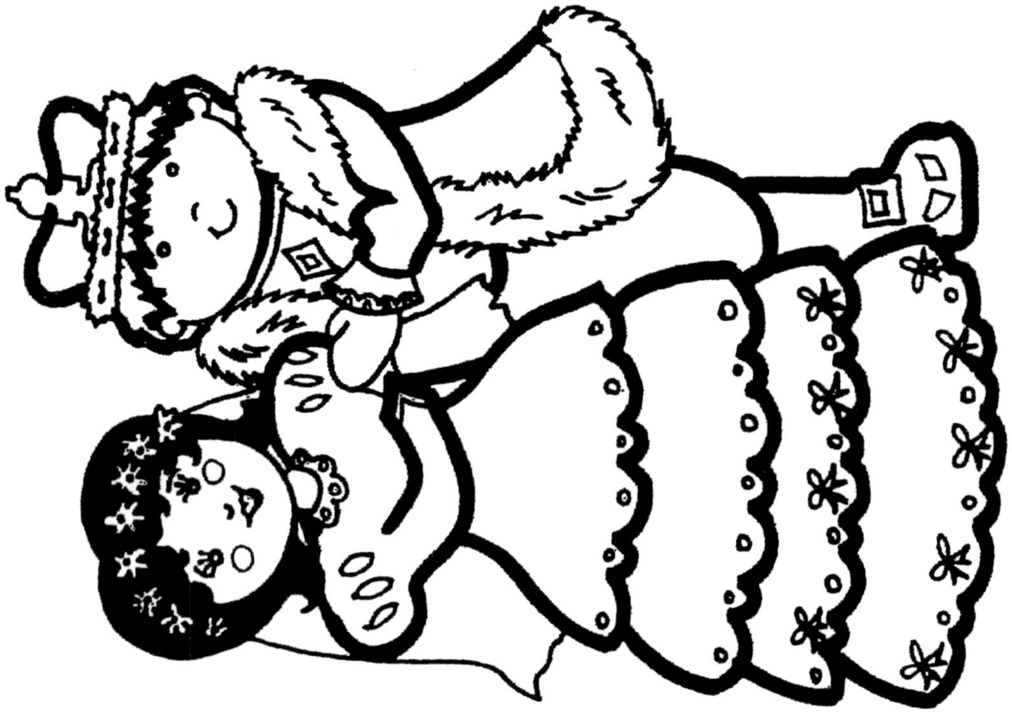

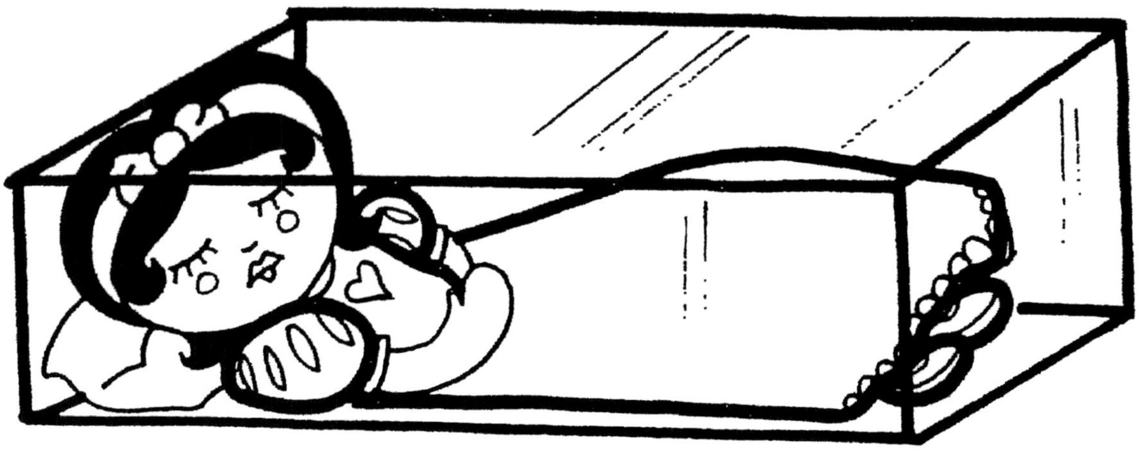

© Janet Rees

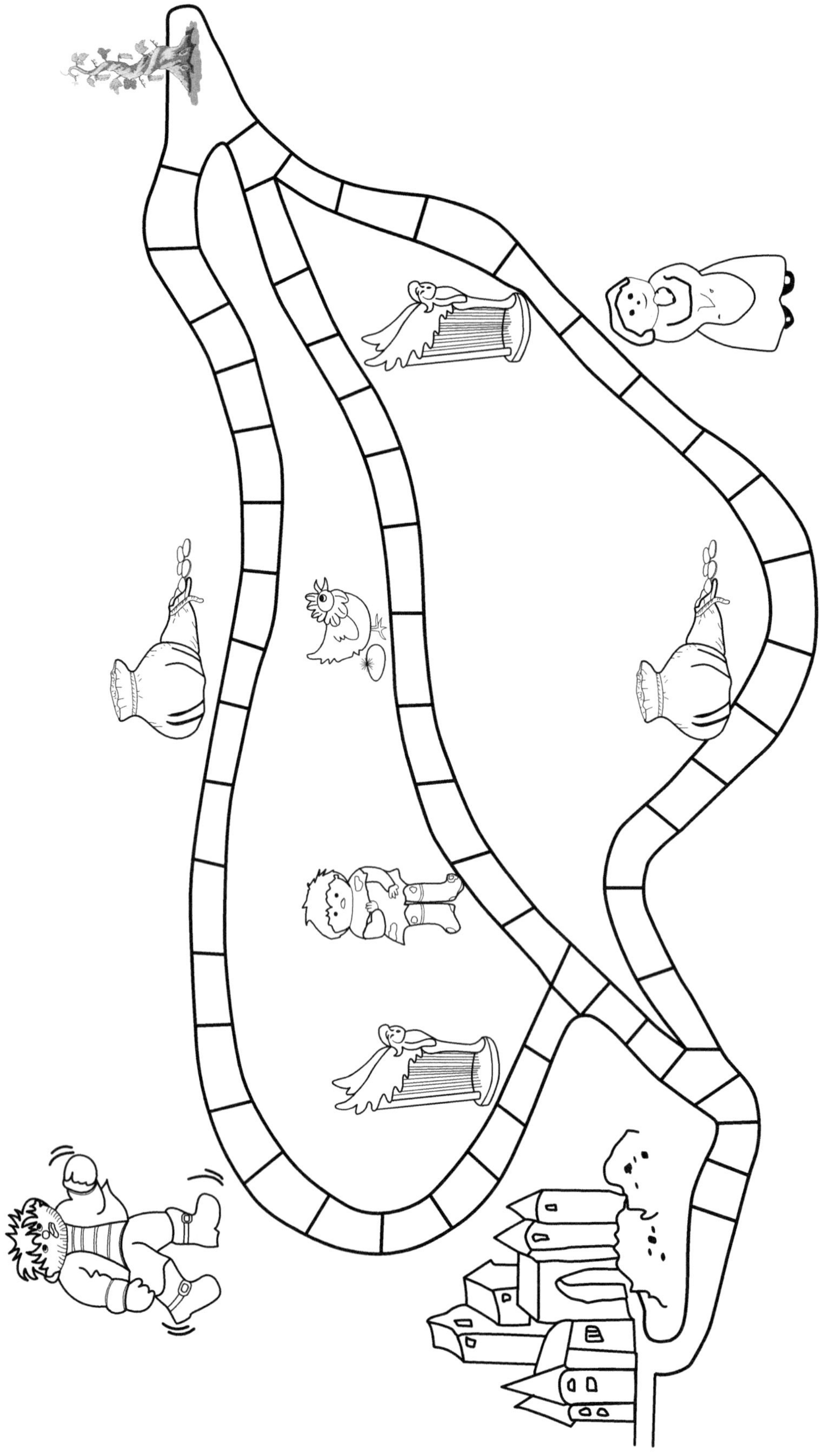

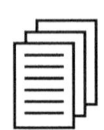

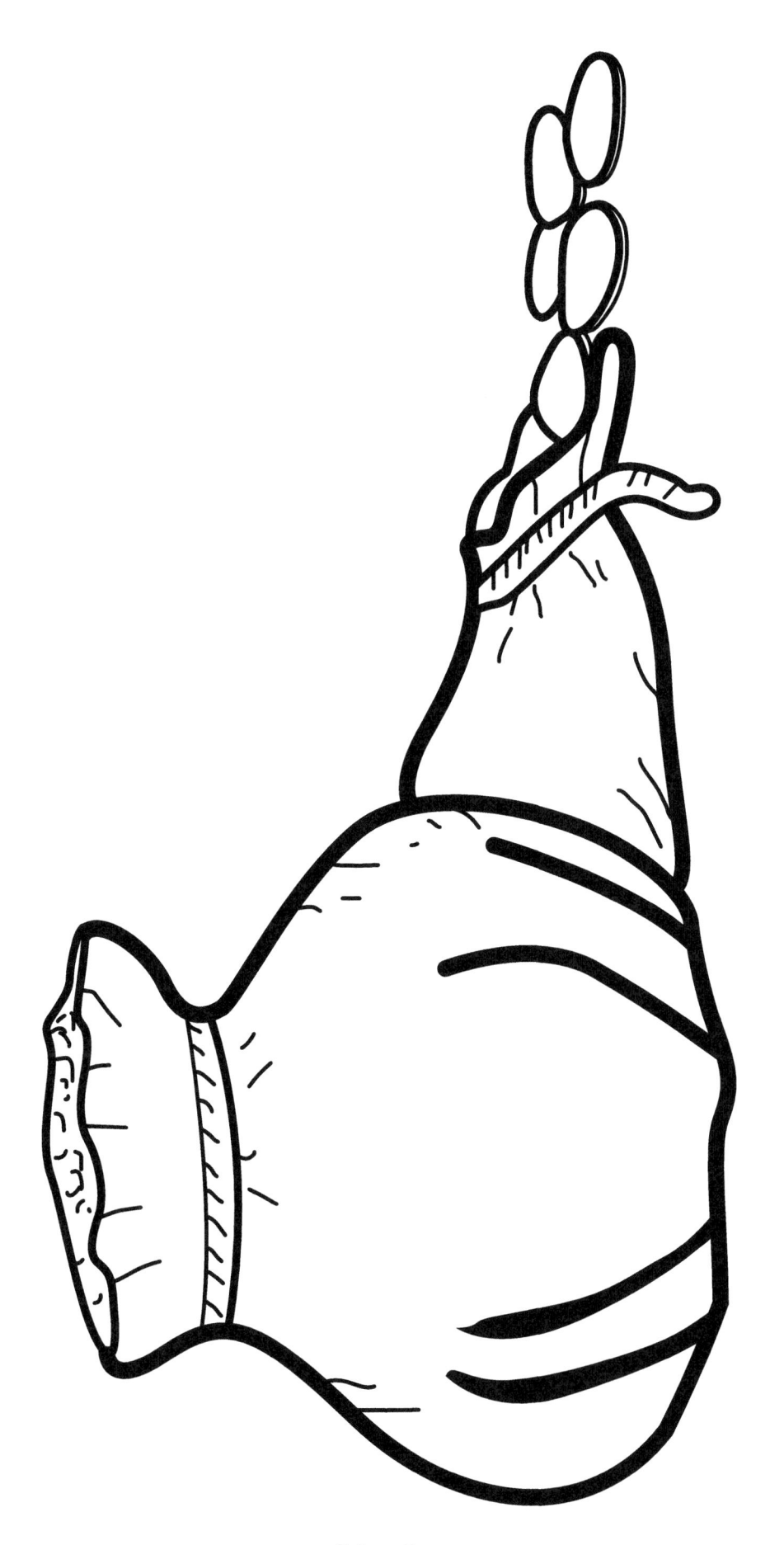

© Janet Rees

© Janet Rees

Seven little dwarves
Standing up like sticks.
One went to wash his shirt.
Then there were six.

Six little dwarves
Glad to be alive.
One went to dig for gold.
Then there were five.

Five little dwarves
Dancing on the floor.
One fell and hurt his knee.
Then there were four.

Four little dwarves
Pleased as pleased could be.
One went to fly a kite.
Then there were three.

Three little dwarves
Thinking what to do.
One went to find Snow White.
Then there were two.

Two little dwarves
Standing in the sun.
One went to get his lunch.
Then there was one.

One little dwarf
Standing all alone.
The rest came back to join him
And they all went home.

© Janet Rees

Chapter 4 resources

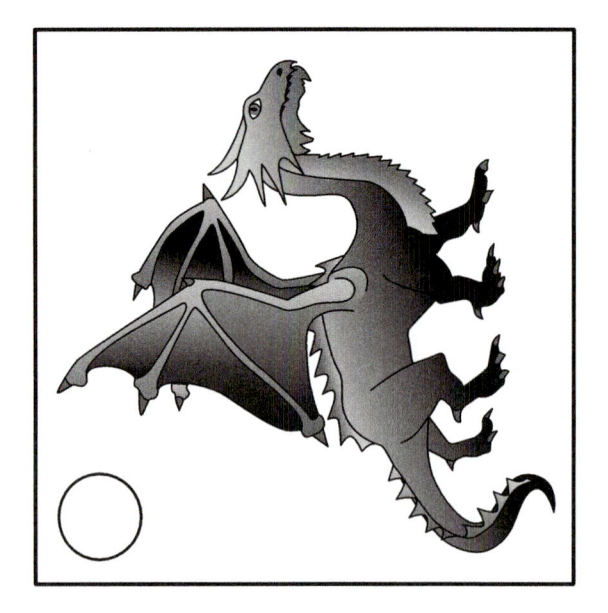

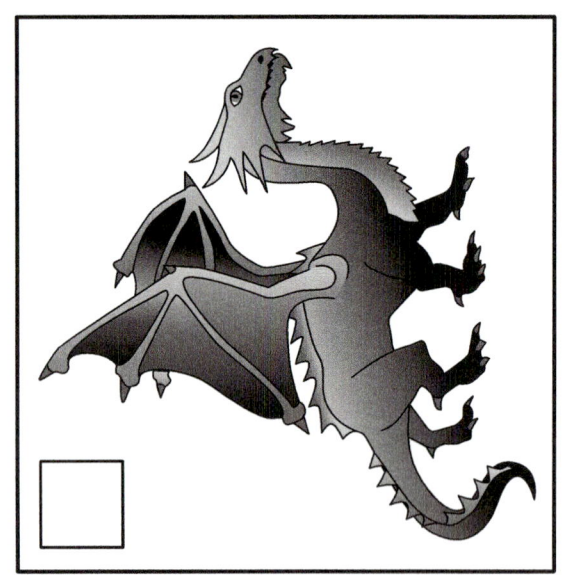

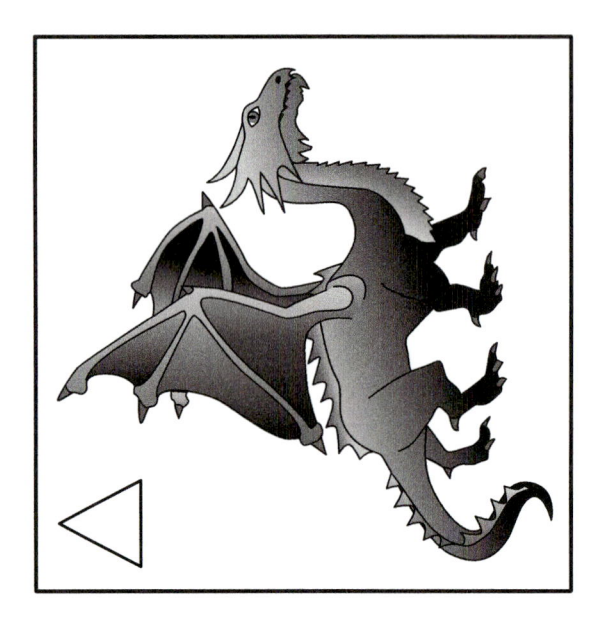

© Janet Rees

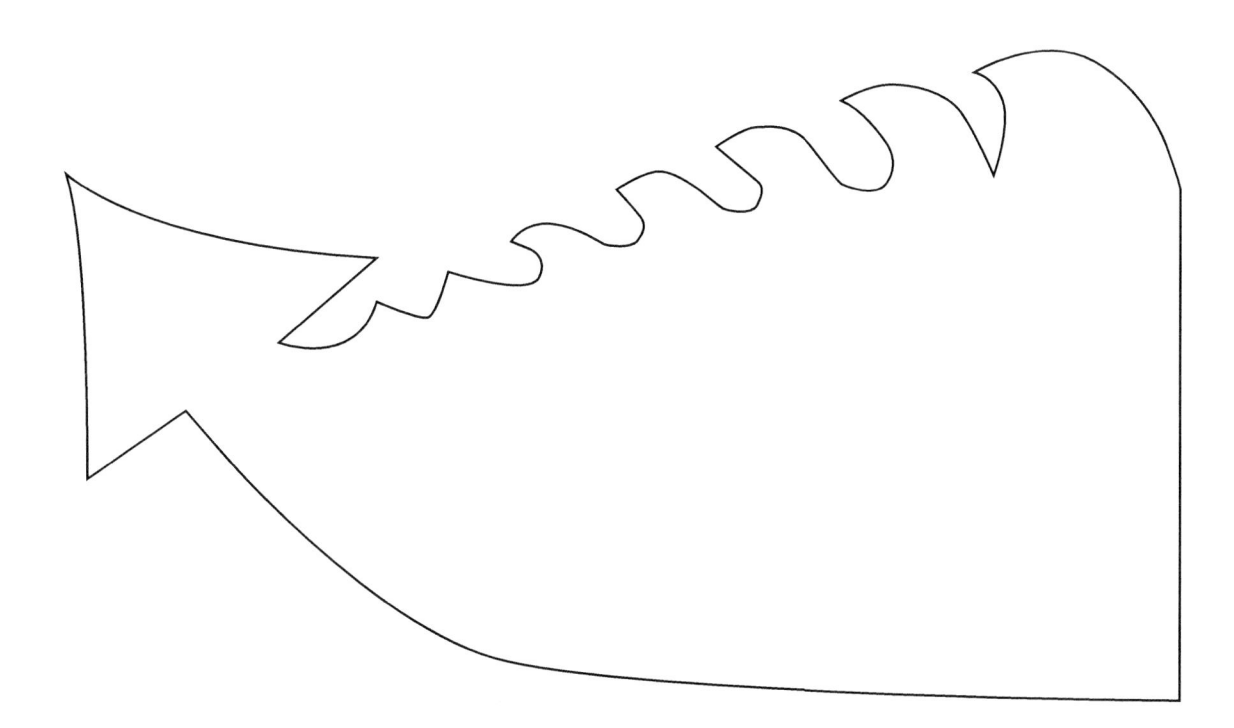

© Janet Rees

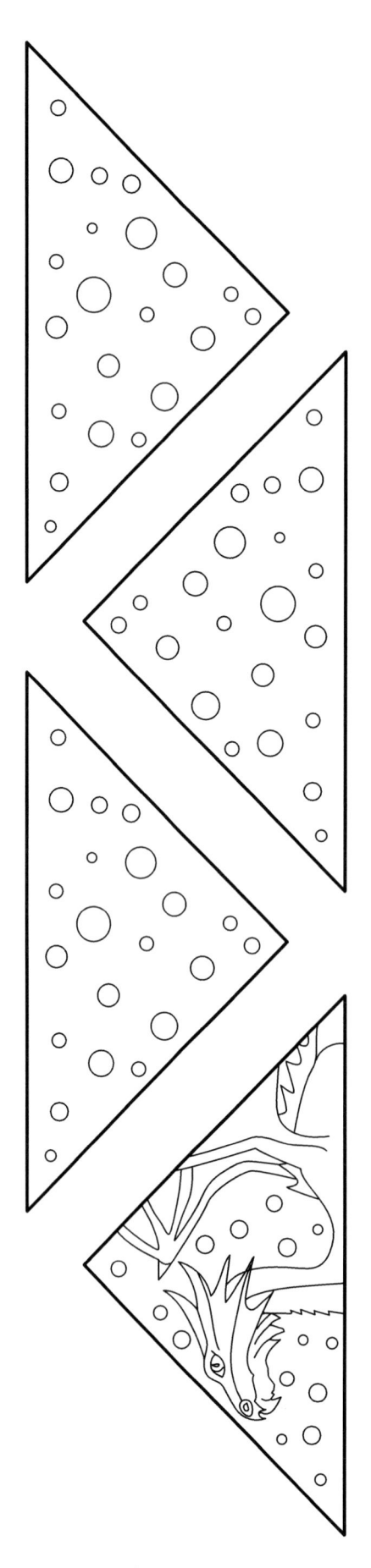

© Janet Rees

© Janet Rees

© Janet Rees

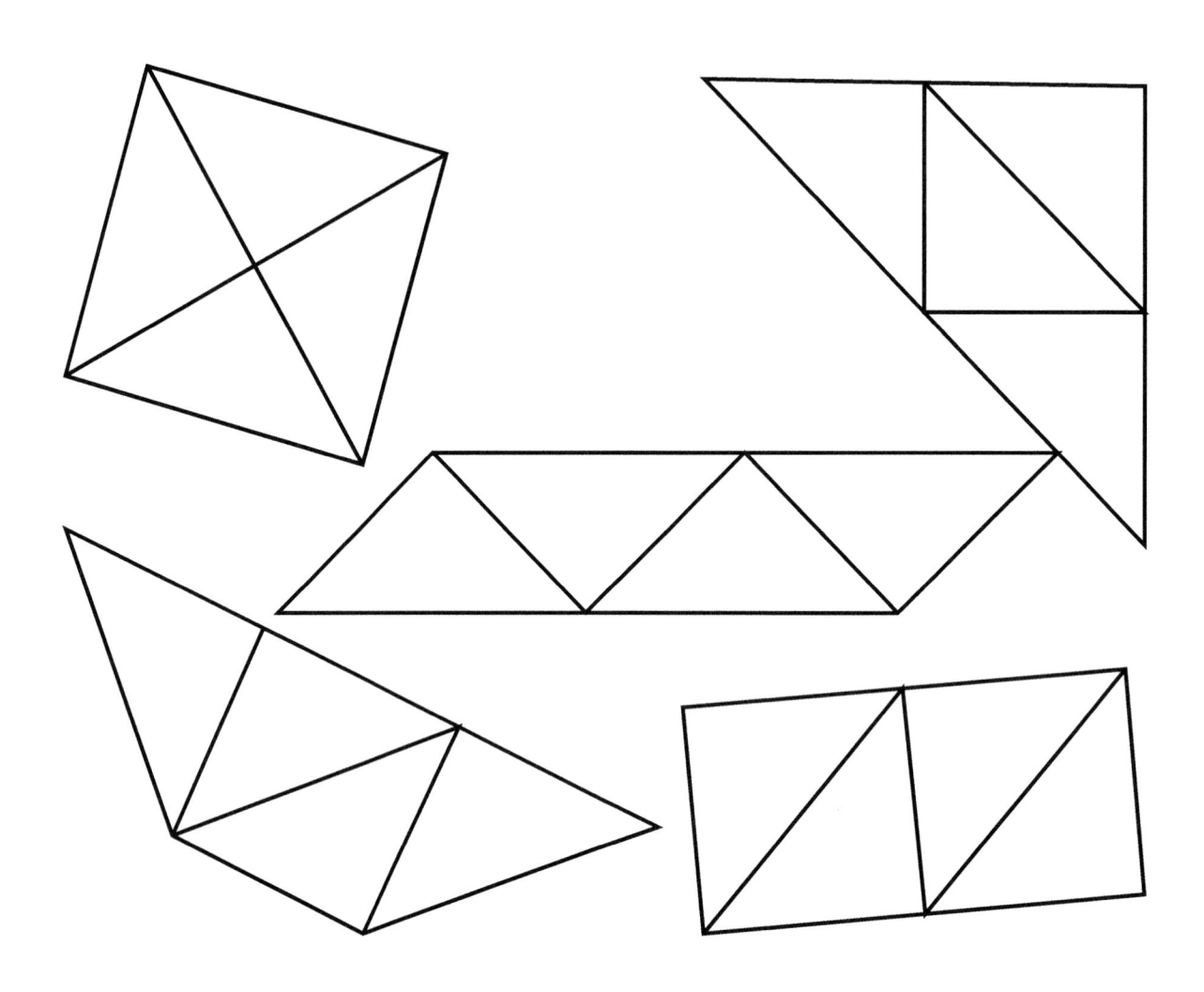

© Janet Rees

Steal the eggs from the dinosaur nest

When playing this game, children are practising team work, playing fairly and following the rules. They are also reinforcing and using their understanding and knowledge of 'one minute'.

Step 1. Place chairs that are face in towards the centre in a square formation, leaving a gap at each corner. The gap should be wide enough for an 'egg stealer' to enter the square and steal a tennis ball (egg) placed in one of two hoops placed on the floor in the middle of the square. Once up to five or six eggs are in place, choose two children to be the parent dinosaurs. Their task is to protect the eggs.

Step 2. Children sit on the chairs whilst the rules are explained.

- The two 'dinosaurs' in the middle are not allowed to leave the square to 'attack' the egg-eating dinosaurs.
- Only one egg can be stolen each time a child enters the square.
- The stolen eggs are taken to a central point at the far end of the room.
- If parent dinosaurs touch the egg eating dinosaurs, the parent has to leave the centre space, leaving just one parent.
- No dinosaur can touch another dinosaur at any time. If they do, they return to their seat and their game is over. The egg stealers have one minute to steal an egg. Use a one-minute timer to make sure that all players have an equal amount of time.
- After that minute, they must leave the nest and the next player enters. The parents have to move and try to block the stealer, but no physical contact is permitted.

Step 3. Check that everyone understands the rules. Choose a child to start the game. After they have had a turn, they return to their seat and the child next to them becomes the egg stealer.

Count to ten and then the game begins.

When all of the eggs have been stolen, play the game again. Choose two different parents and start with a stealer who has not yet had a turn. If the children are finding the game easy, add more eggs and perhaps another parent.

© Janet Rees

© Janet Rees

Chapter 5 resources

© Janet Rees

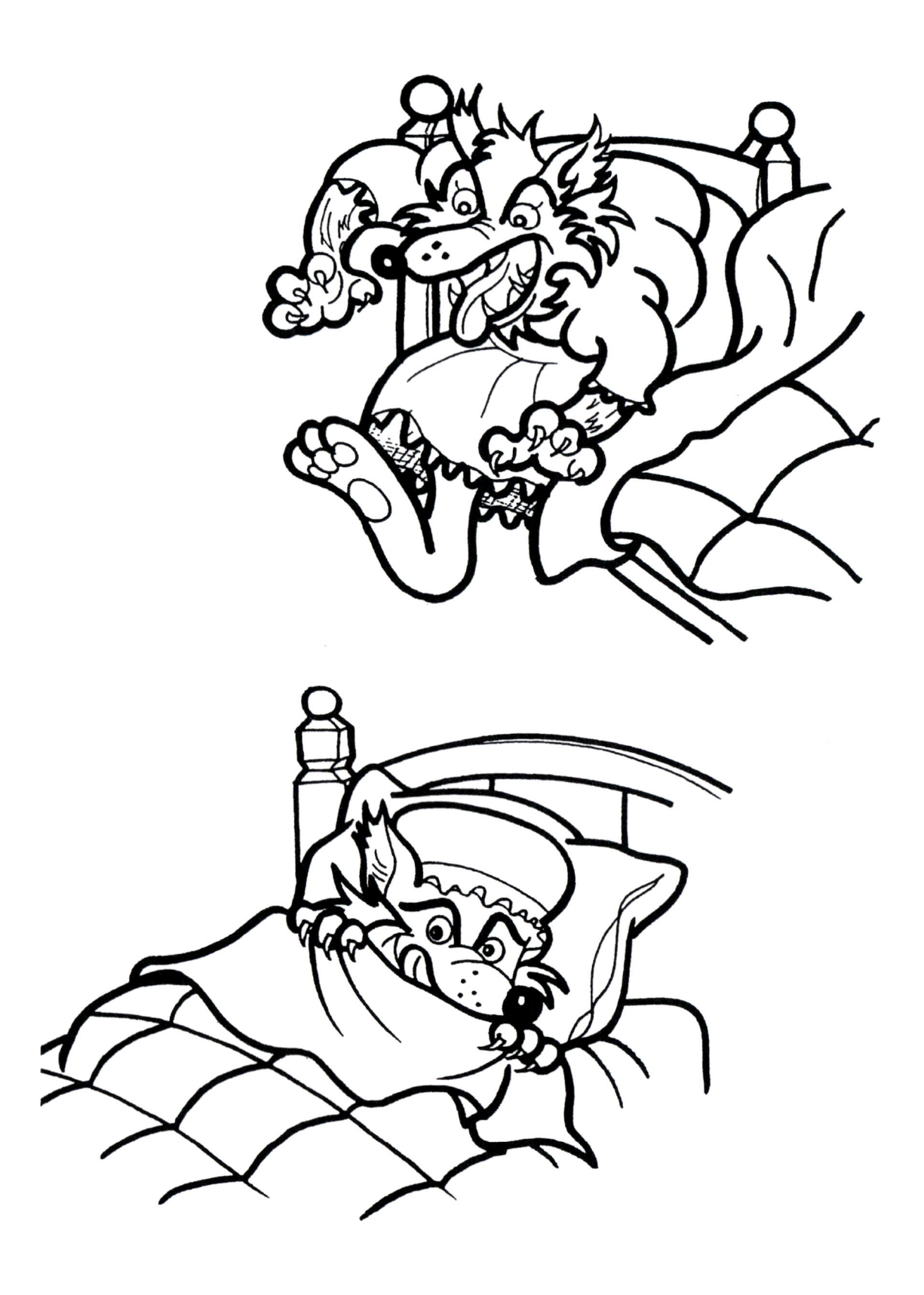

© Janet Rees

© Janet Rees

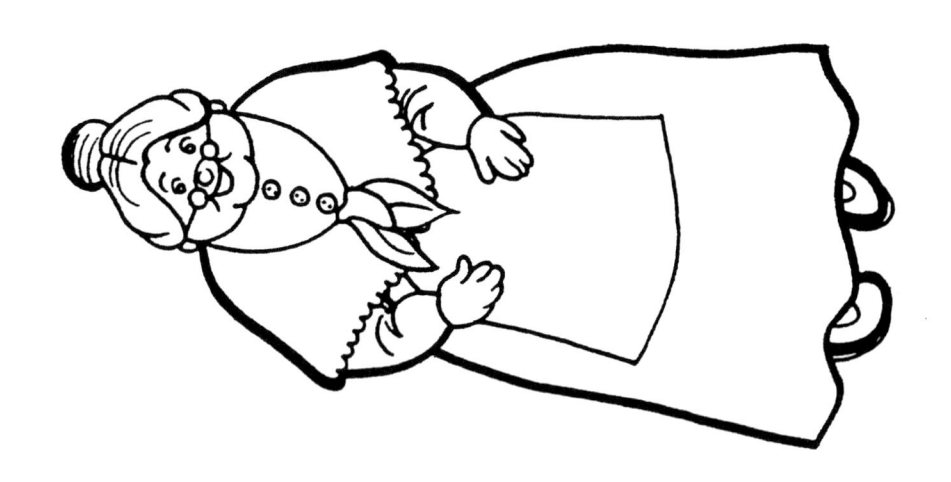

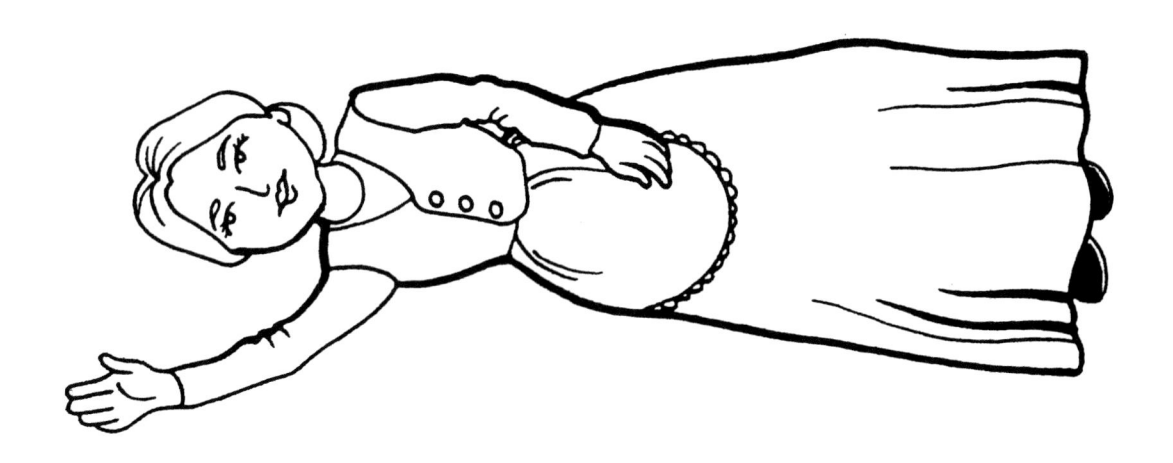

© Janet Rees

© Janet Rees

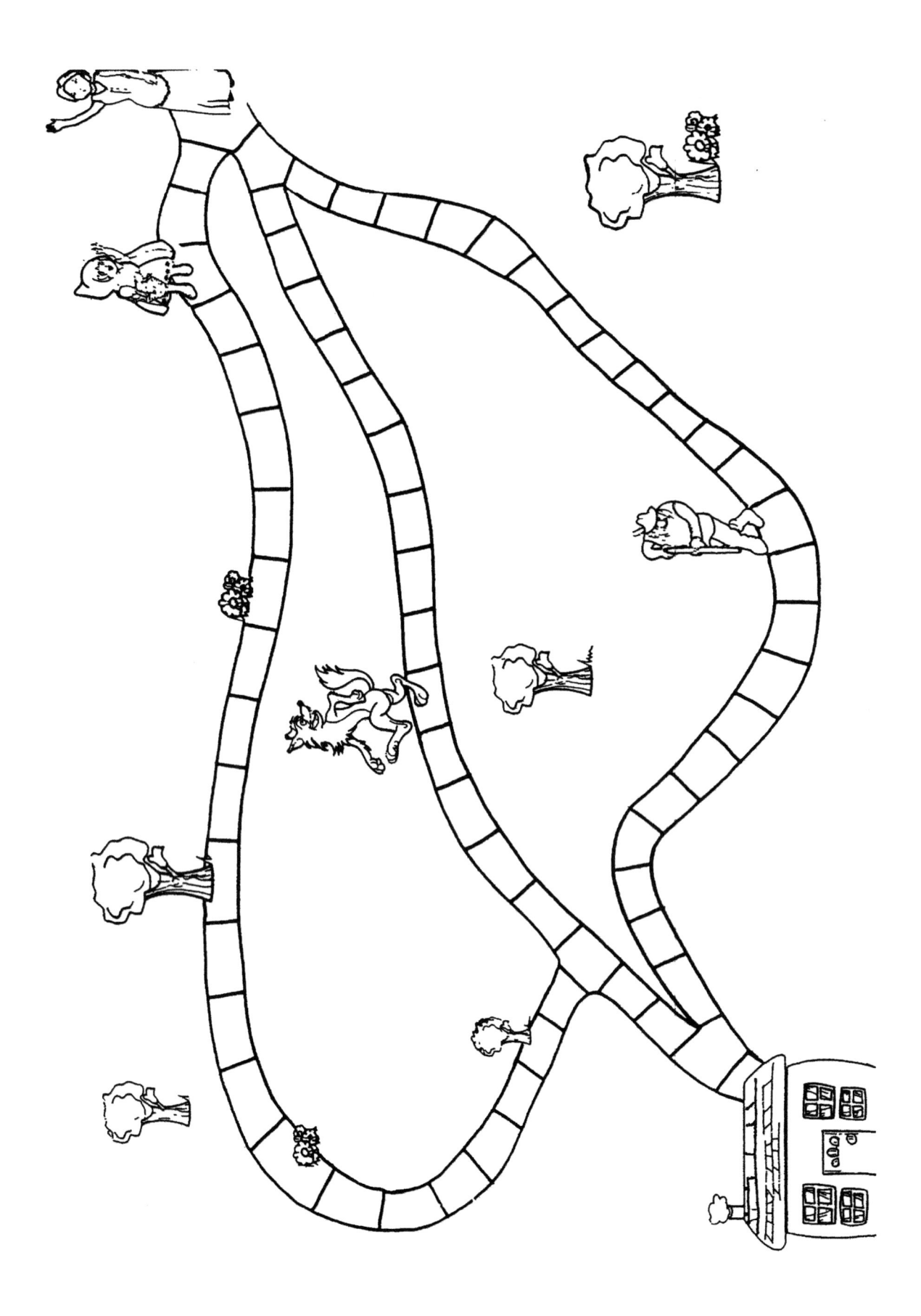

© Janet Rees

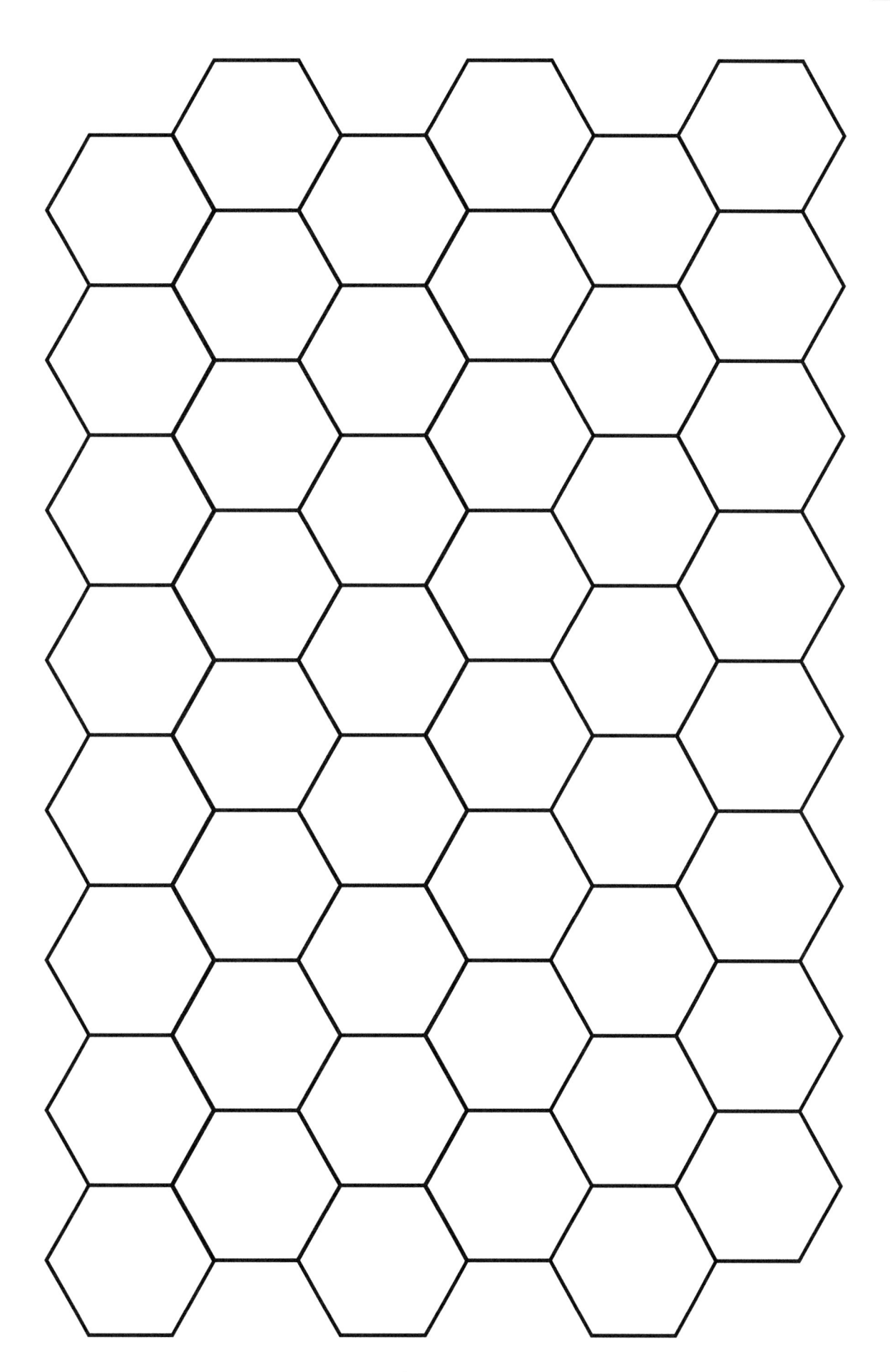

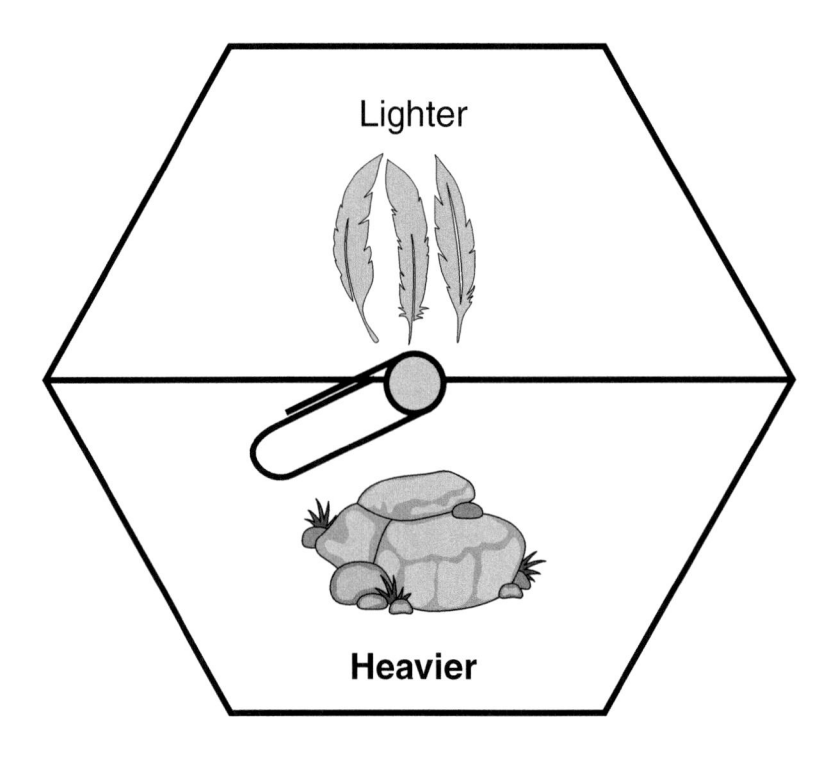

Lighter

Heavier

Spinner-Making Instructions

1. Poke a brass fastener through a ¼" length of drinking straw and a paperclip. Be sure to insert the brad and straw into the large end of the paperclip, as shown.

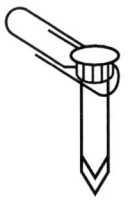

2. Keeping the straw and the paperclip on the brass fastener, insert it into the midpoint hole of the spinner. Once it has been pushed through to the back side, bend each side of the fastener flat against the underside of the gameboard. The section of straw should serve as a spacer so the brad doesn't push the paperclip flat against the gameboard and prevent it from spinning.

3. Give the paperclip a test spin to see if it works.

© Janet Rees

Chapter 6 resources

© Janet Rees

Hedgehog Trail

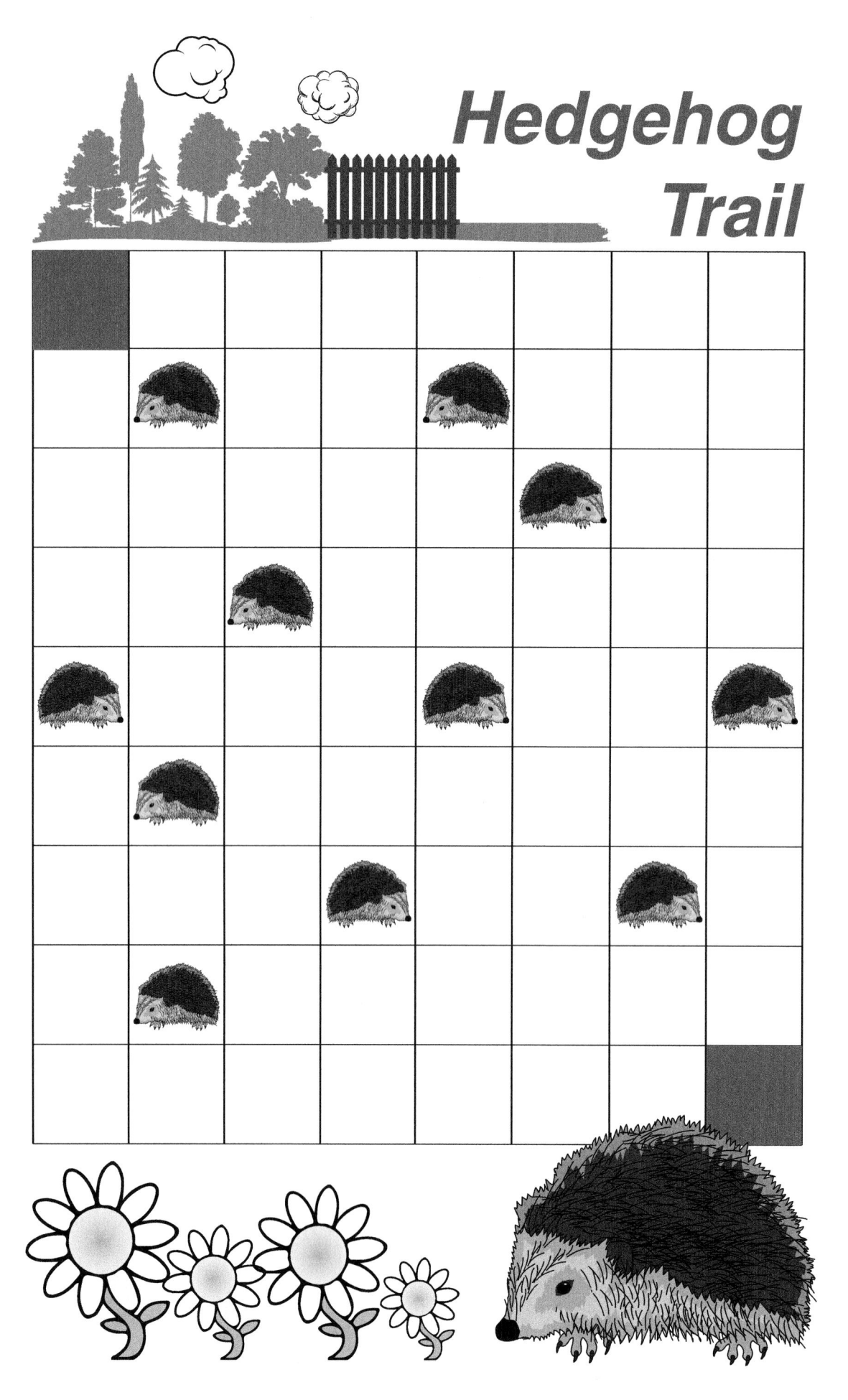

References and bibliography

References

1. Watanabe, R. and Ischinger, B. (2009). *Learning Mathematics for Life: A Perspective From PISA*. Organisation for Economic Co-operation and Development. Retrieved from www.oecd.org/pisa/pisaproducts/pisa2003/44203966.pdf
2. Vappula, H. and Clausen-May, T. (2006). Context in maths test questions: Does it make a difference? *Research in Mathematics Education*, 8(1), pp. 99–115.
3. Egan, K. (1986). *Teaching as Storytelling: An Alternative Approach to Teaching and Curriculum in the Elementary School*. Chicago: University of Chicago Press.
4. Booker, C. (2004). *The Seven Basic Plots: Why We Tell Stories*. London: Bloomsbury Publishing.
5. Griffiths, N. (2001). *A Corner to Learn*. Cheltenham: Nelson Thornes.
6. Oldfield, B. (January 1991). Games in the learning of mathematics. *Mathematics in Schools*, 20(1), pp. 41–43.
7. Davies, B. (1995). The role of games in mathematics. *Square One*, 5(2).
8. Milne, A.A. (n.d.). *Pooh Hears a Buzzing Noise*. Ashland, OR: Blackstone Audio.
9. Danks, F. and Schofield, J. (2005). *Nature's Playground*. London: Frances Lincoln Ltd.
10. Bilton, H. (2007). All about dens. *Nursery World Magazine*, 6 September.

Bibliography

Alborough, J. (2016). *It's the Bear!* Walker.
Alborough, J. (2017). *Where's My Teddy?* Candlewick Press.
Andreae, G. (2005). *Dinosaurs Galore!* Tiger Tales.
Andreae, G. (2014). *Mad About Dinosaurs*. Orchard Books.
Andreae, G. and Wojtowycz, D. (2011). *Mad About Minibeasts*. Orchard Books.
Andreae, G. and Wojtowycz, D. (2011). *Norman: The Slug with a Silly Shell*. Simon & Schuster Children's UK.
Aston, D. H. (2015). *A Butterfly is Patient*. Chronicle Books.
Aston, D. H. (2016). *A Beetle Is Shy*. Chronicle Books.
Baxter, N. (1997). *Big Little Bus (Ladybird Little Stories)*. Ladybird.
Bean, J. (2013). *Building Our House*. Farrar Straus Giroux Books for Young Readers.
Bedford, D. (2015). *Because I Love You*. Nosy Crow.
Bedford, D. (2016). *Big Bear, Little Bear*. Little Tiger Press.
Bently, P. and Oxenbury, H. (2015). *King Jack and the Dragon*. Puffin Books.
Berenstain, S. and Berenstain, J. (1997). *Inside Outside Upside Down*. Random House Books for Young Readers.
Bond, M. (2018). *Paddington Bear*. HarperCollins Children's Books.
Boyd, L. (1992). *Willy and the Cardboard Boxes*. Viking Children's Books.
Bullard, L. (2002). *My Neighbourhood: Places and Faces (All About Me)*. Picture Window Books.
Burton, V. L. (1978). *The Little House*. Houghton Mifflin Company.
Carle, E. (1997). *The Very Quiet Cricket*. Puffin Books.
Carle, E. (2007). *The Very Hungry Caterpillar*. Hachette Children's Group.
Carle, E. (2010). *The Bad Tempered Ladybird*. Puffin Books.
Castor, H. (2002). *The Dinosaurs Next Door*. Usborne Publishing.

Chesanow, N. (1995). *Where Do I Live?* Barrons.
Child, L. (2016). *That Pesky Rat*. Orchard Books.
Collins, R. (2016). *There's a Bear in My Chair*. Nosy Crow.
Cronin, D. and Bliss, H. (2013). *Diary of a Fly*. HarperCollins.
Dahl, R. (2009). *The Minpins*. Puffin Books.
Dodd, E. (2011). *I Love Bugs*. Red Robin Books.
Donaldson, J. (2002). *The Dinosaur's Diary*. Puffin Books.
Ellis, C. (2016). *Home*. Walker Books.
Fletcher, T. and Poynter, D. (2013). *The Dinosaur that Pooped a Planet*. Red Fox.
Fogliano, J. and Smith, L. (2018). *The House that Once Was*. Two Hoots; Main Market Edition.
Foley, G. (2012). *Thank You Bear*. Viking.
French, V. and Ahlberg, J. (2015). *Yucky Worms*. Walker Books.
Funk, J. (2016). *Dear Dragon*. Viking Books for Young Readers.
Garland, M. (2017). *Big and Little Are Best Friends: A Story of Two Friends*. Orchard Books Scholastic.
Gliori, D. (2008). *The Trouble With Dragons*. Bloomsbury Publishing.
Grahame, K. (2005). *The Reluctant Dragon*. Walker Books.
Griffiths, N. (2008). *There's a Spider in the Bath*. Tiger Tales.
Harrison, J. (1996). *Dear Bear*. Picture Lions.
Hart, C. and Eaves, E. (2014). *How to Catch a Dragon*. Simon & Schuster Children's UK.
Hawkins, C. (2002). *The Dance of the Dinosaurs*. Collins Picture Books.
Hayes, S. (1989). *This Is the Bear and the Picnic Lunch*. Walker.
Hendra, S. (2018). *What the Ladybird Heard*. Macmillan Children's Books.
Hepworth, A. (2015). *I Love You to the Moon and Back*. Little Tiger Press.
Hissey, J. (1995). *Old Bear Stories*. Hutchinson.
Hofman, G. (2003). *Who Wants an Old Teddy Bear?* REVERIE.
Hughes, S. (1991). *Moving Molly*. Red Fox Picture Books.
Inkpen, M. (2007). *Billy's Beetle*. Bolinda Audio.
Katz, K. (2006). *Best Ever Big Sister*. Grosset & Dunlap.
Ladybird (2013). *Minibeasts: Ladybird First Fabulous Facts*. Ladybird.
Lamug, K. K. (2011). *A Box Story*. Rabble Box.
Laroche, G. (2011). *If You Lived Here: Houses and Homes of the World*. Houghton Mifflin.
Lehman, B. (2011). *The Secret Box*. HMH Books for Young Readers.
Lively, P. (2004). *Goldilocks and the Three Bears*. Hodder Children's Books.
Maclaren, T. and Damon, E. (2005). *All Kinds of Homes*. Tango Books.
Martin, B. (2006). *Panda Bear, Panda Bear, What Do You See?* Henry Holt and Co.
Martin, B. (2011). *Polar Bear, Polar Bear, What Do You Hear?* Henry Holt and Co.
Martin, B. (2016). *Brown Bear, Brown Bear, What Do You See?* Henry Holt and Co.
Mayo, D. (2007). *The House that Jack Built*. Barefoot Books.
McKee, D. (2015). *Elmer and Butterfly*. Andersen Press.
Merberg, J. (2017). *Turn the Key*. Downtown Bookworks.
Milne, A. A. (2001). *The Complete Tales of Winnie the Pooh*. Dutton Books for Young Readers.
Minarik, E. H. (1978). *Little Bear (An I Can Read Book)*. HarperCollins.
Mitton, T. (2016). *Bumpus Jumpus Dinosaurumpus*. Orchard Books.
Mitton, T. (2016). *Twist and Hop, Minibeast Bop!* Orchard Books.
Moore, J. (2011). *When a Dragon Moves in*. Flashlight Press.
Murphy, J. (2007). *Whatever Next*. MacMillan Children's Books.
Murphy, J. (2013). *Peace at Last*. MacMillan.
Nichols, L. (2014). *Maple*. Nancy Paulsen Books.
Norton, M. (2003). *The Borrowers*. HMH Books for Young Readers.
Patricelli, L. (2009). *The Birthday Box*. Candlewick.
Perkins, C. (2016). *Living in China*. Simon Spotlight.
Priddy, R. (2014). *The Cardboard Box Book*. Priddy Books; Spi edition.
Rawson, C. (2007). *Stories of Dragons*. Usborne Publishing.
Relf, A. (2005). *The Biggest Bear*. Scholastic.

Rosen, M. (2001). *We're Going on a Bear Hunt*. Walker.
Rudy, M. (2017). *City Mouse and Country Mouse*. Henry Holt and Co.
Russo, M. (2000). *The Big Brown Box*. Greenwillow Books.
Schaefer, L. M. (2012). *One Special Day (A Story for Big Brothers and Sisters)*. Disney-Hyperion.
Smith, A. T. (2013). *Home*. Scholastic Books.
Smith, D. K. (2015). *Sophie's Snail*. Holiday House.
Stickland, P. (2000). *Ten Terrible Dinosaurs*. Puffin Books.
Strickland, H. (1998). *Dinosaur Roar!* Scholastic.
Sullivan, S. and Tusa, T. (2010). *Once Upon a Baby Brother*. Farrar, Straus and Giroux.
Sutton, E. (2010). *My Cat Likes to Hide in Boxes*. Puffin Books.
Thomasma, E. and Thomasma, L. (2012). *Sam and the Dragon*. CreateSpace Independent Publishing Platform.
Unmansky, K. and Sharratt, N. (2006). *Stomp, Chomp, Bog Roars! Here Come the Dinosaurs*. Puffin Books.
Waddle, M. (2013). *Can't You Sleep, Little Bear*. Walker.
West, T. (2014). *Rise of the Earth Dragon*. Scholastic.
Willis, J. (2017). *Dinosaur Roar! The Tyrannosaurus Rex*. MacMillan.
Winter, J. (2014). *Mr Cornell's Dream Boxes*. Beach Lane Books.
Woodson, J. and Blackall, S. (2013). *Pecan Pie Baby*. Puffin Books.
Yolen, J. and Sheban, C. (2016). *What to Do With a Box*. Creative Editions.

Index

acorns 159, 196, 198, 201, 209–215; five little acorns rhyme 210
activities: craft 201; favourite 58; independent 165; mandala 187; measuring 18; outdoor 120; problem-solving 89
addition 98–99, 157
aeroplanes 78
Africa/African 171; models 171; necklace 82–83; village 167; women 82
aluminium foil 36–37, 66, 77, 100, 111
angles 25, 73
animals 62, 81, 137, 170–171, 195–196, 207–208, 215
area: castle 65; estimating 50; holiday 84–85; interest 75; local 86; shaded 179; weather 85
avocados 79, 168–169

babies 19, 64, 140, 191, 206
baking 44–45, 162, 170, 186
balance scales 13, 20, 35, 46, 66, 168, 172–173
ball 11, 13, 45, 163, 174, 187, 190
balloons 43, 63, 80–81, 83–84, 88, 163–164
banana loaf 170–171
baskets *see* boxes and baskets
beans 76, 83, 95, 98–99, 103–104; coloured 98; five 98; magic 95; raw 83; white butter 98
beanstalk 5, 97–98, 101–102, 104
bear: baby 14, 17, 19, 21–22; daddy 9, 19, 22; mummy 14, 19, 22
bees: fat 50; imaginary 50; long 50; making 48; making Pooh Bear's 165; short 50; thin 50
Billy's Sunflower (Moon) 104–105
binoculars 34
birds 30–33, 62, 90, 185, 202–203
bird table 33, 96, 107
biscuits 93, 162, 166, 186–187
blocks 20–21, 49, 58, 60, 96, 117, 119–120; big 207; construction 62; green 131; large 24, 59, 119; small 77; wooden 60, 63, 89, 155
board games 23, 85, 128, 159–160, 203, 209
boats 77–78, 144, 166
bones 96, 127, 133
boots 59, 86, 110
bottles 86, 150, 157, 192, 197, 204; clear plastic 150; old plastic 202; sand-filled 150; small plastic 134
bowls, large 125, 171
boxes 88–90, 133, 135–137, 143, 160–162, 173–178, 188–189; biggest 135; child's 178; coloured 175; discovery 133, 136; donate 176; empty 89, 175, 177, 198; enormous 80; feely 214; filled 174; heaviest 175; jewellery 201; junk 69; large 103; letter 72; longest 175; open 65; picture 72; post 88; shiny 201; size 175; sized 127; smaller 133, 161; specimen 188; storage 210; wooden 72, 212
boxes and baskets 5, 65, 149, 153–178, 182, 201, 206
bricks 13, 54, 56–61, 63–65, 73, 198, 212–213
brownies 79
bubbles 146, 193–194

buckets 59, 66, 102, 106, 139, 188
bugs 201, 211
butter 44–46, 162, 170, 186
butterflies 11, 179, 211
buttons 116–117, 148–149, 182

cakes 70, 79, 166
capacity 15–16, 20, 53–54, 94–95, 102, 125, 174–175
cardboard 58, 66, 73, 137–138, 144, 182, 197; coloured 208; cube 85; cylinders 34, 52, 62, 65, 75, 83; hedgehog 209; thin 78; tubes 11, 161
cardboard boxes 10, 20, 36, 56, 77, 146, 174; big 160; large 17–18, 34, 59, 158, 178; strong 66
cardinal numbers 22, 52
carers *see* parents
cars 78
castle 65, 69–70, 95, 97, 103, 119–120, 148
caterpillars 201
chapattis 78
cheese 19, 58, 156
circles 16; actual 25; central 83; matching 211; small 48
clay 80, 91, 105, 133, 144, 152, 209; air-drying 205; coloured 92; divas 76; models 144; rangoli 91; soft 145
clock 80, 123, 128, 150
coins: gold 95; low-value 172; real 106; silver 62; value 62
Come Over to my House (Seuss) 75–76
cone 29, 117, 154, 165, 175–176; fir 21, 196, 198, 200–201, 211; pine 76, 133, 159, 206, 212
conkers 206, 211, 213
containers: large 125; lidded 38; small 193, 197–198; storage 157
cost 16, 54, 73, 111, 172
cotton 88, 90, 111
cotton wool 77, 104, 159
count 15–16, 53–54, 75–76, 121, 142–143, 154–155, 210–211
counters 50–51, 82, 85, 87, 121, 202–204, 207–208
counting 53, 55–56, 113–114, 119–120, 124, 140–141, 210–211
cubes 50–51, 66, 85, 96, 104, 107, 143
cuboid 54, 63, 76, 154, 175, 198
cylinders 50, 59–61, 83–84, 137, 161, 165, 175–176

dice 41, 49–50, 60, 62, 92, 113, 169; blank 92
dice games 92
dice pattern 98; regular 85
dinosaur adventure 144
dinosaurs 122, 139–148, 151–152
dinosaurs and dragons 5, 122–152
diorama 146–147
Divali (Diwali) 80, 91–92; greeting cards 91; prop box 91
divas 80
doilies 199
dolls 10
dough 36–37, 45–46, 48, 144–145, 184, 187–190, 205; animals 62; cookie 176; divas 91; figures 113;

modelling 152; models 40; objects 17; recipe 17; snakes 190; spheres 211
dragons 5, 122–152; bunting 136; puppets 127, 130, 137

Easter 123, 133
Elves and the Shoemaker, The 5, 108–110
Elvira, the Dragon Princess (Shannon) 124
environment: local 52; non-threatening 7; outdoor 7, 12; safe 117
environmental awareness 68

fabrics 21, 46, 58, 62, 77, 206, 208
feely bags 176
fingers 10–11, 48, 176, 182, 185, 189, 191
flour 44–46, 79, 133, 162, 170, 186; plain 162, 186; self-raising 44, 162, 170
flowers 24, 105–108, 155, 157–159, 195, 197, 201
food allergies 44, 80
food colouring 192, 201–202
food, favourite 42, 131
frogs 62, 106, 201, 206–208
fruit 80, 117, 166, 168–170, 172; banned 172; basket of 167–168; buying 172; favourite 168–169; first 170; real 172; second 170

games 7, 49–50, 60–61, 81–82, 85, 92, 99, 108, 113–114, 128–129, 138, 143–144, 151, 159–160, 167, 172–173, 177, 189–190, 202–204, 207–208; developing 11–12, 23, 31–32, 39–41
garden 22, 64, 96, 144, 188
giraffe 168, 170
gloves 11, 34, 59, 89, 106, 128, 133
Goldilocks and the Three Bears 5, 9, 16–17, 19
graph 66, 187, 211

Handa's Surprise (Browne) 167–168
Harry and the Dinosaurs Say 'Raahh' (Whybrow) 139
hats 34
hat shop 28
hedgehog 179, 204–207, 209
height 34–35, 50, 52, 54, 95–96, 100–102, 105–107
hexagon 16
holidays 57–58, 76, 84, 86–87, 92
home/school links 8–9, 22, 24, 32, 39, 60, 84, 106, 144–145, 163, 167, 173, 178, 191, 204, 209, 215
honey 18, 42, 44–45, 50–51
horse chestnuts 206, 214
houses 51–52, 54–58, 60, 62–63, 75–76, 112–113; giant's 97, 101, 103; grandmother's 155, 157–159, 161; making 56, 62–63; round 76, 186
houses and homes 5, 51–92
hundred square, large 117

imagination 26, 127, 140, 173–174, 177–178
In a Minute Mum (Benjamin and East) 148
insects 198, 200–201, 204, 206–207

Jack and the Beanstalk 95–96
jewellery 82–83, 91–92
jewels 71–72, 83, 112

Kalaha 82
kite 76–77

ladybirds 108, 179, 211
language development 7, 22

learning links 30
learning, mathematical 12, 166
leaves 212
length 15–16, 36, 73–74, 101–102, 107–108, 122–123, 174
Lighthouse Keeper's Lunch, The (Armitage) 163
Little Red Riding Hood 5, 154–161

magnifying glasses 34, 136, 164, 188, 196, 211
making: bear puppets 25; books for stories 72; chapattis 91; flags 84; games 99; kites 76; lanterns 69; picture books 72; shortbread for grandmother 162; spiders 200; spoon puppets 57; sunflower stick puppets 108; worms 194
making and testing hypotheses 94, 123, 153, 180
making and testing predictions 53, 94, 123, 153, 180
Mancala 81; game board 82
mandala 187–188
maps 37–39, 70–71, 81, 85–86, 144, 170, 195; large 85, 195; making 37, 195
margarine 44, 186
mass 16
materials, junk 17
mathematical: development 12; ideas 17, 52, 55, 97, 122, 148; investigations 12; language 44, 56, 70, 105, 153; learning objectives 12; problems identifying 89; processes 15, 52–53, 94, 195; towers 73; vocabulary 13, 60, 69, 93, 194
mathematical language: correct 24; practice 96
maths trails 7–8; best 8
maze 207, 214
measure/measures 16, 31; non-standard 13
minibeasts: fiction and non-fiction books on 188; imitation 196, 201; plastic examples 188; real 212
minutes 45, 149, 162, 166, 170–171, 187, 190
money 16; real 28, 46, 88, 106, 110
moon 140
mountain 143, 173
mouse 102, 209
Mr Brown's Fantastic Hat (Imai) 27–28
mugs 46, 181
musical instruments 18, 84, 90, 138, 171

newspaper 77, 88, 103, 135, 144
Not a Box (Portis) 173–174
number(s) 45, 97–99, 121–124, 166–167, 189–190, 203–206, 211; activities 117; bond activities 98; bonds 65, 113, 190; cards 113; correct 118, 206; die 60; last 45, 210; line 28, 32, 62, 95, 97–99, 117, 143; match 129; mats 206; odd 97, 116; rhymes 210; square 119; system 205

oblongs 153, 156, 165
one-to-one correspondence 15, 21, 51, 104, 203
ordering 52; height 21; numbers 15
ordinal 22, 52, 55, 122, 170, 180

Paddington Bear 14
paper bags 25, 58
paper chains 130, 194
paper cup 99, 163–164
paper plates 24, 146, 165–166, 197, 200; circular 83, 197
papier-mâché 127, 133
parents 7–9, 18, 32–33, 39, 84, 172–173
patterns 53–54, 94–95, 116–117, 121–125, 180–182, 188–189, 199–200; making 30, 204; repeating 107, 188; and shapes 94, 122
pegs 72, 196, 206
Peppa Pig 72

Index

pictogram 31, 34, 58, 169, 187
picture books 72–73, 136
picture dice 203
pictures: appropriate 10, 195; dwarf 114, 119; matching 31, 85; next 108, 114; smaller 114
pipe cleaners 52, 75, 191, 199–200
plants 102, 105–108, 179, 182, 197, 201, 207
poems 140–143, 185–186
Pooh Bear (Winnie-the-Pooh) 41, 42–43, 46, 50
problem-solving 52–53, 69, 113, 116, 122, 153, 156; skills 125, 166, 195; strategies 12, 125
prop box 17–18, 29, 34, 59, 80, 86, 91, 103, 110, 127, 144, 165–166, 171, 176, 188, 201, 206–207, 215
puppets 10–11, 25–26, 36–37, 48, 68–69, 108, 130–131, 137–138, 177, 191, 208–209; finger 11, 161, 191, 215; making 10, 36, 130; peg 69; ready-made 11; shadow 130; sock 11; spoon 57; stick 11, 160; theatre 160–161

quadrilaterals 176
questions: asking 34, 53, 94, 123, 154, 180; closed 93, 205; open 42, 93, 136

Ramadan 80
Rapunzel 52, 64–75; escape 52, 75; hair 66, 70, 75; ideas 78; story 69, 176; tower 74
rectangle 25, 37, 73–74, 153–154
rhymes 3, 43, 64, 66–67, 140; for counting 140; finger 11; nursery 1; short 210; speed 185
rhyming 43; tree 43; wall 71
river 37–38, 47, 142–143, 179
rocket 75, 163–164, 174
role play 7, 18–19, 28, 34, 45–48, 59, 80–81, 87–89, 106, 110–111, 117–118, 126–127, 133–134, 144, 158, 166, 171–172, 177, 188, 201, 207, 215
rulers 35, 59, 110

salt 45, 79, 186
Same, Same but Different (Kostecki-Shaw) 84
sand 20, 36–37, 57, 66, 105–106, 148–150, 196–198
sand timers 148–150, 190
scales 16, 54, 88–89, 126, 168, 173, 175; bucket 175, 196; digital 135, 168
seeds 13, 105, 107, 144, 207, 211, 213–215
semicircles 29, 37, 48
sequence 19
sequencing 55–56, 63, 65, 109–110, 155, 170, 195
shape and space 8, 16, 54, 95, 123, 175, 180–181
shape detectives 13
shapes 39, 61–64, 122–124, 138–140, 153–156, 163–165, 174–177; and patterns 155, 199, 213
shoe boxes 113, 161, 163, 210, 213–214
shoes 63, 72, 104, 108–111, 116, 148, 161; adult's 111; children's 111; giant's 104
shops 28, 86, 96, 110–111, 147, 172, 198
Sikh festival 80, 91
snails 76, 108, 179, 181, 183–191, 201, 206–207
Snail Trail (Brown) 181
snakes 92, 102, 184, 187, 203, 206
Snow White (and the Seven Dwarves) 5, 112–113, 117–118, 121
soft toys 34, 46, 171, 215
solving problems 16, 52, 54, 95, 123, 154, 174

songs 84, 120
spiders 133, 179, 188, 198, 200–201, 204
spider web 198
spinner 49–50, 172–173
spirals 54, 61, 145, 181–184, 187–191, 198–199, 211
spiral shells 179, 182, 188
split book 9–10, 22–23, 55, 115–116
spoons 36–37, 45–46, 79–80, 117–118, 166, 169; wooden 36
squares 31, 95, 97, 113, 153–156, 189
squirrel 179, 210–211
Squirrel's Busy Day (Barnard) 209
stamps 80–81, 88–89, 179
stones 73, 89, 103, 146, 158–159, 179, 188
story books 17, 22, 46, 80, 91, 114
subtracting/subtraction 15, 22, 157; problems 15, 53, 122, 153
sugar 26–27, 45–46, 79, 162, 186
sunflowers 96, 101, 105–108
Superworm (Donaldson) 191–192
Swahili 82
symbols 85, 114, 122
symmetry 13, 58, 116, 155, 181, 188, 211

taller 19, 21, 54, 95–97, 100, 104–105, 123–124
tallying 169–170
tape-measures 28, 59
teddy bear 17
testing hypotheses 94, 123, 153, 180
thinking: children's 12, 39; mathematical 1, 149
Three Little Pigs, The 5, 54–64
time 53–55, 57, 88–90, 104–105, 122–123, 148–150, 173–175
time line 32
timer 121, 148–150, 163, 166
tissue paper 66, 69–70, 74, 161
towers 30, 50–52, 63–66, 70, 73–75, 85, 96
toys 10, 13–14, 40, 125, 140, 151, 159
trails 7–8, 24, 32, 38–39, 60, 71–72, 81, 89–91, 96, 128, 158–159, 177, 188–189, 201, 207, 214; giant 100–101; senses 90–91; snail 189–190; sunflower 105; *see also* maths trails
trains 78, 103, 127, 143
trees 32–33, 37–38, 42–43, 96, 158–159, 161, 179
triangles 16, 24, 54, 75, 95, 97, 153–154; equilateral 25, 134
Tyrannosaurus Rex 146

Venn diagrams 30, 165, 182
Very Helpful Hedgehog, The (Wellesley) 204
vocabulary: correct 13, 114; positional 70, 100

Wake Up Charlie Dragon (Smith) 133
walls 64, 107, 129, 139, 161, 186
water tray 20, 77, 86, 106, 111, 197
weather: symbols 85–86; types 86; words 86
weighing 45, 125
weighing scales 59, 166, 168
weight 20, 35, 88–89, 122, 125, 168, 172
wellies 34
We're Going on a Bear Hunt (Rosen and Oxenbury) 34
woodland animals 5, 179–215
words: position 34, 159; positional 70, 174; rhyming 43, 64, 66
wormery 197, 204
worms 102, 179, 194, 196–197, 201–204